The
MYTHOLOGY
of
GRIMM

The
MYTHOLOGY
of
GRIMM

The Fairy Tale and Folklore Roots
of the Popular TV Show

Nathan Robert Brown

BERKLEY BOULEVARD BOOKS, NEW YORK

THE BERKLEY PUBLISHING GROUP
Published by the Penguin Group
Penguin Group (USA) LLC
375 Hudson Street, New York, New York 10014

USA • Canada • UK • Ireland • Australia • New Zealand • India • South Africa • China

penguin.com

A Penguin Random House Company

This book is an original publication of The Berkley Publishing Group.

Library of Congress Cataloging-in-Publication Data

Brown, Nathan Robert.
The mythology of Grimm : the fairy tale and folklore roots of the popular tv show / Nathan Robert
Brown. —Berkley Boulevard Trade Paperback edition.
pages cm
Includes bibliographical references.
ISBN 978-0-425-27102-5 (paperback)
1. Grimm (Television program)   2. Fairy tales.   3. Mythology.   I. Title.
PN1992.77.G6984B76 2014
791.45'72—dc23
2014021470

PUBLISHING HISTORY
Berkley Boulevard trade paperback edition / October 2014

PRINTED IN THE UNITED STATES OF AMERICA

10 9 8 7 6 5 4 3 2 1

Cover art: Shutterstock.
Cover design by MNStudios.
Interior text design by Laura K. Corless.

Most Berkley Boulevard books are available at special quantity discounts for bulk purchases for sales
promotions, premiums, fund-raising, or educational use. Special books, or book excerpts, can also be
created to fit specific needs. For details, write: Special.Markets@us.penguingroup.com.

For Angie . . .
You are forever the princess of my heart.

And to Monroe's many sweaters, as they give us comfort.

ACKNOWLEDGMENTS

There are so many people to thank for helping make this book happen, and if I miss someone, I apologize wholeheartedly in advance. I assure you that, if I left you out, it was not intentional. First and foremost, I would like to extend my most sincere thanks to the management and staff of the Outlook sports bar in Venice, Florida, for welcoming me in like family and, day after day, giving me an office-away-from-the-office in which to work. Thanks to Jason Bennett for helping me with a number of foreign language translations and giving accurate explanations of many anachronistic words (often preventing me from slamming my face into my desk). Thanks also go out to my good friend Ben Haight (aka "That Squid I Know") for helping me develop a more accurate understanding of the ins and outs of handmade medieval weaponry. To my friend and up-and-coming writer Steve "Stuntman" Winfrey, I would just like to say thanks for the moral support (and congrats on your first book deal). Thanks also go out to another fledgling writer, Michael Arsenault, for helping me remember how blessed I am to live the dream. I would also like to thank my agents, Kim Lionetti and Beth Campbell at BookEnds Literary Agency, as they make it possible for me to do what I love. I'd also like to thank my acquisitions editor, Danielle Stockley, as well as my production editor, Stacy Edwards. I have nothing but love for the lot of you.

Lastly, to anyone and everyone who has ever read my work, I extend a most sincere "Thank you." Without each and every one of you readers, I could not do this job that I love so dearly.

CONTENTS

INTRODUCTION

NO HAPPY ENDINGS

Once upon a time, there was a man who loved writing and mythology . . . and fandoms . . . and *Grimm*. So when this man was given the opportunity to write *The Mythology of Grimm*, he saw it as a win-win situation. He also had no idea what he'd gotten himself into or how this project would completely take over his life.

In case you haven't figured it out yet . . . I am that man.

I'd like to start off by stating that this project has occupied nearly every single day of my life for the last seven months or so. It has also been both a joy and an honor to write . . . and, at times, I worried it might drive me over the edge of madness (but I assure you, it would've been worth it in the end even if it had). As I got into the writing of this book, it soon became apparent to me that it was growing into a beast that could not be fed (or, at least, not fed enough). The manuscript had already gone far beyond its allotted word count before it was even three-quarters finished. As a result, I had no choice but to cut some things during the editing process. While I did my best to omit as little as possible, there were just not enough pages available in the final book (which you now hold) for me to fit in *every* single thing about the *Grimm* universe that might be considered noteworthy. However, I assure you I've taken great pains to be as accurate and thorough as possible. To be honest, I now know any book that covers everything having to do with the mythos of the *Grimm* universe would likely require a multivolume encyclopedia.

As you begin to read, you may notice that the majority of chapters in this book follow a similar format (with a few exceptions here and there). Most include retellings of the original fairy tales on which many *Grimm* episodes have been based. Why create retellings, you may be wondering? Why not just use the original stories, word for word? Well, to be honest, many of the original fairy tales were written down between the seventeenth and nineteenth centuries. To put it simply, people wrote *very* differently in those days. They used words that are no longer in the common vernacular of the English language . . . and some stories include little language quirks of the past that, for many modern readers, can sometimes be confusing or boring—or both. Since one of my main goals with this book was to make it an informative, interesting, and fun/lighthearted read, I decided from the beginning that I would use retellings instead of just quoting the source texts word for word. Anyone can go find the original stories. However, I believe that by retelling these stories I have been able to make them more accessible. Doing so has allowed me to show readers not only the events of these tales, but also the context (and, at times, subtext) of them. I also add a little side comment here and there. Some of these stories have some pretty crazy stuff in them, after all. Why ruin everyone's fun by ignoring it? Having spent much of my life in the South, I have learned it's often better not to hide your crazy relatives in the basement when you could bring them into the living room and show them off.

I fully realize, of course, that certain folks—such as literary loyalists and folklore traditionalists—might be upset with me for retelling these stories in my own words. And I think I'm good with that. I decided long before I took on this project that readability and accessibility were far more important than trying to please any would-be critics by sticking to traditional ideas. After all . . . if *Grimm* teaches us anything, it's that sometimes you've got to shake off the old practices and prejudices of your predecessors and challenge the status quo. So that's what I have tried to do. I took off the reins, as much as possible, in the writing of this book.

In addition to the retellings, most chapters will offer information on the background of each tale, as well as discussions of how these stories have been interpreted by mythologists and folklorists over the years. And, when applicable, mythical and historical points related to some tales will be examined. However, please keep in mind that none of these should be seen as absolutes. As with most things in mythology and folklore studies, it's all open to interpretation. My goal with these sections is to simply introduce you to the metaphors and symbolism related to these stories, so that you might understand them from a broader point of view.

Before I finish up this introduction, I feel that I should make one thing perfectly clear—most of the stories and retellings in this book are *not* appropriate for children. These are *not* the fairy tales Disney lied to us all about when we were kids. There will be sexual innuendos. There will be backstabbing. And, above all else, there *will be bloodshed*. Folks (or, in some cases, animals) are going to die in the stories you read in this book, often in a number of creatively nasty ways that Disney would never even dream of depicting in an animated film (but, apparently, the Brothers Grimm and other fairy-tale writers felt these tales were totally fine for kids . . . and, to be honest, they probably *were* fine for kids who grew up between 1600 and 1900).

Wicked mothers-in-law will meet with ugly and painful ends in tubs full of poisonous serpents.

Children are going to be abandoned and left to die by the parents who are supposed to care for and protect them.

Innocent little girls will be sent alone into the woods to face voracious, salivating creatures that lurk in the shadows . . . looking for the first opportunity to devour them.

The corpses of dead women will be found hanging in forbidden closets.

So, let's just say you might want to give this book a look through before you decide to read it to the kiddies before bedtime. While, yes, a number of the stories I have retold in this book do end with the words "they lived happily ever after," one must understand that this happiness is, more often than not, reserved for a chosen few. In nearly every story, death, horror, and heartbreak await. Because . . . in the true world of fairy tales . . . there is no such thing as a happy ending for *everyone*. It all depends on where you're standing when the tale is over.

[1]

GRIMM ORIGINS

CARLY: *I thought he was gonna kill me.*

HANK: *Why?*

CARLY: *He's a Grimm. It's ... what they do.*

HANK: *A what?*

NICK: *A Grimm ... It's sort of a family problem. Look, I promise I'll explain it later. But right now you just have to trust me.*

—"Kiss of the Muse" (2-20)

Long before the TV show *Grimm* was even an idea in someone's head, there were the OGs—Original Grimms—Jacob and Wilhelm. And, both before and after these two brothers graced the planet with their presences, there were other men and women who served as trailblazers as pioneers in a new genre of literature that we now know as "fairy tales"—men like Charles Perrault and Joseph Jacobs, as well as women like Madame d'Aulnoy. While the Brothers Grimm are certainly the best-known folklorists of the fairy-tale tradition, even they had predecessors (just like Nick Burkhardt) and drew upon the knowledge of those who'd come before them. And they had, as one day Nick presumably shall have, descendents who learned from their examples. In this chapter, we shall look at the ghosts of Grimms past, who have allowed the creation of the present mythos of the *Grimm* universe.

The OGs: Original Grimms

Jacob (YAH-kob in German) Grimm was born in Hanau, Germany, in 1785, and his brother Wilhelm (VIL-helm in German) in 1786. They were the oldest of six children, the first- and second-born sons of Dorothea and Philipp Wilhelm Grimm—a scribe and magistrate to the nearby town of Steinau. Their father's occupation came with a nice salary, allowing him to provide his family with a comfortable middle-class lifestyle (a bit more of a rarity in those days). Jacob and Wilhelm received educations under a private tutor, Herr Zinckhahn, who schooled them in subjects such as Latin, French, geography, botany, and history. Philipp was already grooming his oldest son Jacob for a career in law. Wilhelm was exceedingly intelligent as well, and seemed to have a bright future ahead of him. However, as sometimes happens, fate was about to throw the Grimm family a curveball.

In 1796, when Jacob and Wilhelm were only eleven and ten years old, their father was stricken with pneumonia. The sickness soon took the man's life. Since he'd been too young to qualify for a pension when he died, Dorothea Grimm had no choice but to use the family savings to support them all. They soon had to give up their nice spacious home in Steinau and move into a much smaller place. Within a very short time, the life of the Grimm family was turned on its head.

In 1797, Jacob and Wilhelm were sent to live in Kassel, Germany, with Dorothea's sister, Henriette Zimmer, so they could attend school at the illustrious Lyceum Fredericianum. This was a big opportunity for the brothers, but it by no means meant their lives would get any easier. The school was a rough place for boys like them, who came from neither nobility nor privilege. Jacob often found himself fuming with anger due to the teasing of his socially prejudiced classmates. Wilhelm, on the other hand, was usually too sick to be bothered with such things. He was regularly afflicted with colds, lung/heart illnesses, and fits of asthma. However, the Brothers Grimm persevered through all these hardships and eventually graduated from Lyceum Fredericianum at the top of their classes. Despite this achievement, their experiences with poverty and social prejudice were still not at an end.

In order for the brothers to be allowed to study law at the Philipp University of Marburg (Jacob in 1802 and Wilhelm in 1803), both had to acquire special exemptions and permissions (because they were not from an affluent or noble family). They succeeded in this and gained admission. However, this did not mean they could simply breeze through like the rich kids. Both brothers had to work their rears off while at Marburg, and they were better for the experience. In fact, later in life, Jacob would write in his autobiography of what he learned from his time dealing with poverty at Marburg, saying that such a situation "inspires a healthy sense of pride based on the consciousness of one's own merit by contrast to what is bestowed on others for their rank or wealth." The Brothers Grimm undertook the study of law with little more than their intelligence, work ethic, and diligent study habits. Jacob's first year at university was hard on both Grimm brothers because they were separated. Wilhelm remained at the Lyceum to finish his final year. The brothers never did well when they were apart. Most likely, this was because they could share everything during their times of poverty, and doing so made their difficulties more tolerable.

Unlike their wealthy and/or noble-born classmates, the Brothers Grimm had no choice but to live as modestly as possible. They didn't qualify for stipends, so they had very little money between them—

just enough for essentials like food and rent. They shared a very small living space with a single bed, which they also shared. Some people tend to read a little too much into the fact that the Brothers Grimm often shared a bed, but you shouldn't. This was not uncommon for the time (even Abe Lincoln used to sleep in a bed with multiple men because that's all his presidential campaign could afford). While their upper-crust classmates used their born-into wealth to play, travel, gamble, and pursue other such entertaining distractions, the Grimm boys had their noses in books. It didn't take long before they'd proven themselves far superior—as students, scholars, and just plain old human beings—to their wealthier counterparts. Their obvious academic potential caught the attention of one professor in particular—Friedrich Karl von Savigny, the founder of the German Historical School of Law.

Savigny took the Brothers Grimm under his wing, introducing them to philology (the study of the structure, relationship, and development of languages) and historical research. He also gave them access to his personal library, an impressive collection of records and texts. Savigny was a big influence on the Brothers Grimm—especially Jacob, who dedicated his first philological publication, *Deutsche Grammatik* (German Grammar), to the man.

Savigny's library contained more than just texts on philology and history, however. It also offered many works of romantic literature from as far back as the Middle Ages. The Brothers Grimm, who had loved such tales as children, soon became infatuated with these kinds of stories. Many believe it was this period of their lives that likely sparked the Brothers Grimm's love affair with the folktales that eventually became their legacy.

In the early months of 1805, Savigny invited Jacob, then about twenty years old, to join him in Paris, France, as his research assistant at the University of Paris. Jacob was to assist Savigny in writing a text on the history of Roman law in the Middle Ages. Jacob could not bring Wilhelm with him, unfortunately, which meant the brothers were once again separated.

Jacob Grimm was fluent in French (as was Wilhelm) and did very well for himself while in Paris. He began to cultivate an interest in French law and culture. In 1806, only a year after his move, he was offered a well-paying position at the Hessian War Ministry. Since this job would provide him with the financial means to support his entire family, who'd remained in poverty since his father's death, Jacob immediately accepted the job. However, as already stated, the brothers didn't do well when they were apart. Jacob often wrote of this in the letters he sent to Wilhelm while in Paris. He wrote in one letter that, if in the future either of them planned to be away from the other, "the other must give notice at once. We are so accustomed to being together that the idea of separation causes me great distress." While Jacob's new job could be a bit tedious and boring, he carried out his responsibilities diligently—he needed the money to provide for the rest of his family.

In 1807, Kassel came under the control of Napoleon, who made the city the capital of his newly founded Kingdom of Westphalia and gave it to his younger brother, Jérôme, to rule. During this time, Jacob felt an increasing desire to leave his career in law to pursue his love of literature. He applied for a royal position at the public library in Kassel at the palace of Napoleonshöhe (formerly known as Wilhelmshöhe).

In 1808, King Jérôme of Westphalia offered Jacob a position as a royal librarian at the palace of Napoleonshöhe. This was an event for celebration, allowing Jacob to pursue his love of literature without sacrificing the income he needed to support his mother and siblings. However, good news was often accompanied by bad for the Grimm family. Just before Jacob officially received his new position,

Dorothea Grimm died. This made Jacob solely responsible for his siblings. One can only assume this was a time of conflicting emotions for Jacob Grimm—sadness at the loss of his mother coupled with joy at receiving a position that allowed him to follow his passions.

For a guy like Jacob Grimm, the post of royal librarian at Napoleonshöhe seems to have been the perfect job. He only had to spend a few hours each day doing actual *work*, usually just cataloging new entries and performing other administrative duties. For the rest of the day, the library was his to explore. Jacob was soon given an additional post as auditor to the Council of State for the War Ministry. However, this doesn't seem to have been a very time-consuming job. Perhaps the best part of the deal was that Jacob was able to send for Wilhelm to join him. It was during this period that the Brothers Grimm first began working together to collect various stories of folklore. It is important to note that the Brothers Grimm did not "create" the stories they are known for but collected and recorded them. However, this doesn't belittle their contributions to the literary world in any way.

As seems to have been a theme for those with the Grimm name, their prosperity was mixed with hardship. By 1809, Wilhelm was twenty-three . . . and he was in pretty rough shape. He was in such bad health, in fact, that the family sent him to Halle, Germany, to be treated by Johann Christian Reil, a famous physician at the time. Reil used "magnetic" treatments (which, these days, are known as "junk science"). Wilhelm was given these ridiculously expensive treatments for six months, but they appear to have done nothing to improve his condition. In addition to his asthma, Wilhelm's heart seemed to be ailing as well. He would later write in his autobiography, "The pain, which felt like a fiery arrow was being shot through my heart, left me with a constant sense of anxiety . . . I was not completely distraught by my illness and, when things were tolerable, I was able to work and even find some pleasure in it."

Between Jacob's work obligations and Wilhelm's struggles with illness, the brothers continued to collect their stories—often by interviewing various *volk* (or "folk," in this usage meaning something like "common people") and writing down the stories as they told them. From 1809 to 1811, the Brothers Grimm pursued their work tirelessly as much as time allowed. A pair of inspired men, they hoped to publish a text of the folktales they'd collected. Only a few years after they'd begun their undertaking, this dream became a reality.

In 1812, the Brothers Grimm published their first printing of the folktales and fairy tales they'd collected. The title of their work was *Kinder- und Hausmärchen* (Children's and Household Tales). It would be one of the most well-received books of its time, turning the Brothers Grimm into nearly overnight sensations in the literary world. At a time when the German people found themselves under the foreign rule of Napoleon's French empire, the primarily Germanic nature and origins of the tales in *Kinder- und Hausmärchen* were viewed by some as a kind of cultural resistance, a way to retain a national identity in the face of foreign occupation. It would seem the Brothers Grimm agreed with the sentiment that there was a political element in their efforts to collect these fairy tales. In his autobiography, Wilhelm wrote that "Undoubtedly, the world situation, and the need to withdraw into the tranquility of scholarship, contributed to the reawakening of this long-forgotten literature, but we were not just seeking solace in the past, we also hoped that the course on which we had embarked would contribute somehow to the return of a better day."

Politics aside, the Brothers Grimm saw themselves as stewards of a nearly lost oral tradition of storytelling. With their collections of stories, they hoped to inspire other scholars to do as they had done— preserve such tales in written form (even those with pagan/pre-Christian origins) as accurately and entirely as possible. And, from

1812 to 1815, the Brothers Grimm continued to expand and revise their original *Kinder- und Hausmärchen*, publishing a number of updated editions and related collections of mythology, folklore, and fairy tales. However, the world in which they lived was changing around them (and not exactly in positive ways). In order to put things in context, there is no choice but to give you a bit of a history lesson, dear reader.

During the years in which the Brothers Grimm published their first works on fairy tales, German opposition to Napoleon's occupation had intensified, especially when the occupying government tried to force the German people to speak only French. The German people were getting fed up with their French rulers. Unfortunately for Napoleon, he made a fatal error in 1812 when he attempted to invade and conquer Russia. To put it bluntly, he got his butt kicked. The Russians began a "scorched earth" campaign, setting fire to and then abandoning cities and towns as Napoleon's army advanced into them. As a result, he could not resupply his men with stolen goods from the areas he took. His losses were dire, not only from battle but also from hunger and sickness. Napoleon began his campaign in Russia with roughly 500,000 troops. By December of 1812, roughly 380,000 of these troops were dead. About another 100,000 of them were prisoners of war, captured by the Russians. Napoleon fled Russia as fast as he could, even abandoning his surviving troops so he could return to the relative safety of Paris. The epic failure of his Russian campaign greatly weakened Napoleon's military might, and just about all of his enemies (of which there were many) now smelled blood in the water . . . and they were beginning to circle.

In October 1813, a coalition army made up of Russian, German/Prussian, Austrian, and Swedish troops engaged what was left of Napoleon's army at Leipzig in what would be the largest battle in European history until World War I. Roughly 600,000 troops took the field. The battle that followed is referred to as *Völkerschlacht* (Nation Battle or People's Battle) by Germans. In the English-speaking world, this event is commonly known as the Battle of Leipzig or the Battle of the Nations. Overwhelmingly outmanned, outgunned, and outmaneuvered, Napoleon suffered a crippling defeat and retreated (yet again) back to France with his tail between his legs. Unlike the Russians, however, the coalition forces pursued him relentlessly, and by 1814, France was under siege. Napoleon was captured, forced to give up his throne, and exiled to the Mediterranean island of Elba.

The French had already been ousted from Kassel in 1813, when Jacob Grimm was given a diplomatic position in the Hessian Peace Delegation. He traveled to both Vienna and Paris to aid in the drafting of peace treaties. While this, once again, required the Brothers Grimm to be separated, it was well worth it to both if the distance meant an end to Napoleon's empire. Once the necessary treaties were drafted and signed, Jacob rejoined Wilhelm in Kassel and resumed his position as a librarian. The next ten years would be, according to Jacob Grimm, "the quietest, most industrious . . . and most fruitful period" he'd ever known. Jacob and Wilhelm worked side by side as writers, chroniclers, and scholars. Both became incredibly prolific writers and published many more works over the years, such as *Deutsche Mythologie* (German Mythology), *Deutsche Rechtsalterthumer* (Ancient German Law), and *Deutsche Sagen* (German Heroic Legends), among others.

While Jacob and Wilhelm were undoubtedly delighted to finally be reunited at the end of Napoleon's rule, everything between them wasn't always all unicorns and roses. As brothers tend to do, they often disagreed, had heated arguments, and just generally got on each other's nerves. Jacob had always been the more ambitious and aggressive of the two brothers. As they grew older, though, Wilhelm began to feel his life had been overly dominated by his older sibling. He also grew increasingly intolerant of Jacob's temperamental attitude, which made him a bit difficult to deal with at times. For example, in a letter Wilhelm wrote to his friend Ludwig Achim von Arnim (a German poet and novelist), he complained of often feeling frustrated with Jacob's negativity: "He tends by nature to engage in criticism, and has nurtured this tendency, so that he always sees the worst side of things . . . I often worry about this condition, but then he is always extremely sensitive, often believing he's been abandoned or neglected. He acts unhappy about it, but the truth is he is the one who alienates people with his testy nature." Despite the occasional disagreement between them, the Brothers Grimm remained close their entire lives.

In 1825, Wilhelm married a woman named Henriette Dorothea Wild. Known by her nickname Dortchen, she was the daughter of a pharmacist living in Kassel and the great-granddaughter of a renowned philologist. Married life seemed to agree with Wilhelm, who is quoted as having referred to marriage as "God's best blessing." Jacob, on the other hand, remained a lifelong bachelor. In April 1826, Wilhelm and Dortchen had their first child. They named him Jacob. Sadly, the boy died that December. Infant mortality rates were far higher in those days, of course. They would have other children, but one can imagine how heartbreaking the loss of their firstborn must have been for the couple.

Even though Wilhelm was married, the Brothers Grimm continued to live under the same roof and worked together by day as librarians. In 1829, the chief librarian of the Royal Library died. An elector was chosen to select a new chief librarian and, unfortunately, neither Jacob nor Wilhelm got the job. The elector wasn't too fond of Jacob and felt that he'd neglected his duties because he'd published his text *German Grammar* while working as a royal librarian. Poor

Wilhelm just seems to have been viewed as guilty by association. Realizing they'd likely never be promoted now, both brothers resigned from their positions. Upon their departure, the elector is often said to have made the following (sarcastic) remark: "The Grimms are leaving? What a loss! They've never done anything for me." FYI—the elector also seems to have shortly thereafter realized what a terrible mistake he'd made. Only a few weeks later, he made generous job offers to both Jacob and Wilhelm . . . which they declined.

The Brothers Grimm now moved to Göttingen, where Jacob took a job at the university as a professor of German linguistics and law. He was also given the additional appointment of head librarian. Wilhelm, as he often did, relied on his older brother and acquired a job as a librarian under Jacob. Later on, he was given a post as a professor. The reason the Brothers Grimm chose Göttingen most likely had to do with the fact that it had one of the largest and most coveted collections of texts in the world at the time. In addition, it was the first lending library in all of Germany.

By 1833, the world was transforming around the Brothers Grimm yet again. Germany had drafted a new constitution and elected its own parliament. The winds of change seemed ready to blow away the monarchical past. Unfortunately, when Ernst August I assumed the throne in 1837, the first thing he did was abolish the constitution and get rid of parliament, making himself the sole authoritative power. He also required all civil servants (which, at that time, included university professors like the Brothers Grimm) to swear oaths of allegiance to him. Seven professors resisted, among them Jacob and Wilhelm Grimm.

These seven professors (eventually known as the Göttingen Seven) collectively drafted a document that stated they were loyal to the 1833 constitution and that the king had no right to abolish it. As one might imagine, the king didn't take the news very well. Within a few weeks, all seven were dismissed from their jobs. Three professors were singled out as the ringleaders of the whole thing, Jacob Grimm among them (big surprise). The king ordered all three to leave the lands he ruled within three days or be arrested and thrown in prison. However, their strong resolve and willingness to stand against the tyranny of the king's decree (who'd made it obvious he cared nothing for the will of his subjects) made them champions of the people . . . sort of.

Before being forced into exile, Jacob Grimm publicly addressed an assembly of students and professors: "The freedom of Christian men," he said, quoting Martin Luther, "must give us the courage to resist our ruler if it turns out he acts against the Spirit of God and if he offends human rights." Unfortunately for Jacob, many of his colleagues at Göttingen had sided with the king on this particular issue, choosing job security over freedom. There was no outcry among their fellow scholars for the king to repeal his decision. Sadly, as time passed, a certain amount of the German population came to view Jacob Grimm as a traitor to Germany instead of a hero of the people. Even their old mentor, Friedrich Karl von Savigny, refused to give his endorsement to their protest. Some dissidents remained, though, continuing to support the rebellious professors, and a group even tried to raise money to help the Göttingen Seven. However, after the professors made their very public protest, the university experienced a series of hardships that were blamed on the Göttingen Seven. The king stepped in and provided financial aid, later remarking that money was all he needed, all anyone needed, in order to secure the obedience of "dancers, prostitutes, and professors." This guy was a real peach, wasn't he?

Jacob returned to Kassel, followed shortly thereafter by Wilhelm and his beloved Dortchen. The brothers were greeted as heroes by the inhabitants of Kassel but, while everyone seemed willing to give them a pat on the back, no one was willing to offer them employment. Stripped of their incomes, they had no choice but to rely on savings, the generosity of friends, and the sporadic earnings they made from publishing. During this time, they immersed themselves in a new project that had never before been attempted—creating a comprehensive German dictionary. These were, yet again, difficult times for the Brothers Grimm. They weren't strangers to difficulty, however, and they muddled through as they always had—together.

In 1840, both Jacob and Wilhelm were offered positions at the University of Berlin and the Academy of Sciences by the newly crowned Frederick William IV of Prussia (while Berlin is now part of Germany, it was in the Prussian Empire at that time) thanks to friends such as Savigny and Bettina von Arnim, who appealed to the king on their behalf. These positions came with very generous stipends, finally bringing an end to the brothers' financial difficulty. This also allowed them to continue working on their comprehensive dictionary of the German language, which had turned out to be an even more time-consuming and monumental undertaking than they'd originally anticipated. They were able to move from their modest accommodations in Kassel to luxurious living quarters in Berlin (along with Dortchen, of course).

By 1848, the world of the Brothers Grimm seemed ready for transformation yet again. Many German states were changed by the large protests in Berlin and around the country, in what came to be called the Märzrevolution (March Revolution), known to most English speakers as the Revolution of 1848. The protestors insisted the king meet their demands—the establishment of a parliament, a new constitution, freedom of the press, and a return to a unified German nation. Frederick William IV, caught entirely off guard by the appearance of such a giant mob of protestors, verbally conceded to all their demands. While this moment was followed by a period of turbulence and occasional bloodshed, as such transitions often are, things finally began to change for Germany . . . and they changed for Jacob, as well.

Jacob Grimm was elected to the new parliament in 1848, which was comprised of 95 judges, 81 lawyers, 103 teachers, 17 merchants, 15 physicians, and 40 wealthy landowners. Needless to say, he was in excellent company among so many of his fellow intellectuals. At the time, in fact, many referred to it as the Professors' Parliament because the vast majority of those who'd been elected were academics, scholars, and otherwise well-educated men. Jacob had always dreamed of changing many of the social prejudices and ills he'd experienced in his youth, and he undertook his new duties with great enthusiasm. However, his enthusiasm soon turned to disenchantment as the monarchy took steps to diminish the power of the parliament . . . eventually to such a degree that its members were impotent to do much of anything. Before the end of 1848, Jacob was through with politics. He left parliament, saddened by feelings that he'd failed to affect any real change. He also resigned from the university that year. In 1852, Wilhelm did the same.

By that time, both of the Brothers Grimm were in their mid-to-late sixties. At a time when the average life expectancy was just over sixty (for those who survived infancy), this meant they were old men. Now in their retirement years, they continued working together on their German dictionary. One can't really claim either of the Brothers Grimm ever really "retired" in the modern sense of the word.

Jacob undertook a German translation of the epic "Reynard the Fox" (a folklore story tradition found in the Dutch, English, French, and German culture groups that follows the adventures of the trickster, anthropomorphic fox named Reynard) and wrote comparative analyses of its renditions in various languages and cultures. Wilhelm translated a number of old Scottish songs as well as various ballads, songs, and folktales from Denmark. The two worked together on a new translation of *The Elder Edda*, an ancient poetic epic of Norse mythology, as well as many other epics and works of romantic literature from other languages and cultures. The brothers befriended a number of well-known writers—Edgar Taylor (who translated many of their tales into English), Peter Christen Asbjørnsen (a renowned Norwegian folklorist), and Sir Walter Scott (the famous Scottish playwright, poet, and novelist who penned *Ivanhoe* and *The Lady of the Lake*).

Despite his regular illnesses, Wilhelm beat the odds (something the Brothers Grimm were rather talented at doing) and lived to the ripe old age of seventy-three. However, his history of poor health finally caught up with him and, on December 16, 1859, he died from ailments of the heart and liver. Jacob, who one can only imagine was heartbroken by the loss, gave a eulogy at Wilhelm's funeral. He expressed his love for his little brother, calling him his *Märchenbruder* (roughly translated, "fairy-tale brother").

After the death of Wilhelm, Jacob continued working diligently on that accursed German dictionary both he and Wilhelm had begun together so many years before. Even when he was so old and frail he could scarcely move, it is said he would prop himself up with a pillow and work on it late into the night. Ironically enough, the project would never be finished . . . not even halfway. The German dictionary only ever got as far as the letter *F*, to the word "*Frucht*" (fruit). As Mark Twain once remarked of German in his essay "The Awful German Language," "Surely there is not another language that is so slipshod and systemless, and so slippery and elusive to grasp. One is washed about in it, hither and thither, in the most helpless way; and when at last he thinks he has captured a rule which offers him firm ground to take a rest on amid the general rage and turmoil of the ten parts of speech, he turns over the page and reads, 'Let the pupil make careful note of the following exceptions.'" It seems German can be one seriously maddening language . . . even for native speakers like the Brothers Grimm.

Jacob Grimm left this world four years behind his beloved little brother. On September 20, 1863, Jacob passed away from an unspecified illness. The two brothers were buried as they had lived—side by side—in Berlin. Both requested their tombstones bear a simple inscription:

"Here lies Wilhelm Grimm."

"Here lies Jacob Grimm."

While the Brothers Grimm are undoubtedly the best-known pioneers of the fairy-tale genre, they are by no means the only ones. In fact, other trailblazers in the field came both before and after the brothers chose to put pen to paper. And so, let us next look at one predecessor to the Grimm tradition—Charles Perrault—followed by a later folklorist by the name of Joseph Jacobs.

Charles Perrault: The "French Grimm"

Born in Paris, France, on January 12, 1628, Charles Perrault grew up to become one of the most talented and influential men of his time. While he spent much of his life making a living as a civil servant, he was also a renowned writer and poet. Like the Grimm brothers, who came after him, Perrault began his professional career studying law. He also served as secretary for his brother Pierre. A tax collector at the time, Pierre later became a scientist and is credited with developing the concept of the water cycle or hydrological cycle. When he finished school, Perrault took a job working for one of Louis XIV's most influential ministers—Jean-Baptiste Colbert. Colbert appointed Perrault to the post of secretary of the Petite Académie, making him responsible for monument inscriptions and any inscriptions placed on medals in honor of the Sun King (an alternative title for Louis XIV).

In 1671, Perrault was made a member of the Académie Française (French Academy) and had by then proven himself a talented bureaucrat in the royal administration. In 1672, he married a woman named Marie Guichon. He did this despite Colbert's objections that the girl's dowry was too small. In fact, Perrault's marriage to Marie resulted in a rift in his friendship with Colbert. Despite this, Perrault was promoted to the post of surveyor general of His Majesty's Works later that same year. Sadly, his beloved Marie died in 1678 due to complications during the birth of their first daughter (they'd already had three sons). Perrault was shattered by the loss but pulled it together and continued to provide for his family.

In 1683, Perrault's longtime benefactor Jean-Baptiste Colbert died. The year before, he'd made one of his sons the new surveyor general of His Majesty's Works, and Perrault had been forced out of the position. The man who replaced Colbert as minister, unfortunately, had long disliked both Colbert and Perrault. As soon as he was granted authority as minister, he stripped Perrault of all his posts and had him excluded from the Académie Française. Left to provide for his family without the pensions and stipends that had always been his financial support, Perrault turned to writing (and used it as a weapon against his opponents at the Académie Française).

In January 1687, he published *Le siècle de Louis de Grand* (The Century of Louis the Great), which started a number of heated debates between the intellectuals in France (later known as the quarrel of the Ancients and the Moderns). The Moderns rallied around Perrault, who argued that the unnecessary veneration of ancient authors and the critical judgment of women in the arts had to stop. The "quarrel" sparked a time of progressive thought and change in France—in arts, literature, and women's rights.

Shortly after his little war with the Académie Française, Perrault found himself newly inspired by folklore. Years passed as he sought to create a new genre of literature—fairy tales. In February 1696, he published his first fairy tale—"La belle au bois dormant" ("Sleeping Beauty")—in the French literary magazine *Mercure galant*. This was only the beginning. Based on the positive reception of this tale (and likely in desperate need of money), Perrault published a collection of fairy tales under the rather long title *Histoires ou contes du temps passé, avec des moralités* (Tales and Stories from the Past, with Morals) in 1697. Today this work is more commonly known by its subtitle—*Tales of Mother Goose*. That's right . . . Mother Goose was a Frenchman (just ponder that for a second). The collection includes a number of fairy tales that remain well-known to this very day—"Cinderella," "Puss in Boots," "Tom Thumb," and "Little Red Riding Hood" (a German version of which would later be recorded by the Brothers Grimm).

On May 16, 1703, Charles Perrault's life ended where it began— Paris, France. He was seventy-five years old. This is pretty impressive, considering the average life expectancy at the time was around thirty-six (factoring in infant mortality, of course).

Joseph Jacobs: The "English Grimm"

Joseph Jacobs was born on August 29, 1854, in Sydney, Australia. In 1872, at the age of only eighteen, Jacobs immigrated to England in search of a better life. Interestingly enough, he began his career (like both Perrault and the Brothers Grimm) studying law . . . though he did so at the University of Cambridge. Eventually, however, he began to pursue subjects in the humanities—anthropology, history, literature, and philosophy. Jacobs soon came to be a learned and well-respected folklorist, and from 1889 to 1900, he was editor of the journal of the Folk-Lore Society of London—*Folk-Lore*.

While Jacobs penned a number of texts on the subject of folklore, he is best known for his collections of fairy tales (many of which were illustrated by John Dickson Batten). In 1890, Jacobs published his first collection—*English Fairy Tales*. The positive reception of this work led him to create two new collections, *Indian Fairy Tales* (containing tales from Hindu Dharma mythology) and *Celtic Fairy Tales*, in 1892. Two years later, in 1894, he expanded on two of his past works by publishing *More English Fairy Tales* and *More Celtic Fairy Tales*.

While his collections of tales were popular, many of Jacobs's theories on folklore were *not*. During the late nineteenth century, an overwhelming majority of folklorists favored the theory of polygenesis—that similar fairy tales are found in different cultures due to the universality of the human psyche. Jacobs, however, believed in a theory of monogenesis—that each story was created by a single person or culture and then spread throughout the world, from one culture to another, modified to fit into each by the new culture groups who adopted them. He also tended to focus more on the historical and sociological contexts of tales in his analyses, ignoring any psychological and/or spiritual points of view. While many of his ideas are accepted by folklorists of today, they often put him at odds with those of his own time.

In 1916, Jacobs published his last collection of stories—*Europa's Fairy Book* (or *European Folk and Fairy Tales*)—and dedicated it to his *many* granddaughters. He was living in New York at the time, having moved there in 1900 in order to work as the revising editor on *The Jewish Encyclopedia*. Joseph Jacobs passed from this world on January

30, 1916, just after the publication of *Europa's Fairy Book*. He was sixty-one years old. Many of the stories he collected and recorded, however, survive to this very day.

So, in a way, Joseph Jacobs is immortal, as his name and spirit live on in the works he left behind, as do those of the Brothers Grimm and Charles Perrault, who came before him, and as do the names and spirits of others who chose to record the folk and fairy tales of days past for future generations (such as Robert Southey, Peter Christen Asbjørnsen, Madame d'Aulnoy, and Hans Christian Anderson). Without such men and women, it is quite possible that these stories would have been lost to the passage of time.

Classifying Fairy Tales: The Aarne-Thompson-Uther System

When it comes to classifying and categorizing folktales and fairy tales, the Aarne-Thompson (or Aarne-Thompson-Uther) tale type index has been the standard for many decades. This system was first created by a man named Antti Aarne, who published it in 1910 as *Verzeichnis der Märchentypen* (Directory/Index of Story/Tale Types). In 1928, this system was expanded and revised by Stith Thompson and came to be referred to as the "Aarne-Thompson Tale Type Index." Thompson again expanded and revised the system in 1961. However, even this would not be the last time someone would add to what Aarne began.

In 2004, Hans-Jörg Uther decided it was time to change the Aarne-Thompson tale type index (by then, it'd come to also be known as the AT number system). Uther, however, did not just expand and revise the original system as Thompson had. He rebuilt the whole thing, from the ground up, and published it as *The Types of*

International Folktales. Uther's new take on the Aarne-Thompson system now came to be known as the Aarne-Thompson-Uther Classification system (or ATU number system for short).

Please understand that what follows is but a condensed version of the ATU number system. Fully explaining each facet of the system would require a book unto itself, and we just don't have enough pages for that. One should also understand that many stories do not fall into just *one* category. As you'll likely begin to notice throughout your reading of this book, many stories overlap and fall into multiple categories. Of course, it would be ridiculous (not to mention nearly impossible) to expect any classification system to cover all possible story types with one category for each.

While there are definitely longer versions with various subcategories, the main categories of the ATU number system are as follows:

I. Animal Tales (1–299)
II. Fairy Tales (300–749)
III. Religious Tales (750–849)
IV. Realistic Tales/Novellas (850–999)
V. Tales of the Stupid Ogre (1000–1199)
VI. Anecdotes and Jokes (1200–1999)
VII. Formulaic Tales (2000–2399)

What the Grimm Did You Say?: Language Issues in *Grimm*

NICK BURKHARDT: *So,* zaubertrank *means "potion"?*
MONROE: *Yup.*
NICK: *Wouldn't it just be easier to say "potion"?*
MONROE: *Yeah.*

NICK: *Then why don't you just say that?*
MONROE: *Because it's so much more than that.*

—"Love Sick" (1-17)

Unfortunately for the writers of *Grimm*, they created a show based on a tradition that stems from the German language . . . which is, undoubtedly, one of the most difficult and confusing languages in the world. As if this didn't make things hard enough, they expanded the mythos of the *Grimm* universe to include other languages—French, Spanish, Latin, Greek, and various Native American dialects, among others. And it would seem this decision has been giving them headaches ever since . . . And online translators are just making the problem worse.

One need only go online to discover that many folks have been scrutinizing the linguistics mistakes on *Grimm* ever since the beginning. And, in their defense, there are plenty to be found. In fact, when *Grimm* is shown in Germany, the German words for certain Wesen often have to be retranslated into *different* German words. Take the word "Fuchsbau," for example. While English-speaking audiences have no problem accepting this term as meaning a fox-type of Wesen, for a native German speaker it becomes confusing because to them that word just means "a fox burrow" or the place where a fox lives. Therefore, for German audiences the name of this Wesen is changed to Fuchsteufel (Fox Devil) to avoid confusion.

The name of the rhino-type Wesen called Dickfellig is also problematic. The *ig* at the end of the word makes it an adjective for native German speakers, whereas it is used as a noun on the show. Then there are problems of context, like when Monroe claims that his people refer to the Murciélago as Geölterblitz and says that it means "Literally, bat out of hell"—it doesn't. It *literally* means "greased lightning."

So . . . what's the takeaway from this? Should Grimmsters just abandon the universe of their beloved show, simply due to a bunch of foreign language issues? No. The takeaway from this should be that *Grimm*, in a sense, has a language all its own . . . one known only to those familiar with its mythos. Have the writers made mistakes in linguistics? Sure. Do the foreign languages on the show often need to be retranslated in the countries where they are natively spoken? Yes. Does any of this affect the story in any crucial way? Well, that's up to you.

While the origins and language of *Grimm* are interesting, there is another element of the show that is far cooler—weapons. And *Grimm* is full of them. From the "castration blade" and Siegbarste Gewehr of Aunt Marie's trailer to the brutal, skull-bashing maces and morning stars of the Löwen Games, there are plenty of ways to kill—or be killed—in the life of a Grimm.

Time to arm yourself.

[2]

THE TRAILER:
WEAPONRY OF *GRIMM*

Yeah, it's a veritable museum of Wesenology, chronicling the Grimms'
proud tradition of hunting and beheading people like us.

—Monroe, "Kiss of the Muse" (2-20)

Weapons are pretty important to a Grimm, one would assume. After all, taking down a rogue Wesen is hard enough as it is. Doing so empty-handed, even more so. However, as Nick Burkhardt has learned during his time as a Grimm (sometimes, the hard way), equipping himself with the right weapon can mean the difference between life and death. After all, you wouldn't want to bring a doppelarmbrust to a Siegbarste Gewehr fight—would you? That'd just be embarrassing.

Aside from providing Nick with "the books," centuries of Wesen-hunting know-how written by the Grimms of years past, Aunt Marie's trailer also contains a vast arsenal of interesting weaponry. Some of the weapons found in the trailer are just generically useful (for example, the *kanabo*), while others have been designed for taking out specific types of Wesen (such as the Siegbarste Gewehr and Murciélago Matraca).

One side note before we begin—not every weapon discussed in this chapter has necessarily been *used* on the show. However, the inside of the weapons cabinet has been shown enough times for most (if not all) of its contents to be identified. In this chapter, we intend to discuss as many of the more interesting weapons seen in *Grimm* as possible, both those that have been used and those that have not (well . . . not *yet*, anyway).

So, let's begin our journey into the weaponry of *Grimm* with one of the first Wesen-specific weapons to be introduced on the show—the doppelarmbrust.

Doppelarmbrust: When Just One Shot . . . Just Won't Do

> *You know these were designed specifically to stop Blutbaden? I suppose*
> *I should take that as sort of a backhanded compliment, huh?*
> —Monroe, "Leave It to Beavers" (1-19)

When Nick Burkhardt first tangled with a rogue Blutbad in the "Pilot" episode of *Grimm* (1-01), he probably would've found it useful to know there was a doppelarmbrust in Aunt Marie's trailer. Unfortunately for Nick, he hadn't started making use of the trailer's arsenal just yet. So instead, his partner, Hank Griffin, just busted some caps in the creepy postman of a Blutbad—which appears to have been just as effective (but not nearly as awesome).

The doppelarmbrust is not introduced to the audience of *Grimm* until the episode "Leave It to Beavers" (1-19), when Nick discovers this double-loaded piece of hardware in the trailer weapons cabinet. With a little assistance from Monroe (which is just a little awkward, since he's a Blutbad), Nick manages to master this anti-Blutbad weapon.

The term "doppelarmbrust" comes from German and, roughly translated, means "double crossbow" (*doppel* = twin/double; *armbrust*

= crossbow). This weapon is designed to allow the wielder to fire two bolts (or crossbow arrows) one after the other, without the need to reload for the second shot. In *Grimm*, the bolts are specifically designed and loaded with herbs that are problematic for Blutbaden—hellebore and hemlock extract.

The first bolt, loaded with hellebore, has a sedative-like effect on Blutbaden (in one Greek myth, hellebore is used to cure a king's daughters from "lunacy," which originally meant something like "moon madness," so one can see how its use against Blutbaden kind of makes sense). This would come in handy if, for example, a Grimm needed to interrogate a Blutbad without killing him/her (or, at least, without killing him/her right away). The second bolt, on the other hand, is loaded with hemlock, which is a poison that's deadly to just about anyone (whether they be Wesen or human). One would imagine the second bolt was intended to deliver a fatal shot to a Blutbad after interrogation, or just to be a more lethal secondary shot after the initial bolt had slowed him/her down.

While you're unlikely to find an *exact* duplicate of the *Grimm* doppelarmbrust in historical arsenals, a crossbow that fires multiple bolts is not an unheard of concept. Various innovations on the original crossbow design can be found throughout history, in fact, from Europe to Asia. In keeping with the German roots of the *Grimm* mythos, let's first look at an extremely powerful crossbow from that part of the world—the *wallarmbrust*.

Wallarmbrust roughly translates from German as "wall crossbow," and it is aptly named. The wallarmbrust was a beast among crossbows, even as large crossbows go, and was primarily used to defend fortifications from siege attacks. For example, just a few dozen guys armed with wallarmbrusts posted on the walls of a fort or castle could (quite literally) just "go medieval" on the attackers below. Even knights, the elite armored cavalry of the time, could get themselves shot down by this weapon. A wallarmbrust bolt could pierce a knight's armor in some cases. In fact, a well-trained man with a wallarmbrust had the ability to take out an armored knight (even one on horseback) from a distance.

While the wallarmbrust was a specific type of crossbow, it is important to note that not every one of them was the same. Remember, this weapon was used in the days before mass production. Everything was handmade back then, which meant the specifications (such as draw weight and range) varied from one man's wallarmbrust to another's. The general consensus, however, is that your average wallarmbrust had a minimum draw weight of at least 150 pounds. The smaller wallarmbrust models had shorter ranges but could be fired effectively from around 110 yards (about 100 meters). Larger wallarmbrust models, which were far more popular for siege defense due to their increased ranges, had an effective range of 325–435 yards (around 298–398 meters). This wide range difference is due to the fact that, as already stated, each wallarmbrust was made by hand and, oftentimes, with varying materials. For example, the actual bow could be constructed from wood or bone/horn or steel (the most expensive choice), and sometimes it could even be made out of various combinations of these different materials. No matter what materials were used to make a wallarmbrust, however, its use in siege defenses greatly diminished the advantage that plate armor had long provided to knights and nobles.

While the wallarmbrust is a medieval German crossbow, it has little in common with the doppelarmbrust of *Grimm*, which is far smaller and more in the style of what is often called a pistol crossbow. Such weapons are known to have been in use during medieval times, often employed by tower/castle guards as a ranged weapon that could be easily carried. However, these sorts of crossbows were more commonly seen in regions of medieval France and Italy (though it's certainly not impossible that some of them ended up in Germany). However, any

Tasty Morsels

Effective range is the distance at which a ranged weapon can be aimed and fired with an acceptable amount of accuracy. Maximum range, on the other hand, only refers to how far a weapon is capable of sending a fired projectile (without any consideration to factors such as accuracy or lethality).

discussion on crafty and/or innovative crossbow designs should include those that hail from a little farther east—like the Far East.

When it comes to crossbows that can fire multiple bolts before they need to be reloaded, the ancient Chinese were pioneers. One such example of this is a crossbow commonly referred to as the *Zhuge nu* (or Zhuge crossbow). The Zhuge nu was a handheld magazine-fed crossbow that could fire between ten and fifteen bolts before it needed reloading. The oldest one of these repeating crossbows was uncovered during the excavation of a tomb at Qin-Jiu-Zui in China's Hubei province, and has been dated to roughly 500–400 BCE. Before this discovery it had long been believed that this weapon was first invented in the late second or early third century CE, an era in China often referred to as the Three Kingdoms period. As the name of this period suggests, this was a time during which China found itself divided into three separate kingdoms—Cao Wei (sometimes simply called Wei), ruled by the powerful warlord Cao Cao; Shu Han (or Shu), ruled by a loyalist and descendent of the fallen Han Empire named Liu Bei; and Wu, ruled by Sun Quan (a descendent of the legendary strategist Sun Tzu, who penned the famous text *The Art of War*).

While the Three Kingdoms period is certainly interesting, we're not trying to give you a history lesson here. We are here to talk about crossbows.

The ruler of Shu Han, Liu Bei, was aided by a legendary strategist

Tasty Morsels

There are two different texts that describe the events of the Three Kingdoms period. One is called *The Records of the Three Kingdoms*, which is considered a fairly factual account. The other text is called *The Romance of the Three Kingdoms* and is a more sensational and mythical account of what transpired in the conflict between the empires of Wei, Wu, and Shu.

known as Zhuge Liang (pronounced ZHOO-gay Lee-AHNG). According to the records of this period, Zhuge Liang improved upon an old crossbow design by increasing the number of bolts that could be fired with each trigger pull, allowing two to three bolts to be fired at a time. This is why the weapon came to be known as the Zhuge nu, as it was named after him. A well-trained man armed with a Zhuge nu was able to fire off about ten to fifteen bolts in roughly fifteen to eighteen seconds. After each trigger pull, the user needed only to push forward then pull back on the charging handle (located on top of the crossbow), and he was ready to fire again.

While the Zhuge nu repeating crossbow had an unprecedented fire rate when compared to other such weapons of that time period, it couldn't hold a candle to the German wallarmbrust when it came to range. The effective range of a Zhuge nu was only around 65 yards (roughly 60 meters), and its maximum range was a measly 130 yards (roughly 120 meters). Within these ranges, however, the Zhuge nu was still capable of piercing most armor types of that period and region.

In addition to the Zhuge nu, the ancient Chinese also developed a crossbow that was about the size of a coffee table—the *Chuangzi nu* (triple crossbow). Needless to say, this was *not* a handheld weapon. In actuality, it took a small crew of men just to operate the thing. However, don't let the name triple crossbow fool you. It fired only a single projectile at a time. The single bowstring, however, was tied to *three* individual bows . . . and that one projectile was *huge*. The maximum range is said to have been about 1160 yards (about 1060 meters), and its effective range was somewhere between 300 and 500 yards (about 275 to 457 meters). Using three separate bows to fire one projectile greatly increased the draw weight, which meant it could fire a far larger and more devastating projectile.

Crossbows like the doppelarmbrust are pretty handy for those times when a Grimm needs to take down a Wesen from a distance. However, sometimes a Grimm just needs something that's a little more, well, up close and personal. You can't get much more "up close" than a knife . . . and when that knife is a castration blade, things can't get much more "personal" (seriously).

The Castration Blade . . . Yikes!

KELLY: *Your great-great-grandmother Hilda, with this blade, once castrated a rotznasig carcaju.*

NICK BURKHARDT: *That's good times.*

—"Bad Teeth" (2-01)

Grimmsters were first introduced to the nasty little piece of cutlery known as the castration blade during the opening episode of *Grimm* season 2, "Bad Teeth." Awkwardly enough, Nick learns about this creepy little artifact from his own mother. As it turns out, his great-great-granny once used it to chop off the junk of a Wesen we haven't yet seen on the show (but the general theory is that a rotznasig carcaju is probably a wolverine-like Wesen, since the French word for "wolverine" is *carcajou*).

Based solely on the appearance of this bladed weapon, it is most likely a dagger from the Ottoman Empire of Turkey (though at the peak of the Ottoman Empire, their territories spanned far beyond Turkey) that rose to power around 1300 CE and eventually fell at the end of the Turkish War of Independence in 1922. A dagger with the sort of backward curving, tapered blade seen on the castration blade, as well as the intricate details on the blades and/or sheaths, is indicative of the knives that were popular in the Ottoman Empire during its height of power. The design of such a dagger certainly does not indicate that it was specifically *designed* for castration. If one looks a bit more closely at history, however, one finds there was a longstanding tradition of castration in the Ottoman Empire.

In the court of the Ottoman Empire the only male servants allowed to oversee certain duties, such as attending to the royal harem, were eunuchs (which means, to put it simply, they'd had their "man bits" chopped off). These servants were divided into two groups by race—the black eunuchs and the white eunuchs. Black eunuchs were captured, enslaved, and brought in from regions of Africa and, at times, Egypt. White eunuchs, on the other hand, were brought in from places such as the Balkan Peninsula of southeast Europe. Black or white, they had one thing in common—they were all slaves of the Ottoman imperial family.

The black eunuchs were assigned to serve the harem of royal wives, as well as any concubines they had on the side. The white eunuchs were used as servants at the Palace School, where young members of the ruling elite were educated. Both groups had their own appointed leader—the chief black eunuch and chief white eunuch. To be honest, there isn't anything all that incredible to mention about the white eunuchs or their chief. The chief black eunuch, however, was a very interesting figure.

The first thing one needs to realize is that the differences between the white and black eunuchs were more than just skin deep.

GRIMM WORDS

Harem: In modern language, people often use this word to refer to a group of wives in general. The word had a more specific meaning in the Ottoman Empire, however, and referred to a house, or separate area of a large household, in which a man's wives were cared for and kept.

While the members of both groups were castrated (obviously), the black eunuchs underwent a far more traumatizing ordeal than their white counterparts.

Whenever young male slaves were captured, any who were younger than eight years old (by at least a few years or more) were first brought to the Abou-Gerghe monastery, located on Mount Ghebel Eter in Egypt (a peak on Mount Sinai). Until they reached roughly the age of eight, they were trained to serve their future masters. Once they reached the age of eight, however . . .

FYI—If you get squeamish easily, you might want to skip the next paragraph. Things are about to get a little graphic.

At the age of eight (or thereabouts, if exact age could not be determined), the boys would be taken to a room and chained down to tables. The priests of the monastery would then come in with knives and slice off their sexual organs (*all* of them . . . the "twig" as well as the "berries," if you get the idea). What is even worse is that the boys were *not* sedated. They were awake and able to feel everything that was being done to them, which is enough to send chills up your spine. Once that was over, the priests shoved a sharpened piece of bamboo into the raw flesh of each boy as a "replacement" phallus. And even then their torment was not over. Next, they took the boys out to the desert and buried them neck deep in the burning sand. It is estimated that roughly 90 percent of the boys put through this ordeal did not survive it—which is just horrifying. This means that for each black eunuch who lived to be enslaved, nine other young boys had died. Those who did survive, however, were worth a small fortune as slaves.

The position of chief black eunuch eventually became, in many ways, one of the most powerful positions in the Ottoman Empire. In time, the black eunuchs grew into a very effective network of spies. They rarely spoke, but they were always listening . . . and almost nothing that happened in the empire escaped their attention. They knew which wife or concubine certain Ottoman royals were favoring at the moment. They also knew which wives or concubines these men wished would just "go away." They knew everyone's vices, weaknesses, past mistakes, insecurities, and an assortment of other dirty little secrets. They learned about every skeleton in every closet, and they reported all of it to the chief black eunuch.

As you've seen, the fact that the castration blade is of the Ottoman design seems fitting when one considers the role castration played in the land of its origin. While the castration blade might allow a Grimm to get up close and *very* personal, he or she would have to be crazy to use one against a Siegbarste. For that, a Grimm needs a BFG (Big Freaking Gun).

BFG: The Siegbarste Gewehr

That is a big *rifle*.   —Monroe, "Game Ogre" (1-08)

The good old Siegbarste Gewehr—when you absolutely, positively have to kill every ogre in the room, accept no substitute. When Grimms need to bring down a BFO (Big Freaking Ogre), they need a BFG, and that's a fitting description for the Siegbarste Gewehr. As

Hank Griffin asks in "Game Ogre" (1-08), however, "Who the hell would own a gun like that?"

A Grimm . . . that's who.

Like an impressive amount of the weapons used on *Grimm*, the Siegbarste Gewehr (*Siegbarste* = an ogre-type Wesen; *Gewehr* = rifle) has foundations in reality. To be honest, the only thing that makes this weapon unique is the ammunition—coated in Siegbarste Gift (in German, *Gift* means "poison"). Without this unique ammunition, it is just a three-barreled model of a very high-caliber rifle, commonly referred to as an "elephant gun" . . . which is exactly what it sounds like—a rifle designed to bring down an elephant. Such weapons became increasingly popular during the late nineteenth and early twentieth centuries, when the African ivory market was at its peak (these days, hunting elephants for ivory is *very illegal*).

While there have been many different elephant gun models, the writers of *Grimm* were kind enough to provide some specifics in the episode. These clues came in the form of a ballistics report explained by Captain Renard in "Game Ogre" (1-08): "Now, these are the bullets pulled out of Stark's body. According to ballistics, one .577- and two .600-caliber Nitro Express rifle bullets—made in England over one hundred years ago."

When it comes to early twentieth-century elephant guns, the three largest calibers available were .577, .600, and .700. And the Nitro Express series of ammunition produced all of these. Just to give you an idea of the rounds used to put down Oleg Stark (a rogue Siegbarste), let's take a look at the specifications of the .577 and .600 rounds used in the Siegbarste Gewehr.

For just the smaller .577 round, the projectile alone is .585 inches thick (14.9 mm), and the casing is 2.75 inches long (70 mm). The entire round is a combined 3.70 inches long (94 mm). Depending on the grain weight (the amount of powder used to propel the projectile), it had a velocity of between 1,850 and 2,050 feet per second (between 560 and 620 meters per second). If a normal human being were to be shot in the chest with this round, as Stark was, he or she would likely just fly into a number of very bloody pieces.

The projectile of the larger .600 round has a diameter of .62 inches (15.75 mm), and the casing is 3.00 inches long (7.62 cm). The .600-caliber Nitro Express rounds have only ever been manufactured in 900-grain weight, with a velocity of 2,050 feet per second (625 meters per second). An elephant that was hit in a vital organ with this round would go down for good. If a normal human being was to be hit in the torso (or anywhere, for that matter) with this sort of round . . . well . . . they'd almost surely be transformed into what could only be described as a very gooey and gory mess of red stuff.

A Siegbarste, however? Well, it depends on whether you remembered to use Siegbarste Gift on your ammo.

While most elephant guns are either single- or double-barreled, a number of three-barreled models are known to exist (using any sort of weapon to hunt elephants has been a crime in Kenya since at least 1973, so elephant guns are now mainly collectibles for firearms enthusiasts). These triple-barreled versions, however, allow rounds of more than 1 caliber to be fired from the same rifle. And, according to the above-mentioned ballistics report, the Siegbarste Gewehr used by Nick's family (and Monroe, on at least one occasion) is also of this design, since both .577- and .600-caliber rounds were recovered from Stark's body. Based on this, it is likely the smaller caliber round was loaded into the center barrel. It was common for such rifles to have one caliber load into the outer two barrels, and the other caliber in the center barrel. The reason for this is simple—to avoid confusion while reloading. Consider the following example: you are a hunter, and you just wasted three rounds shooting at a bull elephant, but you only managed to wound it . . . and now it's charging right at you as you hurry to reload. If the outer barrels are different calibers, you might begin to ask yourself, "Now, was it the right side that I had drilled for the .577-caliber rounds? Or was it the left?" This isn't exactly the kind of question you want to be pondering as a wounded and pissed off bull elephant is charging at you (those tusks aren't just for show, after all). And, one would imagine, the same would be true of a wounded, pissed off Siegbarste.

Some of you may be wondering, "Why use an elephant gun at all, if all you need to do is shoot the guy with a little Siegbarste Gift?"

Well, based on what the show tells us about Siegbarstes, getting a bullet to penetrate their skin isn't exactly easy. Judge Logan Patterson was armed with a pistol when Oleg Stark broke into his home, and it didn't seem to do Patterson much good in preventing his attacker from shoving his own gavel right down his throat. So, based on this little nugget of evidence, Siegbarstes do not appear to be as vulnerable to small arms fire as other Wesen. Based on this rationale, an extremely high-caliber firearm is probably the only thing that can make a hole in the thick skin of a Siegbarste. And, considering that .50-caliber machine guns aren't exactly the kind of thing you can just pick up discreetly at your local hunting supply, a one-hundred-year-old elephant gun would be the most reasonable choice for a Grimm with a Siegbarste problem. However, remember that it is not the bullet that kills the Siegbarste. It's the poison with which the ammunition is coated. Which leaves us wondering: would three *normal* Nitro Express rounds from an elephant gun even *kill* a Siegbarste? We may be better off not knowing the answer to that one.

While a BFG like the Siegbarste Gewehr is helpful when a Grimm needs to take out a Siegbarste from a relatively safe distance, it won't do much good against a Wesen who can shatter eardrums, pop eyeballs, and rupture internal organs before the Grimm can even get a shot off—such as the bat-like Wesen called Murciélago. For that, a Grimm needs a very special kind of weapon.

Tasty Morsels

"Game Ogre" (1-08) is the first episode of *Grimm* in which Nick's role as a Grimm clashes with Hank's past. But it won't be the last. For more, see Chapter 17.

Murciélago Matraca: To the Bat Siren!

In my battles I have discovered that, many times, one does have to pay in kind and, as suspected, loud sounds weaken the Murciélago. Therefore, I'm designing a siren that, at all power, beeps so acutely that it is imperceptible to humans. The sound emitted by the Murciélago Matraca disorients the Murciélago with ultrasonic waves, denying its ability to create its own destructive sound.

—Lopez Diego y Grimm's diary, read by Monroe in
"Happily Ever Aftermath" (1-20)

When Nick finds himself doing battle with a disgruntled "princess" who is actually a Murciélago (bat-like Wesen), he discovers one of his predecessors has already designed a weapon for combating them—the Murciélago Matraca (which, literally translated from Spanish, means "bat rattle" or "bat noisemaker"). As armaments go, the development and use of sound weapons (sometimes referred to as acoustic weaponry) is actually fairly new. However, the use of sound in combat has been around for many years.

The idea of using sound in deception tactics has been around the longest, probably ever since some prehistoric human figured out that throwing a rock in a side direction could temporarily distract a predator or enemy so that the human could flee from a hiding place to safety.

In World War II, in fact, sounds were used in combination with art by a special US Army unit called the Ghost Army. This unique unit, which was comprised almost entirely of artists and engineers, would create tanks, jeeps, etc., out of such materials as rubber and papier-mâché. When these fake units were spotted from the air by Nazi spy planes, or viewed from a distance by ground spies, they caused misinformation and confusion among the enemy. The Ghost Army sometimes even employed recordings, played through loudspeakers, in order to give these "ghost units" a more authentic feel if more closely approached.

In more recent decades, however, the use of sound in combat has evolved into direct forms. Instead of sound being used as a tool for distraction, deception, and/or psychological warfare, today's acoustic weapons are designed to inflict pain, send long-range messages via sound, and (in extreme cases) to kill.

One of the most well-known and widely employed of these acoustic weapons is the Long Range Acoustic Device (LRAD). This device is used in various capacities by military, law enforcement, and private maritime entities. The primary use of the LRAD, according to its creators, is to broadcast acoustic messages over a wide range during emergency situations. While the LRAD is certainly an effective tool for this task, it can also be used for far more destructive purposes.

In June 2009, for example, President Manuel Zelaya fled Honduras when he was overthrown. On September 21 of that year, Zelaya returned to Honduras with his family and took refuge in the Brazilian embassy in Tegucigalpa. When word of his return began to spread on September 22, hundreds of his supporters (along with a small army of journalists) surrounded the embassy. Zelaya emerged briefly and began shouting, "Restitution, Fatherland, or Death!" to the crowd of supporters. Then he returned to the safety of the embassy. The crowd, of course, got riled up because they believed he was encouraging revolution. The Honduran military, many of whom had participated in

Zelaya's unseating, grew fearful and deployed at least two mobile LRAD units. The soldiers operating at least one LRAD cranked it up to full blast and pointed it directly into the crowd. Those who were hit with the concentrated beam of sound waves experienced pain, disorientation, nausea, and (of course) hearing loss. Once hit with the LRAD, the crowd quickly scattered. When another crowd attempted to gather on September 25, the LRADs were again deployed and used to disperse the Zelaya supporters.

At sea, LRADs are used by military and private ships to hail far-off vessels. They are also employed by whaling vessels to prevent anti-whaling activists from coming alongside in smaller motorized rafts (many people have become familiar with the LRAD from seeing it used against the antiwhaling activists on the Animal Planet show *Whale Wars*). Other private vessels use the LRAD in order to prevent pirates from boarding their vessels.

Acoustic weaponry (whether it's the real-world LRAD or the Murciélago Matraca of *Grimm*) can be used to disperse angry mobs or put a pissed off Murciélago into a world of pain. However, there are times when a Grimm just feels like bashing in some skulls. And, when it comes to cranium crushing, few melee weapons can hold a candle to the Japanese kanabo.

Kanabo: Weapon of the Oni

Anyone for some kanabo? —Monroe, "Leave It to Beavers" (1-19)

When it comes to all the lethal toys with which Nick Burkhardt has become proficient since taking over his duties as a Grimm, none has a higher body count than the kanabo. This iron-studded piece of brain-destroying weaponry originated in Japan, and it is perhaps one of the most intimidating and destructive melee weapons ever invented. A lethally simple combination of Japanese white oak and metal spikes or studs, the kanabo is a bludgeoning weapon that just screams, "Don't mess with me unless you want your brains to wind up on the floor!"

The kanabo (literally translated from Japanese as "metal and wood") is a sturdy, long, club-like weapon. The core of the weapon is traditionally constructed from sturdy woods such as Japanese white oak (though similar weapons, such as the *tetsubo*, were forged entirely from iron) and tapered down, becoming increasingly wider from handle to tip (somewhat like a baseball bat from hell). To make this weapon all the more deadly and terrifying, spikes or studs of iron or steel were added to the business end.

While the kanabo is known to have been used on the battlefield by samurai, as well as lower-ranking warrior retainers, it is also associated with frightening figures from Japanese mythology—the demonic monsters known as Oni.

English-speaking Westerners often use a number of various terms as equivalents for Oni—demons, trolls, devils, ogres, and even malevolent spirits. To be honest, there isn't really a proper English equivalent for the word. In regards to the *Grimm* universe, one might say the Oni is the Japanese version of a Siegbarste. However, these two creatures don't quite match up when it comes to the details.

While some Oni are born as monsters, others were once human. According to legend, any human who grows insanely bloodthirsty and/or kills too many people is at risk for becoming an Oni—such as mass murderers, serial killers, and even swordsmen. More or less, the idea is that killing soils the soul—a person does too much killing and his/her soul (as well as the body it inhabits) could transform into an Oni. And it is not a pretty sight. Oni have skin that is red or blue, and devilish horns sprout from their heads.

In statues and pictures that portray the Oni, they are often shown wielding their weapon of choice—the kanabo. In fact, at the Oe Station in Japan one can view a pair of Oni statues. A kanabo sits on the ground behind one of the statues.

One of the most infamous Oni was Shuten-Doji, who lived high on the mountain of Oe-Yama (OH-ay ya-ma), or Oe Mountain, with a ruthless gang of fellow Oni. For years, Shuten-Doji and his fellow Oni raided the surrounding areas, until the emperor eventually ordered the legendary hero Yorimitsu to bring an end to their reign of blood. In fact, there is a Japanese historical record of the battle between Shuten-Doji and Yorimitsu's band of legendary warriors known as Shittenou. According to these official records, the clash took place on January 21 in 990 CE. With a little help from some disguised kami (divine spirits of the Shinto religion) who gave him a special poison called Shinbenkidokushu (*very* roughly translated, "Poisonous liquor of the gods that sends demons to flight") and a magical helmet, Yorimitsu and his Shittenou warriors succeeded in killing Shuten-Doji.

One must admit that a humongous studded club said to have been wielded by Japanese ogre-like monsters seems like a fitting weapon for a Grimm. Speaking of fitting Asian weapons for Grimms, this next one comes not from a monster of myth but from soldiers whose deeds have become legendary—it's called the kukri.

Kukri: Blade of the Gurkha

MONROE: *Dude . . . you have a gun.*

NICK BURKHARDT: *I can't shoot everybody. Plus, I used pepper spray on this kid the other day? Turns out he was a skalengeck. Had no effect.*

MONROE: *Skalengeck . . . he probably enjoyed it.*

—"Leave It to Beavers" (1-19)

If you look at the doors of the weapons cabinet when it is open, you will find various weapons mounted on them. Just below the castration blade (shudder), you will find a very large and unusual looking knife with a strangely shaped blade (some might describe it as boomerang-like in shape)—a kukri. The kukri has its origins in Nepal, a small South Asian country located just between India and Tibet. While the kukri has long been used as both a tool and a weapon among the Nepali people, it is better known for being the signature melee weapon of an elite military unit known as the Gurkha Brigade.

The kukri (sometimes spelled *khukuri*, according to its original Nepali pronunciation) is a large knife with a thick, forward-curving blade that is usually between twelve and eighteen inches in length. This blade design increases the momentum of the edge when the weapon is swung. While better known for its lethalness as a weapon, it is also a popular utility tool in Nepal that can be employed similarly to a machete. While some kukri blades are meant for functional or combat-ready tasks, others are created for purely ceremonial or decorative purposes.

In addition to the kukri's unique blade shape, another distinguishing feature of the weapon is a small notch (called a *kauda* or *kaura*) near the base of the blade. The purposes and/or meanings of this notch vary from one source to another. Some claim it is symbolic of the milk sack of a cow, which is considered a sacred animal in the Hindu Dharma religion, which is the primary faith of Nepal. Other sources claim the kukri's kauda is related to Shiva, God of War and Destruction. Still other sources, however, claim the kukri's kauda serves more functional purposes—to prevent blood from running down the blade onto the handle (causing slippage in grip) and/or to mark a clear stopping point for when a user is sharpening the blade. While the kukri alone is undoubtedly a formidable weapon, its lethality increases a hundredfold when one of these blades is placed in the skilled hands of a trained Gurkha. But who are the Gurkha? Well, let's find out.

Back in the mid to late eighteenth century, the British Empire took great pains to occupy India in order to expand the earnings of the East India Company, a maritime merchant conglomerate formed with the purpose of trading with the Far East in items such as silks, dyes, cotton, tea, and opium. Around 1767, ten years after their initial occupation of India, British troops began having skirmish encounters with fierce fighters from the neighboring country of Nepal. These warriors of the Gorkha Kingdom were being led into battle by their king, Prithvi Narayan Shah. In truth, the Gorkha (the forerunners of the Gurkha, who come from all over the country of Nepal) came from a very small collection of tiny hill villages in what is now western Nepal. The British were only in India at the time, but the Gorkha king figured it was only a matter of time before the Brits set their sights on his lands ... and he didn't take too kindly to the idea of British occupation. So he decided to take the fight to them in the form of raids and guerrilla warfare attacks on the neighboring areas of India and Tibet. Unfortunately, this eventually resulted in British retaliation. In 1814, the British Empire declared war on the entire country of Nepal, sparking the Anglo-Nepalese War. After two years of bloody fighting, the conflict finally came to an end in 1816 when the Sugauli Treaty was signed between Nepal and the East India Company.

During the two years that the British troops spent duking it out with the Gorkha, both sides had developed a mutual respect for each other. Therefore, a condition was added to the Sugauli Treaty—Nepalese troops could volunteer to serve as soldiers for the East India Company in a specially designated unit called the Gurkha Brigade. Members of this elite unit, in modern times, are recruited in Nepal but serve the military of the United Kingdom. They are in service to this very day and have produced some of the most lethal and well-trained warriors ever to take the battlefield. Don't let their size fool you (the average height of a Gurkha soldier is only 5'3")—the Gurkha may not be tall by Western standards, but these guys can and will do some *serious* damage when the situation calls for it.

One of the better known modern examples of Gurkha bravery, and the lethal potential of a kukri in the hands of one, is a man named Corporal Bishnu Shrestha. On the evening of September 2, 2010, the thirty-five-year-old recently discharged Gurkha boarded a train (the Maurya Express) with plans to return home to a life of peace, leaving behind his life of combat. Unfortunately, fate needed him to hold off on his new life of peace for just one more night.

Around midnight, just as the train was reaching the jungles of West Bengal, the locomotive suddenly came to a halt as armed robbers (some of whom were already passengers) took control of the train. Dozens more armed thieves emerged from the jungle and boarded the train. The gang of thugs, wielding weapons such as swords and clubs, began stealing anything of value from the passengers. Shrestha stayed calm and kept his seat.

When some of the bandits asked for his wallet, Shrestha handed it over. As a former soldier who'd survived combat, he knew the value of life. So he did what anyone should do in that situation: gave the robbers what they wanted and let them move on. Unfortunately, some of the criminals decided they weren't satisfied with taking money alone. Three thugs in Shrestha's train car suddenly dragged an eighteen-year-old girl from her seat, threw her to the floor, cut off her shirt, put a knife to her throat, and began attempting to rape her . . . right in front of her parents, no less.

It was at this point that Shrestha decided he'd had just about enough.

"I prevented her from being raped," Shrestha later said during an interview, "thinking of her as my own sister."

As it turned out, the bandits had made a *very* fatal mistake—they'd taken his wallet but not his kukri. Shrestha snatched up one of the would-be rapists, used him as a human shield, and killed all three of them with nothing but his kukri knife. During the chaos, the young girl received only a minor flesh wound to her neck. Realizing he was in a fight for his life, Shrestha armed himself and went from car to car . . . kicking the snot out of any bandits he came across. When it was all over (the whole thing took about twenty minutes), he'd killed three bandits and seriously injured another eight. When the other thugs saw Shrestha coming for them, they ran for their lives despite outnumbering him forty to one. Shrestha didn't come out unscathed, however, receiving a serious wound to his left hand. Honestly, this only makes his feat more impressive. Why? Because his left hand was so injured he couldn't use it, which means he *single-handedly* took on a gang of armed bandits (literally)!

The aftermath of the event is even more incredible. When the authorities arrived, everyone on the train told them what Shrestha had done—he alone had saved the girl from being raped and battled the entire gang of bandits. When the Gurkha Brigade learned what he'd done, they temporarily took Shrestha out of retirement to promote him and award him medals for his deeds. Members of his former unit bought him a silver-plated decorative kukri. The Gurkha Brigade also gave Shrestha a cash award of fifty thousand rupees (in 2010, this amounted to about $1,100). It also turned out the Indian government had a bounty on the robbers Shrestha had killed, of roughly four hundred thousand rupees (in 2010, about $8,850). Shrestha never even bothered to collect it. Lastly, Shrestha was given a generous discount on all travel in India for the rest of his life—buses, trains, you name it. Apparently, the government of India decided his presence on public transport would be a strong deterrent to any future would-be robbers. However, it seems all these rewards and

ucts of fantasy than weapons of reality. While these kinds of axes certainly may have been used in medieval Europe, nearly all of the surviving battle axes known today are single sided. Once again, remember that we are discussing weaponry from the medieval period. There was no such thing as machinery or mass production back then, which means everything (from weapons to horseshoes) was made by hand. So, while certain weapons were indeed of a similar design or type, they were all unique. In those days, each weapon was constructed based on the abilities of the makers and the needs of the users. Therefore, it is entirely possible that someone had a two-sided battle axe made. Axes, of course, have been around since before the development of written recorded history.

Axes have existed as both tools and weapons since the Stone Age (from prehistoric times to roughly 3000 BCE) and continued to be developed well into the Bronze Age (roughly 3000–1200 BCE) and on into the Iron Age (roughly 1200–550 BCE). As is often the case with certain forms of technology, the development of materials used to construct axes advanced due to the needs of warfare. The oldest surviving battle axe artifacts date from between 400 BCE and 400 CE, and all of them come from the Scandinavian Vikings who began to expand throughout Europe during this period.

During the Viking Age (775–1050 CE), Scandinavian warriors changed the design of their battle axes to create a broader cutting edge with a more defined curve in the blade. They were able to get around the problem of increased weight by making the axe heads significantly thinner. The strength of iron over bronze allowed them to do this without causing the axe heads to become weak. This style of battle axe would remain in use almost exclusively by the Vikings until between 1000 CE and 1199 CE, when the weapon became popular among the British.

Beginning in the thirteenth century of the medieval period, the

curved edge of battle axes began to change back to a sturdier and
more straight-edged type of design. By the end of the medieval
period (roughly 1450–1520 CE), most of the battle axes still in use had
narrower shafts. On the side opposite of the chopping edge, additional hammerheads (handy for smacking an armored opponent
upside the helm) or armor-piercing picks (useful for slamming
through a chest plate) were added in response to advancements in
plate armor.

The increased usage of plate armor had begun to make swords
less and less effective in battle. In fact, when two knights fought with
broadswords, they would not attempt to cut or stab each other if
both were protected by plate armor. Instead, the general tactic was
to "buffet" (a Middle English term meaning "to hit") one's opponent
upside the helm or helmet with the flat of one's blade. While this was
an effective method for causing concussions, it could also cause a
knight's sword blade to eventually snap. As a result, many began to
carry secondary weapons into battle that were better suited than
swords to the task of battering armored opponents. These instruments were often hung from their horses' saddles and used as backup
weapons, if and when their swords finally broke. In addition to battle
axes, these secondary weapons also included such items as war hammers, morning stars, flails, and maces—the other weapons we'll be
discussing in this section.

War hammers could be employed on the battlefield in much the
same way as battle axes. Instead of cleaving, however, these were
weapons intended to cause blunt-force trauma against an armored
knight (or just a human head in general). A solid strike with an iron- or
steel-headed war hammer could dent, or even cave in, the standard
helm or helmet worn by a knight. The heads of these weapons were
often rather large, usually averaging three inches long by two inches
wide and deep. The face of the hammerhead was often toothed in

order to improve its armor piercing ability. Handles for these weapons were usually between two and two-and-a-half feet long, constructed from steel or wood (or a combination of both), and the bottom halves were commonly wrapped with some form of cording to improve grip. The war hammer was an improvement over its predecessors, which were far more crude and intimidating blunt instruments—the mace and the morning star.

In the early days of the Stone Age, of course, clubs were likely one of the first weapons ever invented by humans. A clubbed piece of wood, needless to say, is an effective tool for caving in another man's skull. Even the ancient Egyptians appear to have been fond of clubs made from wood or stone. To be honest, whether made from wood, stone, bronze, or iron, the design of such weapons hasn't changed much over the years—a handle of varying size with a heavy blunt weight at the end. By the Medieval Period, however, iron had given rise to a far sturdier (and even more intimidating) form of this weapon—the mace. The type of weapon now referred to as a "mace" is believed to have been a weapon of warriors as far back as 800 BCE. Among the knights of Europe, however, this weapon likely came into use between 1230 and 1350 CE. It also ceased to be made of wood or stone, even the handles, instead coming to be a whole piece of iron or steel.

By the mid to late fifteenth century, maces had evolved into clubbed weapons made entirely of metal. During this period, they also became far more ornate and shapely in appearance. Between 1440 and 1510 CE, many agree, the art of mace making reached its height. During these years, the mace became a small weapon (often between one and two feet in total length) forged entirely of metal (after 1450 CE), with an intimidating-looking flanged head. In contrast to the more round-headed or flat-edged maces of the past, these new maces had heavily pointed flanges on their heads. While these were highly effective for piercing armor, they had a serious flaw. When the flanges punched through an opponent's armor, they often got stuck. This required the user to either abandon the weapon completely or waste time trying to pry it loose. With warriors finding functionality preferable to intimidation, this flaw led to the weapon being changed yet again by the sixteenth century.

By 1500 CE, the armor piercing flanges of maces were gone and replaced by smoother-headed designs. These non-flanged heads were still ornate in design, though. And they were both bigger and heavier. Some maces still had flanges, but they were far smaller and less likely to get stuck in an opponent's armor. While the mace was indeed a frightening weapon on the medieval battlefield, few instruments of death were capable of striking fear into the hearts of warriors like its close relative—the morning star.

The morning star, to be honest, is not all that different from a mace when it comes to usage—hit a guy in the head with one, armored or not, and he'll go down. The main difference between the two, by the medieval period, had to do with how they were constructed. While maces after 1450 CE were solid pieces of metal, morning stars had wooden handles mounted with iron or steel spiked heads. This made them more readily replaceable weapons, since a broken handle of wood was far easier to repair than a snapped piece of metal. This design also allowed for modification. And it seems many chose to get creative. For example, a morning star could be given a flail configuration . . . allowing its spike head to be attached to a chain. This is the form of the morning star that is seen in *Grimm*, a wooden handle with a chained/flail head at the end.

The flail, in medieval Germany, was not an unfamiliar sight. A weapon known as the *kreigsflegel* (war flail) had been around for centuries by then. It was as simple in design as it was lethal in use—a long shaft of wood with a piece of iron or wood (or a combination) attached to the end by a short chain. The wielder needed but to swing the "business end" at an armored opponent to do damage. The striking end, honestly, could be just about anything—a spiked iron ball, an iron bar (or multiple iron bars), a spiked iron bar, or even a heavy piece of wood reinforced with iron (sometimes with spikes on it). Needless to say, such weapons made their wielders fearsome opponents to face . . . even for armored nobles and knights.

While we have spent this chapter discussing the weapons that a Grimm uses to take down rogue Wesen, we haven't said much about the Wesen themselves. Well, that's about to change, dear reader. The following chapters in this book are meant to familiarize you with the fairy- and folktales on which *Grimm* has been based . . . and, by doing so, educate you in the study of Wesenology.

[3]

RED HOODIES AND CROSS-DRESSING BLUTBADEN

NICK BURKHARDT: *Don't you need silver bullets?*
MONROE: *What are you, an idiot?*

—"Pilot" (1-01)

Just about anyone who was told a fairy tale or bedtime story as a child is familiar with the iconic figure of the Big Bad Wolf—bane of both girls in red headwear and pigs alike. So it should not be much of a surprise that the writers of *Grimm* chose the story of Little Red Riding Hood as the basis for the show's pilot episode.

While most of us know this tale by the common title "Little Red Riding Hood," the Brothers Grimm actually called it "Little Red-Cap." Some alternative versions of the story bear the title "Red Riding Hood" (sans the "little"). You may be wondering, why the differentiation between "hood" and "cap"? Well, it's likely because, as with many folktales, this story was first spread from one culture group to another throughout Europe via word of mouth. The earliest orally transmitted versions of these stories existed in France and Italy, where the hooded cloak (or "riding hood") was more commonly worn. In Germany, the primary region from which the Brothers Grimm compiled the main body of their stories, the cap was more common. Therefore, the young girl in the story went from having a "red riding hood" to a "red cap."

As will be the case with a number of the stories retold throughout this book, we will be sticking to the Brothers Grimm version when it comes to the original folktale. While frequently odd, sometimes laughable, and admittedly riddled with more factual holes than a block of Swiss cheese, the Brothers Grimm version of "Little Red-Cap" has stood the test of time as one of the world's most popular children's cautionary tales. As explained in the introduction, what follows is only a *retelling* of the original Brothers Grimm story. For the original version, see the suggestions in the Further Reading section of the Bibliography.

Little Red-Cap: A Retelling

HANK GRIFFIN: *What do we know?*
SERGEANT WU: *Little girl on her way to her grandfather's house and never showed up.*

—"Pilot" (1-01)

Once upon a time (so far, so good, right?), there was a pretty young girl who was the apple of just about every eye that looked upon her. Of all those who adored the girl, none loved her as much as her grandmother. And the little girl loved her grandmother dearly. At one time, the grandmother had given the girl a special gift—a red velvet cap. As kids tend to do when they are fond of something, the little girl almost never took the thing off

Tasty Morsels

In wine, there is truth. In beer, there is strength. In water, there is bacteria.   —*Old German Proverb*

her head. For this reason, people took to calling the girl Little Red-Cap, as she was never seen without her head adorned by her beloved piece of crimson headwear.

One day, Little Red-Cap's mother came to her and said, "Come take this basket, which has a piece of cake and a bottle of wine in it. Take them to your grandmother, since she has grown ill and weak these days." (Because, you know . . . cake and wine can make just about anyone feel better.) "These will strengthen her."

"Yes, Mother," replied Little Red-Cap.

"You should leave early in the morning," her mother continued, "before it gets too hot outside. When you travel, walk calmly and stick to the path. Otherwise, you might stumble or drop the basket. You could break the bottle, and then you'll have no wine for your grandmother.

"And when you arrive at her cottage, be polite. Don't forget to say 'good morning' as you enter, and don't go running about the place and nosing through her things."

"Yes, Mother," replied Little Red-Cap. "I will do as you say and take care to stay on the path."

Now you see, Little Red-Cap's grandmother didn't live in the village for some reason. Instead, she lived in a small cottage deep in the woods ("half a league from the village," according to the original text—a league being the distance an average person can usually walk in an hour, or about two to three miles). There could

Tasty Morsels

After the spread of Christianity throughout Europe, many of the pre-Christian religious practices were deemed to be "witchcraft" or "devil worship" by the church. Since older people tended to follow the old traditions more than younger folks, they were sometimes branded as witches and forced to live away from the village proper.

be any number of reasons for grandmother not living in the village—insanity, people fearing that she might be a "witch" (seriously . . . it happened a lot back then), or maybe she just smelled bad or had especially offensive flatulence. The original story doesn't really give any specifics.

The next morning, Little Red-Cap hit the path into the woods. Just as she lost sight of the village, a wolf (or, in *Grimm* terms, a Blutbad) met her on the trail. Apparently, Little Red-Cap had never encountered one before and so was totally ignorant to the danger he posed. She had no knowledge of the wickedness of which such a creature was capable. As a result, she exhibited no fear and, oddly enough, struck up a conversation with him.

"Good day, Red-Cap," said the wolf.

"Holy crap, a talking wolf! And it knows my name!" replied Red-Cap.

[Okay, not really . . . I made that part up.]

"Thank you, Mr. Wolf," is what she really said, which is even weirder, in some respects.

"Where are you off to so early in the morning?" asked the wolf.

GRIMM WORDS

Blutbad (*Blutbaden*, pl.): This term doesn't actually mean "wolf." It is literally translated as "bloodbath" in English, meaning violence or slaughter. In the context of its *Grimm* usage, it refers to the murderous tendencies of the creature to which the label is given.

"I'm off to visit my grandmother."

"What's that you're carrying with you?"

"Cake and wine. Yesterday was my mother's baking day"—because, apparently, that was a real thing back then: baking day—"so I am taking cake and wine to my poor sick grandmother, to make her stronger."

"And where does your grandmother live?" asked the wolf.

"Oh, she lives at least another quarter of a league down the path. It's the small cottage that sits under the three large oak trees, with some nut trees sitting just below it. Since you live in the woods, you must surely know of it."

It seems that Little Red-Cap wasn't familiar with the whole "stranger danger" concept. She did just about everything but draw the guy a map. Though a pretty and kindhearted girl, one might say Little Red-Cap wasn't the sharpest crayon in the box.

The wheels were turning in the wolf's head all this time. After meeting the naïve Little Red-Cap, he started thinking to himself: *This girl is young and plump! She'll make a far tastier meal than her grandmother, the withered old bag of bones I've been planning to eat. If I play this right, I'll be able to fill my belly with the both of them!*

The wolf and Little Red-Cap kept walking down the path together for a time—him still scheming, her still clueless. Then,

Tasty Morsels

In the original Brothers Grimm version of this story, Little Red-Cap actually carries the cake and wine in her apron. This is a deviation from the basket with which most are familiar in this story. We've stuck to the basket in this retelling, for the sake of familiarity (and because, honestly, it's a lot harder to visualize her carrying all that stuff in her apron).

the wolf finally seized the opportunity to speak up and enact his deceitful plan.

"Red-Cap, you work too hard," he said. "Do you not even see how pretty the flowers are that line the path? Why not take some time to stop and smell the flowers? On top of that, do you not hear the sweet songs of the birds? You trudge along this path like a sad child forced to walk to school. And yet, all around you the woods are merry and bright!"

Red-Cap, of course, heeded the wolf's ill-given advice. She took a look around her and, like a poster child for Attention Deficit Disorder, was immediately distracted—the sweet smell of the flowers and the beautiful serenade of the songbirds was just more temptation than she could ignore. *Well*, she thought to herself, *it would be nice to bring Grandmother a fresh nosegay. That would make her happy too. I left home plenty early this morning, so it's not like I'm going to be late.*

So there went Little Red-Cap, running off the path and into the woods—doing exactly as her mother told her not to do. As soon as she put together one bouquet of flowers, she saw others that seemed even better and started the process all over again. Before long, she was deep in the woods, her arms full of flowers,

GRIMM WORDS

Nosegay: The term comes from Middle English (the vernacular of English spoken during much of the Middle Ages, between the late twelfth and late fifteenth centuries). It is a combination of the root words "nose" (nose) and "gay" (happy/joyous), and more or less means "happy nose" or something that makes a person's nose happy. The term specifically refers to a small bouquet of sweet-smelling flowers, such as those still used today in wedding ceremonies (though, originally, a wedding nosegay was used to mask the bride's body odor—because most people only bathed once or twice a year back then . . . which is gross).

and so far off the path that her mother likely would've slapped her if she were present.

Unfortunately, Red-Cap's mother *wasn't* present . . . and things were about to go from bad to worse.

While Little Red-Cap was distracted by her ADD-fueled bout of flower-laden insanity, the wolf was making a beeline for poor old Grandmother's house. He arrived and knocked on the door (which must've been difficult, considering how small and soft wolf knuckles are).

"Who is there?" called Grandmother from her bed.

"It's Little Red-Cap," replied the wolf, in his best girly voice. "I've brought you cake and wine. Let me in."

"All you have to do is lift the latch. The door isn't barred," explained the grandmother. "I'm too weak to come open it myself."

The wolf lifted the latch and stepped across the threshold. Silently, he stalked into the grandmother's bedroom and swallowed her whole (which must've been hell on his digestion . . .

what good are all those teeth if he isn't even going to chew his food?). The wolf then participated in a little gender-bending, dressing up in the grandmother's clothes. He lay down in her bed and waited for the arrival of Little Red-Cap.

Meanwhile, Little Red-Cap was finishing up with her flower gathering. In fact, she gathered so many flowers that she couldn't physically carry any more. Luckily, this somehow helped her remember that her poor old grandmother was still waiting for her. So she returned to the path and continued on her way to Grandmother's cottage. However, when she finally arrived, she found it odd that the door to the cottage was wide open. For once, her instincts told her something wasn't right.

"Oh, dear," she said to herself. "I feel so unnerved. Usually, I feel at peace when I visit Grandmother."

Just to be safe, she called out to her grandmother from outside the door.

"Good morning!" she called, just as her mother had instructed.

But there was no reply. So what did Little Red-Cap do? She completely ignored her instincts and went inside the house anyway. Upon entering, she headed immediately for the bedroom, remembering her mother's instruction not to snoop about the place (*now* she decides to listen to her mother!). She saw what appeared to be her grandmother, bed cap pulled low over her face, in the bed.

In the first intelligent move she'd made thus far, Little Red-Cap realized strange things were afoot in Grandmother's house. She stayed just out of reach and observed the situation.

"Oh, Grandmother," she said. "What big ears you have!"

"The better to hear you with, my dear," the wolf replied in his best old-lady voice.

"But, Grandmother! What big eyes you have!"

"The better to see you with!"

"Oh! But, dear Grandmother! What a terribly big mouth you have!"

(She just *had* to say it, didn't she?)

"The better to *eat* you with!"

And with a sudden leap forward, the wolf lunged from the bed and swallowed Little Red-Cap whole (again, no chewing for this bad boy).

His belly now filled to bursting with the entire bodies of both an old lady and a little girl, the wolf decided this was a good opportunity for a little naptime. He went back to bed and drifted off to sleep. Luckily for these two ladies, the wolf was a snorer.

It's at this point that we learn of a huntsman who lives in the woods. His name? The huntsman. That's it. Poor guy is the hero of the story, and he doesn't even get a name. He's just "the huntsman." How messed up is that?

The huntsman passed by the cabin and heard the wolf's crazy loud snoring.

"Wow! How that old woman snores! I should visit her and see if she is in need of anything," said the huntsman.

Finding the door open, the huntsman just let himself in. He approached the bedroom and found the slumbering wolf, snoring away with his swollen belly. Now you see, the huntsman had long been trying to kill the wolf—both for its valuable wolfskin and to rid the area of a violent nuisance.

"I've found you, you old sinner," the huntsman whispered as he began to shoulder his musket and take aim on his target. However, just as he was about to pull the trigger, it occurred to him the wolf may have eaten the old woman. So he grabbed up a pair of scissors and started cutting open the wolf's stomach! And what did the wolf do? Nothing! He just kept on sleeping. The huntsman made two snips and was able to see the crimson of Red-Cap's favorite piece of headwear. He made two more snips, and the girl came bursting out like a newborn baby.

"I was so scared," Little Red-Cap cried. "It was really *dark* in there!"

The huntsman did a little more snipping and out came Red-Cap's grandmother. She was alive but barely breathing. Too bad CPR had yet to be invented. But she was a tough old bird. It wasn't anything a little cake and wine couldn't remedy.

The huntsman sent Little Red-Cap off to bring him as many heavy stones as she could find. He shoved the stones into the wolf's belly, once again not disturbing the wolf's slumber, in place of Red-Cap and her grandmother. Then the huntsman stitched everything back up.

And *now* the wolf decided to wake up!

The wolf, upon seeing the huntsman, tried to bail from there like a bat out of hell. Unfortunately for him, his belly was full of heavy stones that weighed him down and impeded his escape. In fact, the stones were so heavy they caused the wolf to collapse on the floor of the cottage—dead as a doornail.

Little Red-Cap then solemnly vowed, "I'll never again stray from the path and run into the woods against my mother's orders." At this point, everybody celebrated. They were alive, and the wolf was dead. Red-Cap and her beloved grandmother were reunited. The huntsman got the prize of the wolf's skin as well as the satisfaction of knowing he'd done his good deed for the day. So, all's well that ends well . . . right?

Not just yet.

Wait for it . . .

This wasn't the last time Little Red-Cap had a run-in with a Blutbad. Not long after the aforementioned incident, Red-Cap's grandmother again grew ill and weak. Thank goodness for cake and wine. Red-Cap's mother gave her another basket of these life-saving items before sending her yet again to face the perils of the path in the woods. Since things went so well the last time.

Once again, brave Little Red-Cap started her way down the path. Like before, she was met by a (different) wolf. However, she was a bit more wary this time. She stuck to the path and ignored the wolf's deceptive words. Like an upper-class couple confronted by a homeless guy at night, she just avoided eye contact and kept on walking.

When Red-Cap arrived at her grandmother's cottage, she told the old woman what happened.

"Well, shut the front door," Grandmother told her. "That will keep him out."

Shortly thereafter, they heard a knock at the door.

"Who's there?" the grandmother called out.

"Open the door," replied the wolf. "It's Little Red-Cap. I've come to bring you cake and wine."

However, Red-Cap's and Grandmother's bellies were assumedly already full of cake and their heads full of wine. They knew the true nature of the wolf's trickery and did not reply. The wolf circled the house—once, twice, three times he circled. Realizing they'd seen through his deception, he went up on the roof and planned to pounce on Little Red-Cap when she left to return home. But Grandmother was a crafty old hag and was able to predict what the wolf was planning.

We only now learn that in front of the house was a large stone trough.

"Get a pail," Grandmother told Red-Cap. "I boiled sausages yesterday. Take the water from the pot and pour it outside into the trough."

So Little Red-Cap did as her grandmother said (the story doesn't really explain how Red-Cap accomplished this without exposing herself to the wolf . . . but honestly, that's one of the smaller holes in the story). Soon, the trough was filled with water that smelled of sausages. It didn't take long for the scent to waft up to the wolf. He craned his neck more and more over the edge of the roof. He eventually went just a little too far and lost his footing. The wolf slipped from the roof, fell into the stone trough full of "sausage water," and drowned in it . . . because, apparently, he was the only wolf in history that couldn't swim . . . or stand up in about a foot or two of water.

And from that day forward, Little Red-Cap lived a blessed life, and "no one ever did anything to harm her again."

The Path to Grandma's: Background of "Little Red-Cap/Riding Hood"

Blutbad? Vulgarized by your *ancestors as the Big Bad Wolf? What'd you just get the books tonight?* —Monroe, "Pilot" (1-01)

As mentioned previously, the story the Brothers Grimm called "Little Red-Cap" had already been around for quite a while. The tale is believed to have originated in France and was spread via word of mouth across Europe, possibly for centuries, before finally being written down. In the oral tradition versions of this tale, told long before it was ever written down and published, the creature that confronts the girl on the path wasn't always said to be a wolf. Some versions claimed it was an ogre or giant, while others claimed it was a man (although an evil and murderous one, possibly a rapist or cannibal of some sort). Some stories, depending on the time period, even claimed it was a werewolf (as opposed to just an ordinary anthropomorphic wolf). Also, older versions of the tale often had the wolf butchering the grandmother like an animal and leaving behind her flesh ("Granny steaks," you might call them) for the girl to find. When she arrives and sees the delicious-looking steaks, the girl cooks them up and eats them. She doesn't realize, of course, she is cannibalizing her own dear grandmother. It's also important to note that in most of these early oral versions, the girl did manage to escape. The grandmother, however, usually didn't fare as well.

While the Brothers Grimm did chronicle a German version of this folktale, it's important to note that they certainly were *not* the first ones to write down and publish the story. The credit for being the first person to publish the tale goes to Charles Perrault (you learned about him in chapter 1), who first published the story back in 1697 as part of his larger work *Histoires ou contes du temps passé, avec des moralités*.

The Brothers Grimm did not publish their "Rotkäppchen" ("Little Red-Cap") version of the tale until 1812, as part of their work *Kinder- und Hausmärchen*. While, for the most part, the two versions have the same basic storyline, there is one significant difference between them—the ending.

In Perrault's version, you see, the wolf *wins*. Both Red Riding Hood and her poor sickly grandmother are eaten by the wolf, and that's all she wrote. End of story. Game over. It wasn't until the Brothers Grimm came along that the huntsman was added to the story and came along to rescue them from the belly of the beast with a pair of scissors. It is not certain if the Brothers Grimm added this on their own, perhaps to make the story more readable for children (they are known to have done so, on more than one occasion), or if the German version of the story that the Brothers Grimm chronicled had simply been altered over the years to include the huntsman. Those who oppose the latter view often point to the fact that the Brothers Grimm ending to the story is nearly identical to the ending of another folktale—"The Wolf and the Seven Young Kids"—in which the victims are cut from the beast's stomach with a pair of scissors in the same fashion.

The Brothers Grimm version is also the only one to have Red-Cap and her grandmother face a second wolf, and it is the only one in which the two work together to kill a wolf themselves. Again, the Brothers Grimm may have added this part, or it may have been a part of the German version.

When a Blutbad Sees Red: A *Grimm* Comparison

> NICK BURKHARDT: *So . . . How many of you Blutbads are there?*
> MONROE: *First off, the plural is Blutbaden. And . . . I don't know. We don't, uh, socialize much. Bad things happen when we get into a pack. Especially when we see red.*
>
> —"Pilot" (1-01)

In the pilot episode of *Grimm*, Nick Burkhardt and other Grimms are portrayed as being something like supernatural profilers. In Nick's first face-to-face conversation with Monroe (that didn't involve him tackling the guy to the ground, of course), the Blutbad even says of the Grimm legacy: "You people started profiling us over two hundred years ago." As anyone familiar with the work of criminal profilers will tell you, they nearly always begin by studying the victims of a crime in order to identify patterns in the perpetrator's behavior. Based on this, the serial-killer-like behavior of the murderous Blutbad in the pilot episode makes more sense. In fact, victimology can even be applied to the victims seen on the episode:

All the victims are female.

All victims are young but in a wide age range (from preadolescent to young adult).

All are wearing red, and frequently hooded, clothing, which the killer takes as trophies.

They are often attacked while deviating from the path and/or allowing themselves to be distracted.

The victims (the ones viewers are allowed to see in the episode, at least) are always carrying an object of some kind (likely a reference to Riding Hood's basket or apron). And the killer always leaves this object behind, suggesting that it is of no importance to him, just as Red-Cap's cake and wine were of no interest to the wolf in the story.

Based on the above victimology, let's take a look at the two victims we see in the episode:

VICTIM #1: A college-age female wearing a red hooded sweatshirt. She is attacked when she becomes distracted by a small figurine (called a *goebel* in German) she sees on the ground. This figure is presumably placed there by the Blutbad as a lure. Lastly, she has an iPod (an object that, in a manner of speaking, "carries" music). The killer leaves this object behind but takes her red hooded sweatshirt as a trophy.

VICTIM #2: A young girl (possibly between six and eight years of age) also wearing a red hoodie. She is taken by the killer when she deviates from the route set down by her mother and takes a shortcut across a wooded park. She is carrying a small backpack. Again, the killer leaves behind the backpack but hangs up the red hoodie in his "trophy closet."

HANK GRIFFIN: *The old man's house is on the other side of the park, right?*

NICK BURKHARDT: *Right, 4753 Hildebrandt Road, directly across from here.*

HANK: *When I was a kid, I wouldn't have gone all the way around the park.*

NICK: *Well, her mother was very specific about the route.*

HANK: *Yeah, right. Kids always do what their moms tell them to do. I know I did. Come on, Nick.*

—"Pilot" (1-01)

Using the victimology associated with Blutbaden, Nick comes to the conclusion that just such a Wesen is responsible for these crimes. In *Grimm*, however, we quickly learn that simply being a Blutbad doesn't mean you go around kidnapping and/or eating little girls. When Nick first sees Monroe accidentally *woge*, or shift, into his Blutbad form as a pair of little girls pass him by, he immediately jumps to conclusions (as most people probably would), tackling the poor guy through his own front door and slamming him down onto a staircase. When he spies Monroe peeing on his fence ("marking his territory") later that evening, Nick believes his suspicions are confirmed. However, we soon learn the truth when Monroe gets a little payback by tackling Nick after jumping through his own window ("And, by the way, you're paying for that window") then inviting him inside for a beer. Some Blutbaden, he explains, have learned to control

GRIMM WORDS

Wieder (VEE-der): German term that means "again" or "to go back." This makes sense, in a way, seeing as how a reformed Blutbad would have to "go back" to their human nature and reform his or her naturally wild Blutbad urges. Some spellings show this word as *wider* (pronounced, more or less, the same way), which is a term from German that translates as "against/contrary to" or "to go against." Therefore, a wider Blutbad would be a Blutbad who has "gone against" his/her wild tendencies. While *wieder* is the commonly endorsed spelling for its use on *Grimm*, either spelling makes sense.

their wild and often violent natures. Monroe refers to this as being a *wieder* Blutbad. Through a "strict regimen of diet, drugs, and Pilates," Monroe tells Nick that he is "not that big" and "done with the bad thing."

The "creepy postman" Blutbad, on the other hand, is most definitely *not* a wieder Blutbad. As he hangs up the hoodie of his latest victim, we see at least four others hanging there already—suggesting that there are a total of five victims in all. The murderous Blutbad keeps these as trophies in the creepy "fattening up dungeon" he has in his basement. This element may have been included in the episode to explain why the killer left behind the iPod and backpack—the red items of clothing are the only trophies he desires.

In this episode, we also learn that Blutbaden are not werewolves—at least, not in the traditional sense. Killing them doesn't require any special tools such as silver bullets. However, wolfsbane is used by Monroe, Nick, and later Hank to mask their scents from the "creepy postman" Blutbad. Wolfsbane is so-called because it is poisonous to wolves. Some werewolf lore even states that wolfsbane can be used as protection against them. So perhaps this is to show there may be at least a small connection between the existence of the Blutbaden of *Grimm* and certain old legends surrounding werewolves.

Despite his strict regimen, even Monroe isn't completely immune from the wild impulses that come with being a Blutbad. He involuntarily undergoes a woge as he and Nick approach the rural cottage home of the postman Blutbad, and confesses to Nick, "I can't guarantee what'll happen if I go any closer. It's too dangerous. I might be on your side. I might be on his side. I might even go after the girl. I'm sorry, but there's nothing more I can do." And with that, Monroe does the responsible thing and removes himself from the situation.

The wisdom of Monroe's decision becomes evident when Nick has him stand guard over his sick aunt (and fellow Grimm) Marie in "Bears Will Be Bears" (1-02). This is the first time we see Monroe lose control, when he goes all Blutbad crazy on a pair of human would-be assassins. He picks one guy off the ground and slams him into the ceiling. When the other pulls a gun, Monroe actually rips the man's entire arm completely from his body. Admittedly, one could argue he had it coming. *They* attacked *him*, after all. But even Monroe admits, "Okay . . . that went a little too far."

Luckily for the kidnapped little girl in the *Grimm* pilot episode, the postman Blutbad is taking a few days to fatten her up by feeding her chicken pot pies. So Nick doesn't have to cut her out of the Blutbad's belly with a pair of scissors like the huntsman in the Brothers Grimm story. Instead of cutting her from the belly of the beast, he rescues her from the *basement* of the beast—a far less messy option. And, unlike in the Brothers Grimm story, this Blutbad gets shot to death by Nick's police partner Hank as opposed to being killed via death by belly rocks or drowned in a trough full of sausage water (which, admittedly, would've been pretty difficult for the writers and producers of *Grimm* to work into the episode in a believable way).

Now that we've seen both the original Brothers Grimm story as well as it's comparison to the *Grimm* pilot episode, let's take a look at the mythology, psychology, and history of this age-old tale.

Sometimes a Red Hood Is Just a Red Hood: Mythology and "Little Red-Cap/Riding Hood"

NICK BURKHARDT: *What's that?*

MONROE: *Wolfsbane . . . so he won't sense us.*

NICK: *You're kidding me, right?*

MONROE: *Not if you want to stay alive.*

—"Pilot" (1-01)

There exists an impressively large body of analysis when it comes to the mythological and/or psychological significance of this age-old folktale. And (as is often the case with such stories), depending on the school of thought being used, the meaning of the tale differs from one interpretation to another.

While they tend to differ in the minor details, many theorists see this story as being a metaphor for sexual maturity. The first element such scholars usually point to is the color of the girl's cap/hood/cloak—red (although, it appears the whole "red-colored headwear" thing wasn't actually a part of the earlier oral versions). Since red is the color of blood, this analysis claims the girl's red cap/hood symbolizes the blood of menstruation that marks the point where a female biologically reaches sexual maturity. Some such analyses have even claimed that Red Riding Hood's head poking out through the opening of her cloak symbolizes the phallic penetration of a virgin's hymen. This interpretation fails to take into consideration the fact that (as already mentioned) her hood/cloak wasn't red in the original oral versions, if it was present at all (sometimes, her head was bare).

Tasty Morsels

Sigmund Freud (1856–1939), known as the "father of psycho-analysis," was very much the creator of the modern school of psychology with which most are familiar these days. He developed such techniques as dream analysis and word association. Freud viewed sex (libido) as the primary human motivator. Freud's star pupil, **Carl Jung**, looked at psychology from a more spiritual/mythological based perspective. Jung acknowledged the role of sex in psychoanalysis but didn't view it as the sole primary motivator. Jung also created the term "archetype," meaning a recurring image, figure, or symbol seen in both myths and dreams. This term is still used by both mythologists and purveyors of depth psychology.

The Big Bad Wolf, according to this kind of analysis, represents the threat of rape, the temptation of adultery, or the seductive lure of premarital sex. The girl must resist the wolf in order to sexually mature within the proper social confines of her world. This view is clearly influenced by the theories of Sigmund Freud. His stuff always seems to come back to sex, in one way or another.

While some mythologists and folklorists at least partially agree with the abovementioned "sexual maturity" interpretation, their analyses of the tale often look at the story as a whole, taking into account its usage, history, and place in various cultural traditions. They also look at as many renditions of the story as possible, both the early oral versions as well as the later written ones (such as those from Perrault, the Brothers Grimm, and, later on, Andrew Lang).

Mythologists and folklorists tend to look at the cyclical and ritualistic elements of the tale. While they may indeed see it as related to sexual maturity, mythologists often feel that such sex-centered analyses are missing the larger picture. The tale isn't about just reaching sexual maturity on a biological level but passing from the innocence of girlhood to the responsibilities of womanhood. And it is from this point of view that mythologists and folklorists commonly approach the story. Some have even theorized that this story might be a metaphoric telling of an ancient, possibly prehistoric, ritual or female rite of passage.

In the prehistoric and ancient worlds, both men and women commonly participated in rites of passage that symbolically recognized their transitions from childhood to adulthood. Such rituals often involved the uninitiated person being sent out from the village or away from the main group in order to endure some form of test, trial, and/or ceremony that proved their readiness for the difficulties and responsibilities of adulthood. In fact, one's right to take a spouse sometimes depended on whether one could successfully pass such rites. Some have theorized the "Red Riding Hood" tale is based on such a tradition—the girl was forced to travel away from the safety of the village to walk a predetermined path. The first test, perhaps, was that the girl could not leave the path. As she walked, she would be tempted to come into the woods by males from her village. Her testers' identities may have even been concealed beneath guises made from wolfskins. The path would have led her to a ceremonial hut in which she'd have been greeted by her village matriarch, a female oracle, some form of priestess, or perhaps just an elder female from her immediate family. Such a ritual seems plausible and most certainly bears similarities to the "Little Red-Cap/Riding Hood" stories. However, until conclusive evidence of such a rite's existence is found, it all remains little more than an interesting theory.

The above idea seems even more plausible when one considers the fact that a group of "wolf-men" existed in the Norse Viking regions of Europe from ancient times until they were finally banned back in the early eleventh century. These "wolf-men" were actually an elite

unit of Viking warriors known as the *ulfheðnar*. As you learn more
about their role among the ancient Norse, the above theory may not
seem so far-fetched after all.

Ulfheðnar: The Warriors Who Became Wolves

MONROE: *I'm a reformed Blutbad . . . a wieder Blutbad. It's a different*
    church altogether.

NICK BURKHARDT: *But . . . you guys go to church?*

MONROE: *Sure . . . don't you?*

—"Pilot" (1-01)

Among the warrior tribes of the Norse Vikings, the ulfheðnar (pronounced ulf-heth-nar) were considered some of the more highly valued shock troops any chieftain could hope to have in his employ. The
ulfheðnar, or "wolf wearers," were one of the most feared elite fighting units of the Norse Vikings, along with their more well-known
"bear-warrior" counterparts the berserkers (for more, see chapter 4).
Whenever a chieftain needed a surefire way to strike fear into the
hearts of his enemies, he sought out and hired ulfheðnar.

While during their later years the ulfheðnar became warriors for
hire, it is believed that they were originally a type of priesthood that
oversaw certain ancient religious rites related to wolves. Wolves were
a sacred animal related to the very popular Norse deity Odin, god of
mead, poetry, death, battle, wisdom, and a very long list of other
things. Unlike the berserkers, who were thought of as men who
behaved as bears, ulfheðnar were men who *became* wolves. Members
of the ulfheðnar darkened their fair Icelandic skin with black dye
and covered their bodies in wolfskins. This made them appear more
like beasts than men to those who met them on the battlefield.

Before a battle, ulfheðnar would carry out ritualistic dances and chants in order to work themselves into a state of homicidal frenzy. By the time their preparatory rituals were concluded, it's said they were no longer men—their human natures completely replaced by the madness of the wolf trance. Norse chieftains and warriors alike appear to have truly believed that, after these rituals, the ulfheðnar became nearly unkillable in battle.

The Norse Vikings were big fans of amphibious assaults, often attacking from the sea in groupings of small ships. As a Norse conquest party approached the shore, ulfheðnar were placed in the most forward ships and were the first to hit land. They'd stand near the prows of their ships as they came near, howling and snarling. They wore no armor. They carried no shields. They wielded only basic weaponry such as daggers, short swords, and battle axes. And, to a unit tasked with holding the shoreline against the landing forces, they must have been absolutely terrifying to behold. The psychotic trance the ulfheðnar entered was so deep and powerful that they ignored almost any injury—even the loss of a limb didn't seem enough to stop an ulfheðnar.

According to the old legends surrounding ulfheðnar, they could not be brought down with arrows, swords could not kill them, and they would advance right through a fire attack. In fact, the Norse claimed the only way to put down an ulfheðnar once and for all was to bash in his skull with a club. However, this probably wasn't considered very comforting. A club is a close-range weapon, after all. This meant that, if one was going to crush the head of an ulfheðnar, one had to go toe-to-toe with him in close-quarters combat. Needless to say, standing your ground against the advance of a maniacal psychopath required a level of bravery that goes beyond that of an ordinary person.

Of course, there were times when these encounters didn't even require battle. Sometimes, just the sight of an approaching ulfheðnar landing party was enough to so utterly demoralize the defenders that they abandoned their posts and ran for their lives without even putting up a fight.

In the nineteenth century, however, when the Brothers Grimm were compiling their tales, it's unlikely that many people would have been thinking of the ulfheðnar. Peter Stubbe, on the other hand . . . he was a wolf-man for the times, as you'll see in the next section.

Peter and His Stumps: Scapegoat or Blutbad?

Look, I don't want any more trouble. I'm not that kind of Blutbad.
—Monroe, "Pilot" (1-01)

The story of Peter Stubbe (his first name is sometimes spelled Peeter, and his last name has a bunch of alternate spellings—Stub, Stumpf, Stumpp, or Stump) is one of the more well-known among the many cases of "werewolf trials" held over a period between the early fourteenth and late eighteenth centuries. This particular event took place in 1589 somewhere near the village of Bedburg just outside of Cologne, Germany, and involved the "trial" of a farmer named Peter Stubbe. The only surviving documentation of the incident comes from a pamphlet that was published in England on June 11, 1590, by one George Bores, who claims that he did "both see and hear" the events recorded in his account. There appears to have been, at some point, supporting documentation for this pamphlet. However, most if not all of it was destroyed sometime between 1618 and 1648, during the Thirty Years' War.

Since Bore's pamphlet is the only surviving *official* record, much of what he wrote cannot be verified. First and foremost, there's nothing to confirm the details of how Peter Stubbe came to be in the custody of local authorities. According to Bore's account, a werewolf (or just a very large wolf) had been seen around the village. Normally, this wouldn't be such an odd sight. However, this particular wolf appeared to be wearing a belt or girdle around its midsection. Just how the evil nature of this belt-wearing monster was uncovered is not really explained, aside from the fact that some people saw a wolf with a belt on.

Some of the village men claimed that they chased the wolf down, surrounded the creature, and ripped off the belt. Suddenly, according to these men, the beast transformed into the man they all knew as Peter Stubbe. They dragged the accused man before the local court, where he is recorded as having confessed to a horrifying list of assorted atrocities.

The nature of his confession is never explained in any detail. Did he confess under threat of torture? Did he confess *because* he was tortured? Or did he first confess and *then* was tortured? We may never know. But one thing seems pretty certain—he *was* tortured. Man, was this poor guy tortured. And, in the end, he confessed to just about everything but kidnapping the Lindbergh baby (probably because that hadn't happened yet).

When all was said and done, Stubbe confessed before the court that he had murdered fourteen local children, two pregnant women (along with their unborn babies), and an undisclosed number of assorted livestock. He also confessed to a sexual relationship with his own teenage daughter and, as a result, a charge of incest was added to the list of his crimes. From here, his confessions start getting even weirder. He claimed to have eaten the unborn children of his pregnant murder victims and admitted to keeping a succubus demon as a familiar and sexual partner (thus adding devil worship to his charges). He also admitted to adultery, which is probably the only crime of which he was actually guilty. Stubbe is confirmed as having kept a mistress, who was the mother of his teenage daughter.

GRIMM WORDS

Succubus (*succubi* or *succubae*, pl.): A female demon that usually spends its time seducing men. The concept likely came from the Lilith figure of Judaic folklore. In Jewish lore, men are told not to sleep alone, to avoid being seduced by Lilith.

Is it plausible that Peter Stubbe was a demented serial killer? Sure. Could it be possible that the local authorities used him as a scapegoat so they had someone to prosecute for a bunch of unsolved crimes? Yes, it could be. But Peter Stubbe confessed, plain and simple, and for that his fate was sealed. He was convicted of sixteen murders, two counts of cannibalism and infanticide, as well as adultery, incest, rape, killing livestock, devil worship, and (let's not forget the original charge) running about town in the form of a belt-wearing wolf. If Peter Stubbe was, in fact, guilty of all these horrendous acts, his punishment certainly fit his crime.

First, Stubbe was stripped down to his drawers and tied down to a large wooden wagon wheel. Next, a big pair of iron pincers was placed in a fire until the metal glowed red-hot. The searing pincers were then used to tear the flesh from his body in ten different places. And the pain didn't stop there. After this, they took a heavy wooden axe or hammer (or just the blunt side of a normal axe) to every major bone in his body—one by excruciating one—until none of his long bones remained unbroken. Only after this was he given the sweet release of death, which came in the form of being beheaded. After they chopped off his head, they tossed what was left of Peter Stubbe into a fire.

You'd think that would've been the end of it . . . wouldn't you?

It wasn't.

Their thirst for retribution not yet satiated, the court brought to trial Stubbe's teenage daughter and his mistress. They were charged as accessories in the crimes to which Stubbe had already confessed, and since his confession was already on record, the two women were immediately deemed guilty and sentenced to death. They were either strangled and then thrown into the fire like Peter Stubbe or burned at the stake. Take your pick. Neither end was pretty.

What about that belt? After all, isn't that what got the craziness ball rolling? In his confession, Stubbe claimed that he'd received the magical item when he'd made a deal with the devil. However, all attempts to locate the thing by the local authorities met with failure, which is odd since his captors claimed to have ripped the belt from Stubbe's wolf form with their own hands. And what was the official explanation for the missing belt?

The devil took it back.

Clinical Lycanthropy: Mentally Ill or Real-World Blutbaden?

> NICK BURKHARDT: *Can you really smell him?*
> MONROE: *Dude . . . You have no idea.*
>
> —"Pilot" (1-01)

If Monroe were ever to go see a therapist, he'd probably be diagnosed with a condition called clinical lycanthropy—unless, of course, the therapist was Wesen. Then again, if he decided to woge it probably wouldn't matter whether the therapist was Wesen or human. In either case, he or she would likely need a new set of undies.

Unlike many documented mental disorders, clinical lycanthropy is still kind of new—it's only been known of for well under a century, in fact. While a number of cases have been closely documented over the last few decades, not a lot is known about exactly why this condition occurs. This is mainly due to the fact that clinical lycanthropy is a *symptomatic* disorder, meaning that it is usually a symptom of some other underlying form of mental illness or brain defect. It's defined, more or less, as a condition in which the sufferers exhibit wolf-like behaviors and/or believe they are under the control of some secondary wolf presence (usually manifesting in the belief that they are possessed by a demon). Sufferers may even believe they are werewolves. The symptomatic condition of clinical lycanthropy has been linked to a number of different main causes—schizophrenia, long-term psychedelic drug use, an unidentified brain defect, or post-traumatic stress disorder.

The most common behaviors and delusions associated with clinical lycanthropy read like a Blutbad's version of a fun night out:

Socially inappropriate displays of nudity

An overwhelming urge to be in the woods (sounds like the night Monroe went into the woods with Angelina, doesn't it?)

Sleeping in graveyards

Mimicking the sexual postures of wolves or other animalistic behaviors, especially in public surroundings (where butt sniffing is usually *not* appreciated)

Belief one is not in control of one's own actions or is under the control of some secondary force (they should try a strict regimen of diet, drugs, and Pilates . . . seems to work for Monroe)

Preoccupation with eyes or belief in the "evil eye" (Blutbaden do have red eyes, though they don't seem to be preoccupied by this)

While normally those who suffer from clinical lycanthropy are relatively harmless, in some serious cases the condition has been

[4]

BEARS, BLONDES, AND BUTCHERY

NICK BURKHARDT: *What do you know about Jägerbars?*
MONROE: *What am I, your personal Grimm-opedia?*
NICK: *No, you're a Blutbad. And I'm assuming Blutbaden know about Jägerbaden?*
MONROE: *It's just Jägerbars.*

—"Bears Will Be Bears" (1-02)

When a young woman comes into the station to report that her boyfriend went missing after the two broke into an empty house, Nick Burkhardt's investigation leads him to encounter a well-to-do family of Jägerbars (bear-type Wesen) during the episode "Bears Will Be Bears" (1-02). When she then goes missing after saying she was going back to the same house, the rookie Grimm finds himself in a race against time to keep the teens of the family from ripping the couple to shreds in an ancient and savage Jägerbar rite of passage known as *Roh-Hatz*.

In truth, a family of angry Jägerbars who wish to observe a violent old tradition by chasing a couple of delinquent adult lovers through the woods might not seem to have much in common with the usual

GRIMM WORDS

Jägerbar: German for "hunter bear." In *Grimm*, this refers to a bear-type Wesen.

Roh-Hatz: German for "raw hunt" or "barbarous hunt," depending on interpretation. In *Grimm*, this refers to an old rite of passage once performed by male Jägerbars in which they would hunt down humans. However, this tradition is rarely observed by the majority of modern Jägerbars.

"Goldilocks and the Three Bears" story with which most people are familiar. However, it does bear a number of similarities to the original written version of the tale that was penned by British author and poet Robert Southey. So as to display these similarities, the retelling of this chapter is based on Southey's original version—"The Story of the Three Bears." Before we talk about the background or get into the episode comparison, let's get familiar with Southey's version.

The Story of the Three Bears: A Retelling

Mr. and Mrs. Rabe got back from Seattle a couple hours ago. Found their house broken into. Somebody raided the fridge, hit the liquor cabinet, tried on some clothes, and test-drove a couple of beds.
—Sergeant Wu, "Bears Will Be Bears" (1-02)

Once upon a time, there were three bears (and none of them were related in the original version). They lived together happily in a house deep in the woods and never tried to do harm to anyone.

GRIMM WORDS

Porridge: A soft dish made by boiling oatmeal, or any other kind of meal (such as cornmeal), in water or milk (or a mix of both) until it thickens. The root of this term likely comes from the word "pottage," which in turn came from the word "porray," meaning "soup." The original term "porray" (with varying spellings) can be found in Middle English, Old French, and Latin.

Theirs was a peaceful existence, as bears go—their motto was "Don't start none, won't be none."

One of the bears was Great, Huge Bear; the second was Middle-Sized Bear; and the third was Little, Small, Wee Bear. In their home, they each had a porridge bowl appropriate to their size—a big bowl for the Great, Huge Bear (who, for the sake of brevity, will be referred to from now on as Huge Bear); a middle-sized bowl for Middle-Sized Bear (henceforth referred to as Middle Bear); and a tiny bowl for Little, Small, Wee Bear (but from now on let's just refer to him as Wee Bear, because that original name just has way too many unnecessary synonyms in it). They also had three chairs, each fitted to their sizes—huge, middle, and wee.

One day, the bears decided to make a big kettle of porridge. Once it'd been boiled long enough, they poured out portions into their appropriately sized bowls. Realizing the porridge was still too hot to eat, and not wanting to burn their mouths, the furry trio decided to go for a walk in the woods. A brisk walk is good for building the appetite, most would agree.

While the three bears were out for their stroll in the woods, a little old woman happened across their house. And this woman was most definitely a shady character. She peeped through the windows of the house and, finding the place empty, let herself in through the unlocked door. As mentioned before, these were nice bears. They never barred their doors because it never occurred to them that someone might try to do them harm. On the other hand, one could argue they just never suspected anyone would be dumb enough to come uninvited into a house occupied by *bears*!

When the nasty old woman saw the bowls full of steaming porridge, she was delighted. If she had been a *nice* old lady, she'd have waited for the three bears to return, and they could've *invited* her to join them for breakfast. But instead, the thieving old woman decided to pilfer their meal.

So the woman helped herself to the bears' porridge. Being greedy as she was, she first dug into the giant bowl belonging to Huge Bear. However, it was still too hot to eat, and it burned her mouth (apparently, she was *not* smarter than your average bear). She spat it out and said a curse word about it. Leaving the spoon standing in the huge bowl, she went over to Middle Bear's bowl and had a taste, but this time she found the porridge too cold for her liking . . . so she spat it out too and said another curse word, despite the fact that her mouth didn't get burned this time. She then went to the tiny bowl of Wee Bear, which she found to be just the right temperature. She quickly gobbled it all up. And yet, she still said a curse word about it because the tiny pot didn't hold more porridge.

The naughty, thieving old tramp then decided she'd like to have a sit down and made her way over to the sitting room, where she found three chairs of various size. First she had a seat in the big chair of Huge Bear, but she found it too hard for her wrinkly old butt. Next she tried out Middle Bear's chair . . . but it was too soft. She finally tried the tiny chair of Wee Bear, which she found just right for her oddly sensitive backside. She settled into the tiny chair for a little relaxation (stealing stuff really took it out of the old gal, apparently). Unfortunately, the chair wasn't strong enough to hold the weight of her picky derriere, and the bottom gave out. The naughty old woman fell through and hit the ground with a *thud*, emitting yet *another* curse word! What a potty mouth on this lady!

Feeling like she could do for a nap, the old woman headed upstairs to the bedroom and found the three bears' beds. First she tried out the big bed of Huge Bear . . . but the headboard end was too high for her liking. She went over to the bed of Middle Bear and gave it a test . . . but this one was too high at the foot end. She finally lay down on the tiny bed of Wee Bear. This one she found just right. She snuggled up under the covers and went directly to sleep.

Timing is everything, most of the time. The three bears soon returned home from their walk, thinking their porridge must have cooled by now.

"Someone's been eating my porridge!" said Huge Bear in his loud, gruff voice when he saw his spoon had been moved.

"Someone's been eating my porridge!" said Middle Bear in his middle voice, seeing his spoon was also now in his bowl.

"Someone's been eating my porridge!" said Wee Bear in his wee voice. "And they've eaten it all!"

Realizing someone had been in their house while they were gone, the three bears decided to go check the sitting room.

"Someone's been in my chair!" said Huge Bear in his loud, gruff voice when he saw the cushion had been disturbed.

"Someone's been in my chair!" said Middle Bear in his middle voice (all this "voice" stuff comes into play later on . . . Scout's

GRIMM WORDS

Bolster: As the term is used in this story, it refers to a long, thick, and usually cylindrical style of pillow that is put under the normal head pillow in order to provide neck support. This is where we get the alternate usage of "bolster," meaning "to support/ strengthen" or "to prop up."

honor), seeing the impression of someone else's butt still in the cushion.

"Someone's been in my chair too!" said Wee Bear in his wee voice when he saw the bottom of the chair had fallen out. "And they broke it!"

Their suspicions now confirmed, the three bears decided it best to search the entire house. So they went upstairs and checked the bedroom.

"Someone's been sleeping in my bed!" said Huge Bear in his loud, gruff voice when he saw the pillow out of place.

"Someone's been sleeping in my bed!" said Middle Bear in his middle voice, seeing that the bolster had been disturbed.

Now Wee Bear decided to inspect his own bolster and pillow . . . both were in their proper places. But there was something else there that most definitely was *not* in its proper place— the mean, vulgar, thieving old woman's head!

"Someone's been sleeping in my bed too!" said Wee Bear in his wee voice. "And she's still there!"

While the three bears were speaking, the old woman had been sleeping soundly. When she heard the loud, gruff voice of Huge Bear, she did not wake up since it resembled the rumble of thunder or the roar of the wind. When she heard the middle

Tasty Morsels

The word "window" comes from the Old Norse word *vindauga*, which roughly means "wind-eye." This term entered the English language during the Viking Age. In the days before air-conditioning and electricity, people opened their bedroom windows each morning in order to let light and air come in. Failing to do so would cause a bedroom to reek after a while, especially in a time (such as the Viking Age) when the majority of people only bathed a few times a year.

voice of Middle Bear, she heard it as one hears a voice in a dream. However, when she heard the high-pitched, shrill, wee voice of Wee Bear, it woke her right up since it resembled nothing that occurs in nature.

She saw the three bears and, realizing she'd most definitely made a poor life decision by trespassing in that house, the old woman jumped from the bed and flung herself out the open second-floor window. She fell straight to the ground like Aquaman on a tequila bender.

As for what became of the old woman, no one knows for sure—maybe she broke her neck from her swan dive out the window, maybe she was lost in the woods, or perhaps a local constable took her into custody and put her in a house of corrections where someone like her belongs. Regardless of what befell the old woman who intruded on their home, the three bears saw neither hide nor hair of her ever again. And they all lived happily ever after . . . expect for the delinquent old woman, of course.

Jägerbars and Those Who Anger Them: A *Grimm* Comparison

NICK BURKHARDT: *I know about the hunt.*

FRANK RABE: *What are you talking about?*

NICK: *The Roh-Hatz.*

FRANK: *Nobody does that anymore.*

NICK: *Yes, they do. And when the sun goes down tonight, it's gonna be too late.*

—"Bears Will Be Bears" (1-02)

As you've likely already figured out, Southey's story is a bit different from the "Goldilocks" versions of the tale. The most notable difference, of course, is the portrayal of the character who intrudes into the bears' home. While Goldilocks may selfishly help herself to food and a house that are not hers, she isn't necessarily a *dislikable* character. She's just a foolish little girl, after all. However, Southey's character has no such excuse. She's a mature adult who should know better than to enter a house that is not hers and do as she wishes. And this attribute rings true of the couple that breaks into the house of the Jägerbars in the "Bears Will Be Bears" episode of *Grimm*.

The man and woman in *Grimm* choose to break into a house that isn't theirs and make themselves at home—drinking the owners' wine, eating their food, trying on their clothes, and even attempting to have sex in their bed (before they're interrupted by the owners' unexpected return)—knowing full well that what they're doing is illegal, not to mention just plain old wrong. And, like the delinquent old woman in Southey's version of the tale, the couple tries to make a break for it (out the window, you may note . . . exactly like in Southey's story) when the owners of the house come back. Unfortunately for them, these are *definitely not* the kind of "nice bears" of which Southey wrote. In fact, they are pissed off Jägerbars looking for an excuse to hunt humans. While the woman escapes the initial encounter, her beau isn't so lucky. To be honest, though, it is kind of difficult to feel sorry for either of them . . . just as it's hard to feel sympathy for the nasty old woman in Southey's story.

Not until twelve years after Southey published this tale did the trespassing figure change from an old woman to a little girl. The English writer Joseph Cundall is commonly credited with having made this change when, in 1849, he published the now popular "Goldilocks" version of the story in his collection *A Treasury of Pleasure Books for Young Children*.

While encountering an angry Jägerbar would be, one could assume, a terrifying experience, there were a group of bear warriors among the ancient Norse who were perhaps even more frightening to encounter, especially on the battlefield—berserkers.

Going Berserk: The Bear Warriors of the Norse

NICK BURKHARDT: *You ever seen one of these?*

MONROE: *Not up close, thank God. I think Jägerbars use these for disemboweling. Now I'm hungry.*

—"Bears Will Be Bears" (1-02)

Among the fierce warriors that made up the Norse tribes, there was an elite group of men who covered their bodies in the skins of bears, and the mere sight of their approach was often enough to send less-brave men running in fear—*barserkersgang* (those who act as bears). Commonly known as berserkers these days, these warriors had a reputation for acting with inhuman aggression and brutality on the battlefield. They are considered akin to a similar, wolf-natured group of warriors that you read of in Chapter 3—ulfheðnar. Like the ulf-heðnar, the barserkersgang was coveted by tribal chieftains as war-riors for hire. Over the years, it is believed that the ulfheðnar eventually merged with the berserkers, and the two groups came to be known under the same name (likely due to the fact that many chieftains began to desire the destruction of the ulfheðnar, as opposed to running the risk of having them hired by their enemies).

Unlike the ulfheðnar, who were considered men who actually *became* wolves and are believed to have originated as a kind of ancient wolf-rite priesthood, berserkers are thought to have *always* been war-riors for hire. They were very similar to ulfheðnar in terms of appear-ance, however, also dyeing their skins black (some may have even filed their teeth like fangs) and covering their heads and bodies with bear-skins. They also adopted the same kind of suicidal fighting methods as the ulfheðnar, using neither armor nor shields and carrying only rudimentary close-range melee weapons. Even before they may have merged with the ulfheðnar, there are legends of how their first-wave charges broke the morale of defenders.

Then again, if a bearskin-clad guy with dyed skin and fangs came charging at us with nothing but a short sword . . . most of us would probably run for our lives, as well.

Whereas Blutbaden and Jägerbars rely on power and strength, the Wesen of the following chapter rely on their cunning and talent . . . and a special few of them rely on their music.

[5]

DANCING TO THE PIPER'S TUNE

Death by rat?   —Nick Burkhardt, "Danse Macabre" (1-05)

In the episode "Danse Macabre" (1-05), music teacher Paul Lawson is devoured in his car . . . by rats. Luckily for him, he was already dead; he had a heart attack (apparently the sight of so many furry critters literally scared the guy to death). Earlier that evening, he'd been conducting his students in a playing of Camille Saint-Saëns's symphonic poem *Danse Macabre* (from which the episode takes its name). When Nick Burkhardt finds himself on the case, he suspects the murder was committed by a talented young violinist and Reinigen (rat-type Wesen) named Roddy Geiger (or DJ Retchid Kat, as he's known on the club scene). The boy is special, even among Reinigen, in that he has the ability to control rats with his music.

Interestingly enough, a tale of a man who could control rats (among other types of vermin) with his music—"The Pied Piper of Hamelin"—has roots in both the storytelling tradition of the Brothers Grimm and an actual historical event (which we'll discuss later in this chapter). What follows is a retelling that mixes the plot of the Brothers Grimm version from their 1816 work, *Deutsche Sagen* (German Legends), with the dates of the historical event.

The Pied Piper of Hamelin: A Retelling

You want my weapon?

—Roddy Geiger, "Danse Macabre" (1-05)

Back in the year 1284 CE, in late June, a strange event occurred in the German town of Hamelin. The inhabitants of Hamelin, for the most part, were happy people who lived peacefully in sturdy houses made of gray stone. After many years of prosperity, the town had grown very wealthy. As history often points out, however, good times don't last forever. And a terrible event was about to rock the happy lives of the people of Hamelin.

Over the years, rats had become a problem in Hamelin. However, they'd never been more than a troublesome nuisance. In days past, the cats in the town had always done a fair-enough job of keeping the rats under control. The cats, however, eventually weren't enough to handle the rats' increasing numbers. As a result, the rat population swelled to such a degree that they overran the entire town.

By the time the folks in Hamelin realized what was going on, they were besieged by such a large swarm of rats that, according to the Brothers Grimm, it looked like a "black sea." Every granary and storehouse was ravaged by the rats until hardly a morsel of food was left. Once the food was gone, the rats turned to the buildings themselves and started devouring just about anything they could digest (which, for rats, is an impressively long list)—wood, furniture, clothing, cabinetry . . . you name it. The only things they didn't eat were those made from metal or stone.

Terrified by the sudden influx of swarming rodents, the townspeople quickly turned to their leaders—the mayor and town council. They demanded something be done about the rats. Of course, the mayor had by now convened the town council to a meeting. They were already banging their heads together, hoping to figure out some solution to the pestilence befalling their town.

"We need an army of cats," said one councilman. "They've always kept the rats in check before!" However, it was soon discovered that all the cats in town were already dead (apparently, rat payback is a real bitch).

"We should put down some poisoned food, then," suggested another councilman. "That might kill quite a lot of them."

Unfortunately, they soon realized that just about all of the food in the village was already gone, devoured by the rats. So they decided to just put down poison by itself, and while some of the rodents were killed this way, the others just kept on multiplying.

"This won't do," the mayor told the council. "We need to call in some professional help. Does anyone know of a ratcatcher near here?"

The people of Hamelin were growing increasingly restless outside, but the mayor and town council were out of ideas. They needed to find a ratcatcher soon. Suddenly they heard a loud knocking at the council chamber door.

"Who could that be at a time like this?" said one councilman. "Don't they know we are trying to figure out where to find a rat-catcher?"

GRIMM WORDS

Ratcatcher: An occupation in times past, especially near the end of the fourteenth century when it was eventually figured out that the bubonic plague was being spread by rats (though, technically, it was actually the fleas on the rats that were responsible). Unlike today's modern "exterminators," the original ratcatchers had far less sophisticated techniques. They would commonly capture rats by hand, or by using specially trained dogs or traps. Queen Victoria of England even employed a royal ratcatcher, a man by the name of Jack Black.

"Maybe it's a lynch mob," the mayor suggested, hearing the angry crowd outside.

As the door opened, everyone in the room likely wondered if they were about to be lynched by a mob of disgruntled townspeople wielding torches and pitchforks. Instead, they found a tall and lanky young fellow wearing brightly colored clothes. A matching hat sat upon his head, with a long feather sticking out from one side. In his hands he held a golden pipe, identifying him as a piper by trade.

"I think your town could use a man of my talents," the stranger said, holding up his golden pipe for them to see. "I've rescued many other towns from infestations such as this—beetles, bats, roaches—you name it, I can get rid of it. For a price of only a thousand florins, I can make Hamelin rat free."

"Only a *thousand* florins? We would pay you fifty thousand florins if you can really do as you claim!" the mayor promised.

"Very well," the piper agreed. "It's evening now, but come morning, there won't be a rat remaining in Hamelin."

GRIMM WORDS

Piper: Today, the term usually refers to a specific type of musician, such as a flautist or a bagpipe player. In days past, this word was often used to refer to a traveling musician in general.

Around sunset, the piper placed himself at the far end of town. He put his golden pipe to his lips and began to play. As the sweet sound of his music passed over the streets of Hamelin, he began to walk . . . starting from one end of town and moving toward the other.

Rats soon began to follow the piper. Only a few at first, but soon they began coming out of the woodwork. It was not long before the streets overflowed with rats, all of them following behind the piper as he played his enchanted tune. When he reached the opposite end of town, the piper kept on walking and headed straight for the nearby river of Weser.

Once he reached the banks of the Weser, the piper kept right on walking into the water. He did not stop until the water was up to his chest . . . and the rats followed him right into the rushing river. The entire lot was drowned, their furry little bodies carried off by the current.

By the time the sun broke over the horizon the next morning, the piper had made good on his promise. Not a single rat remained in Hamelin. His job done, the piper went straight to the mayor and town council to collect the payment he was due. They were all overjoyed when, upon a thorough inspection of the town, they found not one living rat.

Then the piper asked to be paid . . . and that's when the story takes a rather dark turn.

GRIMM WORDS

Florin: At one point, a type of British coin that was worth two shillings. At other times in the past, it was used throughout Europe to refer to foreign coinages in general (especially the Dutch guilder, a common coin of gold or silver once used in the Netherlands).

"You expect us to pay you fifty thousand florins?" one councilman said to the piper. "We would never pay such a ridiculously inflated price!"

"Okay," the Piper replied, trying to be reasonable. Fifty thousand florins was a lot of money, after all. "Just pay me the thousand florins I originally asked for, and I'll be on my way."

"We will not pay you even a thousand florins," the mayor of Hamelin told him. "The rats are all dead and gone. It's not like you can bring them back. We will pay you fifty florins and nothing more. Be grateful we are giving you even that much, or you'll get nothing at all."

As most people would be in his position, the piper was livid when the mayor and council stubbornly refused even to pay his original asking price after promising him fifty times that amount.

"You," he replied with rage in his voice, casting a finger at the mayor, "will live to regret this. We had a deal, and you have broken it. Remember that well . . . all of you, remember it. What happens next is *your* fault, not mine."

As the piper left Hamelin empty-handed, some of the councilmen began to reconsider and wondered if perhaps they'd done the wrong thing (or, at least, an *unwise* thing . . . it's pretty obvious what they did was wrong). Besides that, they began to think of what the piper said and feared what he might do in retribution.

GRIMM WORDS

Weser: Actually the name of a very real river located in north-western Germany. The Weser River begins at the union of two other rivers (Fulda and Werra) and flows into the North Sea near Bremerhaven, Germany.

"What a bargain," the mayor guffawed. They all then joined in his laughter and forgot their worries. "We've rid our town of the rats and have saved ourselves fifty thousand florins to boot! I'd call that a job well done!"

Now that Hamelin was free of the menacing rats, the towns-people all slept soundly that night (the date was June 26, 1284, according to most sources). As the adults snoozed contently in their rodent-free homes, however, their children awoke to the sweet sound of the piper's wondrous piping. Drawn to it by the same enchantment that had led the rats to their doom the night before, the children rushed from their beds to follow the Pied Piper as he walked through the streets. According to records, 130 children followed him out of Hamelin that night. They marched to the strange music of the piper, no longer dressed in the color-ful clothing of a musician but in the drab garb of a hunter.

The macabre parade marched to the outskirts of Hamelin and the piper led them on until they reached the base of a nearby mountain. Eventually, they came to an immense stone that sealed the mouth of a large cave. The piper played louder, and the stone rolled away. The children of Hamelin walked into the cave behind the piper. Once the last of them had stepped into the dark cavern, the piper walked back outside and played louder yet again. The giant stone returned to its original spot, sealing the cave shut with the children inside. Next, the piper played louder still until he caused a great landslide that fell over the stone and ensured that the cave remained sealed forever.

Only one boy in Hamelin managed to escape the piper's musical wrath. He was crippled and, therefore, unable to follow the piper, no matter how much he'd felt compelled to do so. It was this boy who explained to the people of Hamelin, to the grieving mothers and fathers who awoke to find their little ones missing, what had happened to their children as the adults all slept soundly in their beds.

In a panic, the townspeople went to the mountain in the hopes their children might still be saved. But it was all in vain. No matter what they tried, the cave remained sealed. An entire generation of children was lost to the people of Hamelin. To this very day, as legend tells it, they all remain entombed within the mountain.

Quite a few years would pass before the sounds of children at play were heard again in the streets of Hamelin. However, the terrible lesson taught to them by the piper was not to be forgotten. The story of what happened that day, so many centuries ago, would be passed down from parent to child in Hamelin . . . and still continues to be.

The moral of this story is simple—you should keep to your agreements with others and stick to contracts when you make them. In the words of philosopher Thomas Hobbes, people must "perform their covenants made; without which, covenants are in vain, and but empty words." If you break your contracts, then you must prepare to endure retribution from those you've wronged. You may have heard a saying people are still known to utter to this very day: "It's time to pay the piper."

Hell Hath No Fury like a Piper Wronged:
A *Grimm* Comparison

You're gonna pay.   —Roddy Geiger, "Danse Macabre" (1-05)

On the surface, the events in "Danse Macabre" might seem quite different from those in "The Pied Piper of Hamelin" story. However, there are still a number of parallels that can be drawn between the two. Perhaps the most obvious similarity is that both the *Grimm* episode and the folktale involve musicians, with special/supernatural abilities over rats, being unjustly wronged by a group. For the piper, the mayor and town council refuse to pay him his promised price (or even his original, much lower, asking price) after he removes all the rats from Hamelin. Roddy Geiger, on the other hand, is twice done wrong—first when fellow students Carter Brimley and Trey Harrison get him suspended from the prestigious Von Hamelin Music Institute by falsely claiming he attacked them (when, in fact, it was they who attacked him), and again when those same boys (along with another student, Marvin) frame him for putting a large number of rats in the vehicle of their teacher Dr. Lawson. Unfortunately, the second wrong causes the man to die of a heart attack.

Both Roddy and the Pied Piper use their music as a means of exacting revenge. Their weapons of choice differ, of course, as do their methods. Roddy Geiger is not a "piper," but instead a very talented violinist (not to mention a pretty sweet rave DJ, as Retchid Kat). Geiger, unlike the piper, cannot control people with his music . . . only rats (which makes sense, in a way, since he is a Reinigen). Whereas the Pied Piper used his music to steal away the children of Hamelin after not being paid for removing the rats, Roddy uses his music to turn the rats into weapons.

Tasty Morsels

In "Danse Macabre," the music school attended by Roddy Geiger (as well as the students who wrong him) is called the Von Hamelin Music Institute. This is an obvious reference to the town of Hamelin, where the revenge of the Pied Piper is said to have occurred.

The last parallel is that in both stories the musicians are successful in dealing out justice against their enemies. The Pied Piper's revenge, however, was far more extreme than Roddy Geiger's. The young Reinigen does not seal Carter, Trey, and Marvin in a mountain. Instead, he lures them to a fake rave with invitations advertising an appearance by Retchid Kat (which is, of course, Roddy's DJ alter ego). After Roddy sets a swarm of rats upon the trio, Nick and Hank arrive to discover none of them have been harmed. Scared out of their minds, the boys admit to putting the rats in Dr. Lawson's car as a prank and claim they only meant to scare the teacher. They also admit to using crates from the pest-control service owned by Roddy's father in order to frame their former classmate for the deed. Unlike "The Pied Piper of Hamelin," this episode of *Grimm* has a bit of a happy ending . . . well . . . not for Dr. Lawson.

The Lost Children of Hamelin: Separating Fact from Fiction

HANK GRIFFIN: *Guess they're gonna have to face the music.*
NICK BURKHARDT: *Really? You went there?*
HANK: *Somebody had to.*

—"Danse Macabre" (1-05)

Tasty Morsels

Roddy Geiger's first name may be a sort of inside joke of the *Grimm* writers. In the heyday of the World Wrestling Federation, there was a popular professional wrestler from Canada who went by the name of "Rowdy" Roddy Piper (real name Roderick Toombs). Perhaps this name choice was their humorous way of hinting that Roddy Geiger was similar to the Pied Piper.

As already mentioned, the story of "The Pied Piper of Hamelin" stemmed from an actual event in history. This is known because, in the town of Hamelin, Germany, there is a house called the Ratten-fängerhaus (Rat Catcher's House, though some refer to it as the Piper's House). However, this is not the house in which the Pied Piper is supposed to have lived. It instead gets its name due to an inscription that was found on one of the house's beams:

> Anno 1284 am Dage Johanni et Pauli war der 26 Junni,
> 130 Kinder verledet, binnen Hameln geborn, dorch einen
> Piper mit allerlei Farve bekledet gewesen to Calvarie Bi
> Den Köppen verloven.

Roughly translated from German, the inscription reads, "In the year 1284, on the day of the Saints Paul and John, June 26, 130 children born in Hamelin were charmed [or seduced] by a piper in multicolored clothing and were lost at [some translations say 'lost to' or 'lost in'] the Calvary near the Köppen." Many believe the reference to "Calvary," or the site of Christ's crucifixion in the New Testament, was intended to designate the location as sacred in some manner.

The beam in which this inscription is etched faces the street in

Tasty Morsels

The element of child murder in the original story of "The Pied Piper of Hamelin" was considered so offensive by some people that revised versions of the tale were created and given less violent endings. Many such versions of the tale have the piper simply use his music to hold the children hostage until he is paid what he's owed. Then the children are safely returned to their parents and everyone learns a valuable lesson.

Hamelin known as Bungelosentraße (The Street Without Drums), where the lost children are said to have last been seen. Even now, in remembrance of that tragic day in Hamelin, dancing and singing are strictly forbidden anywhere on Bungelosentraße or in close proximity to the Rattenfängerhaus.

Another piece of evidence related to the lost children of Hamelin was a stained-glass window, reported to have existed in the Hamelin church back in the 1300s. This window supposedly depicted a man in multicolored garb leading away a mob of children who were all dressed in white. It also bore the same inscription as the one found on the Rattenfängerhaus. Sadly, this window was mysteriously destroyed (or stolen, according to some sources) in or around 1660. However, before it was lost, someone copied the inscription on the beam of Rattenfängerhaus and a painter named Augustin Von Moersperg copied the window's design in a watercolor back in 1592. So at least the spirit of what the window represented was not lost with it.

All of this raises the question—if the story is based on something that actually occurred, then just *who* was this "piper in multicolored clothing" and what *really* happened to the lost children of Hamelin?

There are a number of theories on both the identity of the piper and the fate of Hamelin's children.

One of the least complicated theories claims Hamelin was afflicted with some sort of plague or virus that killed 130 of its children. Rats have long been associated with plagues and disease, of course. In fact, less than a century after the incident in Hamelin, flea-ridden rats would be responsible for spreading the Black Death—also known as bubonic plague—across Europe and creating an epidemic that killed well over seventy-five million people (though some sources estimate the lives lost at as high as two hundred million) by the mid-fourteenth century. According to this theory, the "piper" described in the inscription is believed to be a personification of death (or the grim reaper). This theory is supported by the fact that, in those days, the figure of death is known to have been commonly portrayed in the multicolored garb of a jester.

The next theory claims that perhaps a royal emissary, likely sent by the ruling monarch or nobility, arrived in Hamelin in order to recruit young people for a colonization campaign in which they were attempting to create German settlements in neighboring Moravia in the eastern regions of what was then the Prussian Empire. Such campaigns were often ill planned and poorly executed, and many volunteers died of starvation or illness. Emissaries were frequently fancily dressed, so as to appear prosperous, which may explain the description of the piper in the inscription. However, this theory fails to properly address the final words of the inscription that claim the children were lost at or in a place referred to as "the Calvary near the Köppen."

Another theory points to a phenomenon known as "dance mania" or "dance hysteria" as the culprit for what happened to Hamelin's children. This phenomenon used to be known as the "dance of St. John." In cases where this occurs, groups of people (most commonly youngsters, though not always) are overcome by the compulsion to dance and are unable to stop themselves. Those who experience dance mania will dance to the point of complete physical exhaustion. In extreme cases, people involved in these events have literally danced themselves to death. Perhaps this is what befell the children of Hamelin. The "piper" of the inscription may be, as in the first theory mentioned, a symbolic personification of death. And since the dancing may have been part of the religious celebration related to St. John, this might explain the reference to "Calvary," since the children's deaths may have been seen by some as a form of unintentional sacrifice. One documented case of dance mania is known to have occurred in Erfurt, Germany, in 1237. It is interesting to note that Erfurt is located roughly 168 miles to the southeast of Hamelin. Luckily for the parents of Erfurt, however, they managed to rescue their children. The adults in the town worked together in chasing down their dance-crazed kids and forcibly stopped them from dancing.

A fairly new but interesting theory proposes that the children were led to the nearby town of Coppenbrügge, which was located less than ten miles to the west and, it was recently discovered, was then referred to as Köppenberg (town of Köppen). This would seem to fit with the inscription's mention of Köppen. What of Calvary, however? Scholars in Coppenbrügge have long been aware of the existence of a series of carved stone figurines, many shaped like heads, that litter the areas of the Fahnenstein hill range. One area of the hill range is known as Wall-fahrtsberg (Mount of Pilgrimage), which may explain the reference to Calvary in the inscription. Because of the many "pagan" pre-Christian artifacts found in the area, locals long ago took to calling one area Teufelsküche (Devil's Kitchen). A Coppenbrügge scholar named Gernot Hüsam, director of the museum at the Castle of Coppenbrügge, believes this area once had a wide and flattened stone platform used for seasonal dancing rituals that were performed in the days before Christianity spread through Germany. Shortly after the rulers of a country or region converted to Christianity, any preexisting religious practices that could not be absorbed into the new religion were often vilified and branded as "witchcraft" or "devil worship" and outlawed.

So, perhaps the piper was one of the last remaining keepers of the dwindling traditions related to the "old religion" of the area. Perhaps he came to Hamelin in the hopes of reviving the ways of the past and convinced 130 children to travel with him to Köppenberg/Coppenbrügge to participate in a dance ritual for the summer solstice, which, these days, usually occurs between June 20 and 22. Back then, however, the ritual could easily have been performed on June 26 since methods for keeping track of celestial events were less exact. What happened to the youngsters after they got to their destination, though? Well, perhaps they were all executed by the frightened locals for participating in "devil worship." Perhaps they were all overcome by dance mania and died. Maybe they were unable to go back home after rebelling against their parents and leaving Hamelin. Some even theorize they were the victims of ethnic cleansing. Who knows? The evidence falls a bit short when it comes to this detail.

The truth about what, or who, was responsible for the loss of 130 Hamelin children may never be known for sure. No matter the case, the story that arose from this tragic event remains a strong cautionary tale for adults. For nearly eight centuries, every June 26, the anniversary of this terrible day has been observed. Tourists from all over the world flock to Hamelin every year to take part in the event—taking photographs next to the Rattenfängerhaus and buying Pied Piper–themed trinkets and rat-shaped souvenirs to commemorate their experiences. In fact, the tourism revenue generated by the popularity of the tale has become a crucial part of the local economy.

It is unlikely that the story of "The Pied Piper of Hamelin" will be forgotten anytime soon . . . kind of like the bloody feud between Blutbaden and Bauerschwein.

[6]

ULTIMATE SHOWDOWN—
BLUTBADEN VS. BAUERSCHWEIN

ANGELINA LASSER: *I know who killed Hap and Rolf. It was a cop . . .
a Bauerschwein.*

MONROE: *What?*

ANGELINA: *I picked up his stench at the precinct, and then again at my
place tonight.*

MONROE: *A pig?*

ANGELINA: *Uh-huh.*

MONROE: *Killed one of us? Are you sure?*

—"The Three Bad Wolves" (1-06)

It doesn't take a genius to figure out what would probably happen if
you locked a wild wolf and a feral pig in the same room. At the least,
you could safely assume blood would be spilled. In the realm of fairy
tales, it is usually the wolf doing the spilling. That's not always the
case, however, as Nick Burkhardt learns in the episode "The Three
Bad Wolves" (1-06). Sometimes, it's the pig. Interestingly enough, in
the fairy tale known as "The Three Little Pigs," blood is spilled on
both sides—wolf and pig (or perhaps, Blutbad and Bauerschwein).

The following retelling is based on the version of "The Three

GRIMM WORDS

Bauerschwein: Literally translated from German, this term means "farm pig" or "farmer pig." In the *Grimm* universe, it refers to a pig-like Wesen.

Little Pigs" written down by Joseph Jacobs in his 1890 text, *English Fairy Tales*. The events of this story support the idea that the bloody feud between Blutbaden and Bauerschweins portrayed in *Grimm* has been going on for centuries.

The Story of the Three Little Pigs: A Retelling

HAP LASSER: *Hey, you don't have any schnapps, do you? And what about dinner, huh? You wanna get take-out? Twenty-Four/Seven Pork delivers . . . and if it's more than twenty minutes, it's free!"*

MONROE: *Pork and schnapps? Really?*

HAP: *No . . .* peppermint *schnapps . . . then pork.*

MONROE: *Oh, dude.*

—"The Three Bad Wolves" (1-06)

There was once an old sow (finally, a story that doesn't begin with "Once upon a time") who had three little pigs. Since they'd grown too big for her to keep and care for, she decided to send them out into the world to do what they willed. One by one, the old sow sent her three little pigs away from home.

The first little pig left home and encountered a man who was bundling straw in a field.

"Please, good sir," the first pig said, "may I have some of that straw so I can use it to build a house?"

The man, for reasons unexplained in the original story, gave over some straw, and the first pig used it to build a house for himself. Not long after his new home had been constructed, along came a wolf knocking at his door.

"Little pig, little pig," said the wolf. "Let me come in."

"No," the first pig replied. "No, by the hair of my chinny-chin-chin."

The wolf answered, "Then I'll huff, and I'll puff, and I'll blow your house in!"

So the wolf huffed, and he puffed, and he blew the first pig's house in. And the first pig got eaten by the wolf on his first day on his own (it's a Blutbad-eat-Bauerschwein world, after all).

Now it was the second pig's turn to head out into the world. Like the first pig, he soon encountered a man. Only this man was bundling furze instead of straw.

"Please, sir," the second pig said to the man. "Give me some of that furze so I can use it to build a house."

This man, like the other, gave some of what he had to the second pig. He used it to construct his house and, shortly after it was finished, along came the wolf knocking at his door.

"Little pig, little pig," said the wolf. "Let me come in."

"No," the second pig replied. "No, by the hair of my chinny-chin-chin."

The wolf answered, "Then I'll huff, and I'll puff, and I'll blow your house in!"

So the wolf huffed, and he puffed and puffed and huffed (this house was a bit sturdier than the first pig's, so more effort was

GRIMM WORDS

Furze: The use of the term may be confusing. Most modern translations just say "wood," likely because not many people even know what furze is these days. Furze is actually a spiny and dense evergreen shrub with flowers that are usually gold or yellow in color. Furze is a commonly seen plant in much of western Europe, the region from which this story originated.

required in the huffing and puffing), until at last he blew in the second pig's house. Like his brother before him, the second pig got eaten by the wolf.

And now the third (and final) pig left home to make his way in the big (and, quite obviously, dangerous) world. He, like his ill-fated brothers, soon came across a man. This fellow, however, was in the process of moving a load of bricks.

"Please, good sir," the third pig said. "May I have some of your bricks to use for my house?"

The man (once again without explanation, dialogue, or even a hint that the sight of a *talking pig* fazed him in the slightest) gave the third pig some bricks, which he used to construct a very sturdy house for himself. And, just as with his brothers, the wolf soon came a-knocking at the third pig's door.

"Little pig, little pig," said the wolf. "Let me come in."

"No," the third pig replied. "No, by the hair of my chinny-chin-chin."

The wolf answered, "Then I'll huff, and I'll puff, and I'll blow your house in!"

So the wolf got busy with the huffing and the puffing . . . and the puffing and the huffing . . . and yet more huffing and puffing.

However, this time all he managed to do was hyperventilate. Realizing no amount of huffing and puffing was going to bring down a house of bricks, the wolf shifted tactics from brute strength to deception.

"Little pig," said the wolf. "I know where to find a nice field of turnips, if you'd care to join me."

"Where are they?" said the third pig from the safety of his house.

"Farmer Smith grows them in his field. Be ready tomorrow morning. I'll come calling for you, and we can go together to get some turnips for dinner."

"That sounds nice," said the third pig. "I'm in. Just tell me what time, so I'm ready when you get here."

"Let's say six o'clock in the morning."

"Okay," the third pig agreed. "See you then."

Well, the third pig turned out to be a pretty crafty little guy. He saw right through the wolf's plan and instead headed out at *five* o'clock the next morning. He gathered himself a basket of turnips from Farmer Smith's field and got back home long before the wolf's arrival at six o'clock. And it's a good thing he did, because the wolf showed up at the agreed upon time, salivating in anticipation of a breakfast of raw pork.

"Little pig," called the wolf. "Are you ready to go get some turnips? I hope you aren't still sleeping."

"Ready? I've already gone and come back home again," the third pig told the wolf, chuckling. "I've got myself a pretty little pot full of turnips for my dinner. Thanks for letting me know where to find them, smart guy!"

The wolf, as one would expect, was pretty pissed off when he realized he'd been outwitted by the likes of a pig. However, the wolf decided to soldier on and tried yet again to get his claws on the third pig.

"Little pig," the wolf called out. "Do you like apples? I know where to find an apple tree full of them! Care to join me?"

"Where would we be going?" the third pig called back.

"It's at the Merry Garden," the wolf told him. "As long as you promise not to leave without me again, I'll come calling at five o'clock tomorrow morning. We can go there together and get some tasty apples."

"Done deal," the third pig told him.

This time, as before, the third pig knew the wolf was only trying to get him out of his house so he could eat him. So he left at four o'clock in the morning to gather apples, planning to again be safely home before the wolf got there. However, the Merry Garden was farther from the pig's home than Farmer Smith's field had been. On top of that, he had to climb the tree to get at the ripe apples. All of this took more time than before. Before the third pig finished gathering his apples, the wolf had already discovered he'd been left behind again. As the third pig started down the tree with his basket of apples, he saw the wolf swiftly approaching (this, needless to say, was an "Oh, crap!" moment for the pig).

"Little pig," the wolf growled as he came to the tree. "What the hell, man? Why did you leave without me again? I see you've already got yourself a bunch of apples. Are they nice and ripe?"

"They're absolutely the most delicious and ripe apples I've ever seen," said the third pig. "Here, I'll throw one down to you!"

The pig did not throw the apple *down*, though. Instead, he tossed it as far away from the tree as he could. As the wolf darted off for the apple, the pig climbed down and made a quick break for home. He got safely inside his brick house just as the wolf returned from eating the apple. Wolf boy was *livid* that a pig had, for the second time in as many days, gotten the better of him.

The wolf spent that entire evening concocting a new plan for fooling the pig into leaving the protection of home. The next morning, the wolf showed up at the pig's house for a third and, he hoped, final time.

"Little pig," he called out. "There's going to be a fair at Shanklin Village this afternoon! Want to come with me?"

"Most certainly," the pig replied. "Let's go together. What time should I be ready?"

"At three o'clock this afternoon," said the wolf. "I'll be back to get you then."

Since his usual plan had yet to fail him, the third pig left home an hour ahead of the agreed upon time. He went to the fair (you know . . . like pigs do) and bought a churn for making butter. He was already on his journey back home when he saw the wolf coming on the uphill path. Not knowing what else to do, the third pig jumped inside the butter churn to hide. As he did so, however, he accidentally tipped over the churn, and it started rolling down the hill . . . with him still in it. This was perhaps yet another "Oh, crap!" moment for the pig.

In the meantime, the wolf saw what he'd likely have described as a "big, scary wooden rolling thingy" coming at him fast down the hill. He was so terrified by the sight of it that he ran straight back to his own home and completely abandoned his plans to go to the fair.

The next day, the defeated wolf came by the pig's house and, from outside, told him all about his terrifying encounter with the butter churn.

"Ha, ha, ha," laughed the third pig. "So I frightened a *wolf*, did I? I was in that churn! I was getting in it to hide from you when it tipped over and started rolling! If only you'd been a little braver and not run away with your tail between your legs, you might have finally caught me!"

The wolf was angered to the point of madness when he heard what the pig was saying. He swore that, this time, he would eat that pig if it was the last thing he ever did.

The wolf climbed onto the roof of the pig's house and began to shimmy his way down the chimney to get inside. Once again, the pig figured out what the wolf was up to and started burning wood in the fireplace. He even hung an iron water pot over the flames. The searing fire soon reached the wolf and began turning the bricks around him white-hot, causing him to lose his grip. As he began to fall, the pig removed the lid from the pot of boiling water . . . and in fell the wolf. The pig closed the lid on the pot, and the wolf was boiled alive (a gnarly way to go, one has to admit). Once the wolf was nice and tender, the pig, in a bit of poetic justice for his eaten brothers, made a meal out of his former nemesis and feasted on wolf flesh.

And they all lived happily ever after . . . except for the wolf, of course . . . oh yeah, and the first two pigs that got eaten by him. On second thought, maybe just the third pig lived happily ever after.

When the Bacon Bites Back: A *Grimm* Comparison

MONROE: *Angelina just came by. She says she knows who killed her brothers; says it was a Bauerschwein.*

NICK: *A what?*

MONROE: *A pig. And I don't mean a cop . . . but I* do *mean a cop.*

NICK: *Does she know who?*

MONROE: *No . . . do you?*

NICK: *I can't tell you that.*

MONROE: *Well, you better protect his ass 'cause she's out for blood.*

—"The Three Bad Wolves" (1-06)

A Blutbad once killed a Bauerschwein . . . or two . . . Okay, let's just say that a lot of Blutbaden have killed and eaten a lot of Bauerschweins over the years. And, whether it is in *Grimm* or fairy tales, the pigs eventually get fed up with it and decide it's time for a little payback. Obviously, the *Grimm* episode and the original tale are strikingly different in many respects. Even the comparable elements between the two have been changed up—roles are reversed, names are changed or omitted to protect the innocent, etc. But that doesn't mean there's nothing to compare.

The first and most obvious point of comparison between the *Grimm* episode and the story of "The Three Little Pigs" is the use of the number three. In both stories, there are three siblings—three pigs in the story, three wolves in the episode. Of these three siblings, two are killed/eaten and one survives. In the story, the first two pigs fail to construct houses that are sturdy enough to protect them, and this failure allows the wolf to blow in their houses and devour them. This element of faulty houses was carried over in *Grimm*: it is the way in which the houses are constructed that allows the Bauerschwein arson inspector, Lieutenant Orson, to kill Rolf Lasser and blow up Hap Lasser's house (by a twist of fate, however, Hap runs outside to retrieve his Shake Weight just before the house explodes). Sadly, the happy-go-lucky nature of Hap later causes him to naively open the door to Orson (he thought it was 24/7 Pork), come to avenge the death of his brothers who were murdered by Hap's Blutbad sister, Angelina.

Aside from the whole "three wolves and three pigs" similarity, there is one more commonality to discuss—the "way of the pig," one might say. As would stand to reason, a pig/Bauerschwein would have a rough time going toe-to-toe against a wolf/Blutbad. In folklore, wolves are depicted as being physically superior to pigs in just about every way. Therefore, the pigs must rely on wit and cunning to defeat their wolf predators. In the story, the third pig uses his intellect to fool the wolf by leaving an hour ahead of the agreed upon time. In *Grimm*, Lieutenant Orson (the "third pig," in a way) uses his expertise as an arson investigator to exact his revenge. This also allows him to make Rolf's death and the destruction of Hap's house look like strange accidents of coincidence, covering up his crimes.

Another Wesen who enjoys making his crimes appear as just odd coincidence is the Ziegevolk, namely Billy Capra. These Wesen often seduce women and keep them captive for a time until, eventually, they kill them. This bears a lot in common with a similar figure from a fairy tale by Charles Perrault—"Bluebeard."

[7]

SEXY GOATS AND EAGER BEAVERS

NICK BURKHARDT: *You know anything about Ziegevolk?*

MONROE: *A little . . . They're mostly like preachers . . . game show hosts . . . You know, actor types. You know, guys like to be in the public eye. Why, did one goat out on you?*

NICK: *Yeah . . . Do you know some?*

MONROE: *I knew one in high school—Elvis Greenspan. Got all the chicks. Like, every hottie in school. Okay, kid was 5'4". Weighed in at like 280.*

—"Lonelyhearts" (1-04)

In the episode "Lonelyhearts" (1-04), Grimmsters learn about two new types of Wesen—Ziegevolk (goat-type Wesen) and Hässlich (troll-type Wesen). In this episode, a Ziegevolk uses his powers to lure and imprison young women in the basement of the swanky bed-and-breakfast he runs. While Nick Burkhardt investigates the Ziegevolk, he is also being hunted by a Hässlich reaper. While this is the first time Nick encounters a Hässlich, it certainly won't be the last. In the episode "Leave It to Beavers" (1-19), Grimmsters learn of the long-standing exploitative relationship between the Hässlichen and Eisbibers of Portland.

Due to the overlap between these two episodes, this chapter will have two retellings—Charles Perrault's "Bluebeard" (which applies to the "Lonelyhearts" episode) and Peter Christen Asbjørnsen's "Three Billy Goats Gruff" (which, in a way, applies to both episodes). There will also be two episode comparisons. First, let's take a look at what is perhaps one of the creepiest stories in the fairy-tale tradition—"Bluebeard."

Bluebeard: A Retelling

Germany, 1895—Kitzbuhel Alps, south of Rattenberg. I have followed and observed a goat-like creature for several days now. I've finally been able to identify him as a Ziegevolk, sometimes known as "bluebeards." I now know he is responsible for defiling several women who seem to have fallen under some sort of spell. I have not yet been able to determine how such an oafish man is so attractive to these poor, young women.

—Nick Burkhardt, reading from the Grimm Journals,
"Lonelyhearts" (1-04)

So there was this rich guy way back when. And by "rich," I mean filthily so. He owned a plethora of extravagant homes in various countries, both urban and rural. His vaults overflowed with plates and coins of silver and gold. His homes were furnished with the best finery money could buy—detailed hardwoods, soft cushions, and embroidered fabrics (no particle board junk for this bad boy). When he traveled, he did so in style. Even his horse carriages were

GRIMM WORDS

Gilded: More or less, this refers to a process by which something is coated or covered with a thin layer of gold leaf or paint (in some cases, silver may also be used).

gilded with silver and gold. You'd think such a wealthy guy would have been a hit with the ladies. But alas, the poor (or . . . rich) guy was cursed with a beard of blue (and, appropriately enough, the story refers to him only by the name of Bluebeard).

You'd think a razor could fix that problem fairly easily . . . but whatever.

At the one estate Bluebeard frequented most, he had a neighbor who seemed to him to be a nice enough older lady. However, it wasn't her he was interested in . . . it was her two daughters, both of whom were exceedingly beautiful.

Unfortunately, neither girl wanted anything to do with him or that darn blue beard of his. However, there was another reason for their apprehension. Despite his oddly colored facial hair, it appears Bluebeard had successfully landed wives in the past . . . a *bunch* of them. He'd been married many times before. The most troubling thing was that every last one of his past wives appeared to have left him, and no one knew what had become of any of them.

Bluebeard, however, appears to have been a persistent fellow, not to mention equipped with nearly unlimited financial resources. Hoping to sway the heart of either girl, he invited both to spend a week at one of his luxurious country estates—along with their mother, a bunch of their lady friends, as well as an assortment of young folks from their village.

The trip turned out to be seven days of nothing but pure awesomeness—parties, feasting, dancing, hunting, fishing, bungee jumping (okay, probably not bungee jumping). Bluebeard knew how to throw one heck of a shindig. Nobody slept much that week, either. Instead, they spent most of the nights joking around and playing pranks on each other. It was like summer camp in a 1980s movie.

Needless to say, Bluebeard's plans went swimmingly well. Near the end of the trip, one of the daughters had a change of heart. She decided maybe Bluebeard wasn't such a bad guy. When everyone returned home, Bluebeard and the girl were married right away. And there was much rejoicing.

A month or so after the wedding, Bluebeard was called away on business in the country. The endeavor, he explained to his new wife, was likely to take at least six weeks. Since the business was of an urgent (though unspecified) nature, he had no choice but to leave at once. He encouraged the girl to do whatever she wished to entertain herself while he was gone. He told her she could invite her friends from town to stay over with her at the house, if she wanted. There was no need, he felt, for her to pass the time alone in an empty house. He even suggested she take them to the country estate where they'd had so much fun the week before their wedding.

"Here are all the keys to the mansion," he said, handing her a giant key ring. "These keys are to the rooms where we keep the finest furniture. This one is to the vault that holds the gold and silver plates. This one is to the coin vault. This one opens the jewel cask. This is the master key to the guest house. Lastly, there's this tiny key here."

"And what does the tiny key open?" she said.

"It opens the large closet at the end of the long hallway on the first floor," he told her. "Use any key save this one; enter any room you wish expect that one. If you open that door, I'll be enraged with you. In fact . . . there's no telling what I might do to you if you choose to disobey me."

The girl, apparently unfazed by what was obviously a threat on her life by her new husband, swore she would do as instructed. Bluebeard gave his wife one last hug, boarded his gilded carriage, and rode away to handle his business.

The girl's friends and acquaintances in town, it would seem, were not the sort of folks to wait for an invitation. As soon as they saw Bluebeard's carriage leaving, they came right over. Many of them had long wished to see what sorts of rich furniture were in the grand mansion. Not one had ever dared to visit while Bluebeard was at home. Now that he was gone, however, they went running from room to room, ooh-ing and ahh-ing all the way. Once they'd seen the ground floor, they all went upstairs to the two grandest rooms of the mansion, admiring how beautiful it all was—rich tapestries, embroidered couches, and even a number of giant gilded-frame mirrors so tall that one could see oneself in them from head to toe.

The visitors prattled on about how lucky the girl was to live in such an opulent mansion. They all expressed how envious they were of her and how happy they were for her good fortune. All the while, however, the girl was only thinking one thing: *I wonder what's in that closet he told me not to open?*

Her curiosity overwhelmed her almost as soon as her husband had ridden off. As soon as she could, she abandoned her guests, all of whom were still busy with all the ooh-ing and ahhing. She rushed down a back staircase so quickly and with such

Tasty Morsels

Mirrors weren't always as common as they are these days. In days past, they were considered a luxury item. In times when they were difficult to make, they were incredibly expensive for the average person. Therefore, the presence of several mirrors tall enough to show a person's entire reflection would be considered something that only ridiculously wealthy people (like Bluebeard) would have in their home.

recklessness that she nearly took a tumble several times . . . a fall that would surely have broken her neck.

As the girl approached the closet door, she stopped and pondered whether opening it was a wise move. After all, her husband had warned her of harsh consequences if he found out she'd disobeyed. She even considered what sorts of punishments might be inflicted on her if her husband learned of her disobedience. In the end, however, she figured what the blue-bearded fellow didn't know wouldn't hurt him. He wouldn't find out. How could he? She certainly wasn't going to tell him. He was far away on a six-week-long business trip, right?

And besides all that, she was just so damn *curious* to know what was behind that door!

So, disregarding the terrible things curiosity once did to the cat, she fumbled for the tiny key that opened the door to the forbidden closet. She could barely turn the key in the lock, her fingers trembled so violently. Finally, however, she managed to get the darn thing open.

At first, she could see nothing but darkness.

Then her eyes adjusted, and she was able to make out the floor, which she realized was covered in shiny and clotted blood. Then there was something else, a reflection in the blood—a reflection of bodies.

That's when she looked up.

All along the walls of the closet were hung the dead bodies of a number of women—Bluebeard's former wives. Apparently, they *hadn't* left him. He'd killed each of them and stored their corpses in the closet to hide his crimes.

Now, at this point, you'd think the girl would call out for help. You'd think she would point out the dead bodies to her guests and send one of them to fetch the local magistrate. You'd *think* that she would have done something—*anything*—to reveal the man she was married to as the blue-bearded monster he was.

However, she did *none* of these things. All she did manage to do was drop the key, which fell to the blood-soaked floor. Then she just stood there all catatonic for who knows how long. Then she grabbed the key, closed the door to the closet, locked it, went to her room, and had a total meltdown. She looked at the tiny key and noticed it was stained with blood from when she dropped it. Panic-stricken that Bluebeard would discover what she'd done, she began furiously trying to clean off the blood. She tried everything—soap, polish, even scouring it with sand. Nothing worked. No matter what she did, the blood wouldn't come off.

This was a special key, you see, possessed by a fairy. As a result, the key would never come clean once it had been stained. Whenever the girl scrubbed the bloodstains from one part of the key, they'd just reappear on another part. She scrubbed the key until sundown, but the telltale bloodstains remained.

That night, Bluebeard came home early.

Upon his arrival Bluebeard explained that he'd received certain letters not long after he began traveling, which told him the business matter had been settled to his satisfaction and no longer required his attention. Shocked by his unexpected arrival, the girl did her best to pretend she was overjoyed to see him.

The next morning, Bluebeard asked her to return the keys to him. As she handed over the key ring, her hands trembled so terribly that he guessed right away what she'd done. Bluebeard looked at the key ring and noticed almost immediately that the tiny key to the forbidden closet was missing.

"Why isn't the closet key here?"

"It isn't? Silly me," she replied. "I must've left it on my nightstand."

"Bring it to me right now," Bluebeard demanded.

She did her best to dance around the issue for a few moments. Bluebeard would not be swayed, however, and kept repeating his demands for the key until she had no choice but to fork it over.

"What's this?" Bluebeard said when he saw the stains. "Why is there blood on this key?"

"I have no idea," she told him, lying through her teeth.

"You have no idea? I think you have a very good idea of how this happened," he replied. "You went into the closet, even though I told you it was forbidden. Didn't you? Very well, my dear. If you want to go into that closet so badly . . . you can join my other wives in it!"

In yet another move that defies logic, the girl didn't run. She just threw herself at Bluebeard's feet and begged his forgiveness for having disobeyed his orders. She was so sincere in her pleas, according to how Perrault tells the story, "She would have melted a rock." Unfortunately for her, Bluebeard had the average sympathy level of a textbook psychopath.

"Time to die, my dear," he told her.

"Wait," she begged. "If I must die, at least give me some time to say my final prayers so that my soul is prepared for death."

"If you must," said Bluebeard. "I'll give you fifteen minutes. Go to your room and pray, then come down here and get what's coming to you. A minute longer, and I'll come up after you."

The girl went up to her room. Now that she was alone, she called out to her sister, who had apparently been in the house this entire time (but, for some reason, this is the first we hear of it).

"Sister Anne," she called out. "Go to the top of the tower and see if our brothers are near yet. They promised they'd visit me today. If you see them coming, make a signal to tell them they need to hurry!"

Precious minutes passed, and finally the girl called out to Sister Anne again.

"Sister Anne, are they coming?"

"I don't see anything yet," Anne replied. "I only see the sun shining through the dust and the green grass on the ground."

At this point, Bluebeard became impatient and hollered up from the base of the stairs while he stood there with a giant scimitar in his hand.

"Time for you to die, my dear! Don't make me come up there!"

"Almost done," she called back down. "One more Hail Mary should do it!"

Realizing she was running out of time, she called to her sister again: "Sister Anne, do you see them?"

"Just the sun shining through the dust again," Anne repeated. "And the green grass on the ground."

"Get down here, woman," hollered Bluebeard. "I swear I'll come up there and get you if I have to!"

GRIMM WORDS

Scimitar: A curved bladed sword of Asian origin (specifically Persian). Some translations of this story call the sword Bluebeard carries a "saber," which is more or less the same thing. The scimitar was a very popular weapon in the Ottoman Empire (during the fifteenth and sixteenth centuries, especially) and was long favored as the sword of choice when fighting from horseback.

"Coming," she called back down. "One more Our Father and I'm good!"

Then, once more, she called up to Anne in the tower: "Sister Anne! Do you see them?"

"Wait!" Anne replied. "Something in the distance is churning up a cloud of dust!"

"Oh, thank heaven," the girl sighed. "Our brothers must be approaching."

"Um . . . hang on," Anne replied. "It's just a bunch of sheep. My bad."

One has to think that Anne didn't quite grasp the urgency of her sister's situation.

"Are you coming?" Bluebeard called up, his voice growing louder and more enraged.

"Sister Anne! Do you see *anyone?*"

"Wait," Sister Anne called down. "Yes! Yes, I do! Two horsemen approach! It's our brothers! I'll beckon for them to hurry."

At this point, one might imagine that Sister Anne began flapping her arms and cawing like a bird. "Thank God," the girl said. "My brothers! They will save me!"

Bluebeard's patience had run dry by now, and he let forth with a cry so loud it shook the entire house. Hoping to buy some time, the girl went downstairs and threw herself at Bluebeard's feet—her face all tears, her hair matted to her cheeks—and begged him to spare her life.

"Tears will not save you," said Bluebeard. "You have to die!"

The girl said nothing, but instead just stared into Bluebeard's eyes with a look of despair.

"Commend your soul to God," was Bluebeard's coldhearted response.

He readied his blade to strike, planning to take off her head in one stroke. He snatched his wife by the hair with his free hand and was just about to bring his blade down upon her neck when a loud knocking at the gate interrupted him.

The gate suddenly burst open, and through it rode two men Bluebeard recognized as his wife's brothers—one a dragoon and the other a musketeer (which means her brothers were a couple of total badasses . . . in modern terms, this would be like having a US Marine and a Navy Seal for brothers). Bluebeard released his grip on the girl and made a break for it, but there was nowhere for him to go. The fleeing Bluebeard didn't make it two steps before the girl's battle-hardened brothers caught up to him, ran him through the heart with both their swords, and left him for dead.

Having put an end to Bluebeard, the two brothers rushed to their sister's side. In shock, she could barely stand after they picked her up and put her on her feet. She was too weak even to welcome her brothers. Hopefully they were able to find it in their hearts to forgive her for that.

Bluebeard died without an heir. As a result, the girl inherited every bit of his immense wealth. She used part of it to marry Sis-

GRIMM WORDS

Dragoon: A member of an elite cavalry military unit popular in Europe as far back as 1600. Dragoons were trained to fight with both sword/saber and rifle, and to effectively do so both on horseback and on foot.

Musketeer: There are two possible definitions for this word. Sometimes, it just refers to an infantry soldier armed with a musket. In seventeenth- and eighteenth-century France, however, it referred to a member of the elite royal bodyguard (as made popular in Alexandre Dumas's 1844 classic, *The Three Musketeers*). Like dragoons, they too were trained to be extremely proficient in both swordplay and marksmanship.

ter Anne to a young man she'd long loved. She used another part of her newfound wealth to buy officers' commissions for the two brothers who'd saved her from a grisly fate at the blade of Bluebeard's scimitar. What money remained she used as a dowry and married a nice young gentleman who was kind to her and helped her to forget all the fear and madness she'd experienced in her brief marriage to Bluebeard.

And the moral, according to Perrault? The *girl* is at fault for opening the closet in the first place:

Oh Curiosity, you mortal bane!
In spite of your charms, you cause often pain
And sore regret, of which we daily find
A thousand instances attend mankind:
For you—Oh, may it not displease the fair—
are a fleeting pleasure, but lasting care.

And it always proves too dear, the prize
Which in the moment of possession, dies.

In his defense, Perrault did offer a second, *slightly* less-offensive moral explaining that things have changed since the harsh time period in which the story of Bluebeard is supposedly set:

A very little share of common sense,
And knowledge of the world, will give evidence
That this is a story of a time long passed;
No husbands would now such terrors cast;
Nor ever, with a vain despotic hand,
Ask what is impossible with such a command:
And be they discontented, or have the fire
Of wicked jealousy in their hearts inspire,
They softly sing; and of whatever hue
Their beards may chance to be black or blue,
Red or brown, and it is hard to say
Which of the two, the man or wife, bears sway.

Lady Killers: A *Grimm* Comparison

No way. Dude, I can't be around that guy. He's way too potent. I almost bought him a drink.   —Monroe, "Lonelyhearts" (1-04)

At first glance, you might think that finding similarities between a homicidal maniac with a blue beard and a frog-eating Ziegevolk named Billy Capra who runs a bed-and-breakfast seems problematic.

Tasty Morsels

Billy Capra's name is actually a clue as to his identity as a Wesen. In Latin, *Capra* is the name for the genus of goats and wild goats. Therefore, Billy Capra's name is literally "Billy Goat." At first glance, many saw this as a reference to the tale of "The Three Billy Goats Gruff." As you'll learn later in this chapter, however, this is not the case.

And you would be correct. However, some overlapping points do exist between Perrault's story and the "Lonelyhearts" (1-04) episode of *Grimm*. One just has to know where to look.

The first problem is figuring out why the writers of *Grimm* felt that a goat-type Wesen was appropriately comparable to the character of Bluebeard. The simplest explanation for this is that all goats, both male and female, have beards (they're not blue, of course, unless someone gives a goat a dye job . . . which just opens up a whole other can of crazy worms). Another possibility is that the bearded goat has come to be seen as symbolic of the devil. In many myths, obviously, the devil has been portrayed as a silver-tongued seducer of women who leads them to all sorts of ruin. In Greek myths, the goat-like satyr deity Pan had a voracious sexual appetite and frequently seduced mortal women with his charms (and satyrs in general are often depicted in the same way). One must admit, this description sounds a lot like the Ziegevolk Billy Capra.

Another overlapping element between *Grimm* and Perrault's story is the presence of a "forbidden space." In "Bluebeard," it is the closet to which Bluebeard gives his new wife a key. She opens it, of course, leading to the discovery of her husband's murderous crimes against women. In *Grimm*, the forbidden space is instead Billy

Capra's creepy little "lady dungeon" basement. Again, discovery of this space reveals the Ziegevolk's crimes.

The last point of comparison between the two involves the arrival of two saviors who, in the end, rescue the captives. In *Grimm*, Nick and Hank rescue the drugged females from a fate of certain death (by gassing) in Billy Capra's dungeon. In Perrault's "Bluebeard," the girl's brothers show up and, unfortunately for him, turn out to be a pair of highly trained killing machines who turn him into a blue-bearded human shish kebab.

While Billy Capra is a Ziegevolk, he is also referred to as a "bluebeard." Therefore, it stands to reason that the writers of *Grimm* did not intend for him to be one of the goat characters in "The Three Billy Goats Gruff," in which a trio of goats confront an ogre. However, this story is also a part of the *Grimm* universe, as shown in the episode "Leave It to Beavers" (1-19), in which the Eisbibers of Portland find themselves faced with a choice—continue to be extorted by the Hässlichen, or stand up to their oppressors. Before we compare the two, however, let's take a look at a retelling of the original story. The following retelling is based on the story "The Three Billy Goats Gruff," as it was written in the 1870 book *Popular Tales from the Norse* by Sir George Webbe Dasent (though, in truth, he actually translated most of the stories in the book from tales that were originally collected and recorded by Peter Christen Asbjørnsen and Jørgen Moe).

The Three Billy Goats Gruff: A Retelling

You gotta come quick! The construction site off of 99E, under the Gladstone Bridge! Oh my god, he killed him!
                    —Arnold Rosarot, "Leave It to Beavers" (1-19)

GRIMM WORDS

Billy Goat: A male goat . . . enough said.

Gruff: Abrupt or straightforward in manner, or having a rough voice (such as the biggest Billy Goat Gruff in the story).

Once upon a time there were three billy goats. They were sent up the hillside to graze so they could fatten up. For some strange reason, all three of them had the same name—Gruff (hence, the title of the story).

On their way to the hillside, the three Billy Goats Gruff had to cross a rushing stream by way of a bridge. Under this bridge, however, lived a nasty troll (in *Grimm* terms, a Hässlich), who had a long pointy nose and eyes as big as saucers. As they approached the bridge, the Billy Goats Gruff decided to cross one by one.

The littlest Billy Goat Gruff was the first to cross the bridge. *Clip-clap, trip-trap* went his hooves upon the bridge.

"Who is that, clip-clapping and trip-trapping across my bridge?" growled the angry troll from underneath.

"It's only me, the littlest of the Billy Goats Gruff. I'm going up to the hillside to fatten up," replied the littlest Billy Goat Gruff.

"I should come up there and eat you!" the troll told him.

"Oh, you don't want to eat me," said the littlest Billy Goat Gruff. "I'm hardly a mouthful. But my bigger brother will be coming next. If you'll wait for him, he'll make a far meatier meal."

"Fine," said the troll. "Get out of here before I change my mind. But your brother is mine!"

Next the middle Billy Goat Gruff crossed the bridge. *Clip-clap, trip-trap* went his hooves upon the bridge.

GRIMM WORDS

Hässlich (*Hässlichen*, pl): In *Grimm*, this refers to a troll-type Wesen. Translated from German, however, it just means "ugly" or "hideous" . . . which, one must admit, is a fitting description.

"Who is that, clip-clapping and trip-trapping on my bridge?" growled the angry troll from underneath.

"It's only me, the middle Billy Goat Gruff. I'm going up to the hillside to fatten up," replied the middle Billy Goat Gruff.

"I should come up there and gobble you up!" roared the troll.

"Oh, you don't want to eat me," said the middle Billy Goat Gruff. "If you wait, an even bigger Billy Goat Gruff, my older brother, will be coming along soon. Now, *he* would make a fine feast."

No loyalty amongst goats, it seems . . . or is there?

"Fine," the troll said. "Get going before I lose my patience."

Now the biggest Billy Goat Gruff began to cross the bridge.

Clip-clap-clip, trip-trap-trip went his hooves upon the bridge, which groaned and creaked under his immense size and weight.

"Who is that, clip-clap-clipping and trip-trap-tripping all over my bridge?" growled the troll.

"It is I! I'm the biggest of the Billy Goats Gruff!" replied the biggest Billy Goat Gruff in his strong, coarse voice.

"I'm coming up there to eat you!" announced the troll.

As the troll crawled out from under the bridge, here is what the biggest Billy Goat Gruff, in true badass fashion, said to him (taken from the original folktale, because rewording this won't make it any more awesome):

GRIMM WORDS

Curling stones: Large, polished stones that are fitted on top with an iron handle. These are used in the sport of curling, which involves sliding these stones along ice so as to make them stop in a scored target. You may or may not be familiar with this sport, depending on whether you've ever followed the Winter Olympics. In the story, however, this is likely meant as a metaphor for the biggest Billy Goat Gruff's cloven hooves.

Well, come along! I've got two spears,
And I'll poke your eyeballs out through your ears;
Besides that, I've got two curling stones,
And I'll crush you to pieces, body and bones.

So, more or less, the biggest Billy Goat Gruff's response to the troll was the equivalent of "Come at me, bro!"

As the troll reached the top of the bridge, the biggest Billy Goat Gruff charged the creature at full speed. The goat lowered his head just before impact and stabbed out the troll's enormous eyes with his horns until they, as promised, popped out through his ears. He then trampled the troll to pieces. The biggest Billy Goat Gruff then took what was left of the troll and rolled it off the bridge into the stream below.

The troll now thoroughly blinded, beaten, and tossed into the stream like a fallen mafia don, the Three Billy Goats Gruff continued on until they reached the hillside, where the horned trio grazed until all three of them grew so fat they could barely make it back home again. And, if they haven't yet been sent to slaughter, they are fat to this day. This story traditionally ends with the following words: "Snip, snap, snout. This tale's told out."

You just take that however you want.

Getting Goats and Skewering Trolls: A *Grimm* Comparison

When someone defies the Hässlichen, they send us a message. I don't want my husband or my children to end up being that message.
　　　　　—Female Eisbiber at Lodge, "Leave It to Beavers" (1-19)

There are probably more differences than there are similarities between the *Grimm* episode "Leave It to Beavers" and the original story of "The Three Billy Goats Gruff." First and foremost, there is neither a goat nor Ziegevolk to be found in the *Grimm* episode. Instead of goats, it's the Eisbibers of Portland who are having issues with trolls (and these are not the kind of trolls that just post annoying Internet comments). However, if one gets a little creative, there are some points of comparison to be found.

The murder witnessed by Arnold Rosarot occurs on a site that is owned by a Hässlich. This wouldn't seem all that similar to the original fairy tale if not for the fact that this site is located under a *bridge*, which, as most folklorists would agree, is prime real estate for a troll. Additionally, the trolls of the story are often portrayed as being territorial by nature and taking joy in exacting tolls from those who wish to tread across (or over) their domains. The Hässlichen trolls of *Grimm* appear to have this same trait, extorting exorbitant dues from the Eisbiber workers who are employed at their under-bridge site.

As with the first two Billy Goats Gruff in the original fairy tale, however, the Eisbibers of the Portland lodge have neither the strength nor bravery to stand up against their oppressors. Therefore, a stronger character must enter the picture and deal with the troll. In this case, however, it is not a Chuck Norris–like Third Billy Goat who shows up and dishes out the pain—it's a Grimm.

[8]

WILD CHICKS WITH LONG HAIR

MONROE: *And you think she's been living in the woods for nine years?*
NICK BURKHARDT: *Yeah, we have evidence it was her.*
MONROE: *Well, I mean, if she was only seven years old, you know, society hasn't had much influence on her. So she'd still be a wild child. Her instincts would be working full-time. So, you know, she'd have a decent chance. I'm not sure I'd wanna run into her now, though.*

—"Let Down Your Hair" (1-07)

In the episode "Let Down Your Hair" (1-07), the DNA of a little girl named Holly Clark, who'd been given up for dead after disappearing nine years earlier, turns up in a hair found at a woodland crime scene where a drug manufacturer had his neck broken by an unseen assailant just before he was about to savagely murder a pair of innocent hikers. It's just another day on the job for Detective Nick Burkhardt and his partner, Hank. When Nick learns Holly Clark has grown into a long-haired Blutbad in full-on wild mode, however, he brings in Monroe to help him find the girl and return her to civilization . . . as well as reunite her with the adopted human mother who still mourns her loss. This episode has its roots in a well-known fairy tale, "Rapunzel," penned by the Brothers Grimm in their 1812 *Kinder- und Hausmärchen*.

Rapunzel: A Retelling

SERGEANT WU: *Hold on to your . . . whatever you hold on to.*
You're not gonna believe this. We just got the lab report
back on the brunette hair you found at the scene.

HANK GRIFFIN: *Holly Clark? You sure?*

WU: *We got a preliminary match. They're running the tests*
again to make sure.

HANK: *One of the more depressing cases I ever worked. Little*
girl playing in her mother's backyard just vanished. Mas-
sive search turned up nothing.

—"Let Your Hair Down" (1-07)

A man and a woman once wished for a child for many years but were unable to conceive. That is until the day came when the woman began to feel their prayers were about to be answered (this is just a long-winded way of saying "she thought she was pregnant" . . . remember, they didn't have over-the-counter pregnancy tests back in the day). The couple was so happy to be expecting their first child, and there was nothing the husband would not do to care for his newly pregnant wife.

In the house where the couple lived, they had a little window high at the back through which could be seen an amazing garden filled with all sorts of beautiful flowers and rich herbs. However, they never dared to venture into it. There were two reasons for this. First of all, the garden was surrounded by a high wall. Secondly, the garden belonged to a very old and powerful enchantress (or fairy, in some versions) who was not very nice when it came to trespassers.

GRIMM WORDS

Rapunzel: Known to botanists as *Campanula rapunculus* (*Campanula* = bellflower; *rapunculus* = little turnip), is a species of bellflower. It's common throughout Europe, with edible leaves that can be used in salads and are similar to spinach. The second part of its botanical name actually refers to the roots, which are edible and often compared to turnips or radishes. So . . . yeah . . . the girl is named after a plant. This isn't so strange, when you think about it. After all, most of us know someone named Daisy or Violet.

One day, as the wife was sitting by the window looking out at the wondrous garden, she noticed a flowerbed full of rapunzel. Suddenly, she started to feel that it looked like the most delicious thing she had ever seen. From that moment on, day in and day out, she did nothing but long for a bite of that rapunzel. Within days, she grew pale and thin which, of course, made her husband concerned for her well-being.

"What is bothering you, my dear wife?" he said.

"Oh," she replied, "if I don't have a bite of that rapunzel from the garden behind our house, I fear I shall surely die."

"Well, I can't have that," the husband said to himself. "I'll get her some of that rapunzel, no matter what the cost or consequence."

The man waited until evening, and under cover of darkness he snuck over the wall into the enchantress's garden. He quickly collected some of the rapunzel and brought it home to his ailing wife. As soon as she had it, the woman wasted no time. She immediately made a salad with it and gobbled it down as if she was about to starve to death. It was even more delicious than she had imagined. However, it would seem as if this rapunzel had the same effect on the woman as potato chips have on most people—she couldn't stop with just one.

The next day, the wife desired the rapunzel three times as much as she had before. She begged her husband to bring her more of it, and the man knew not a moment of peace until he agreed to once again venture into the forbidden garden.

As before, the man waited until evening to scale the garden wall. This time, however, the enchantress was standing there waiting for him when he descended on the other side. Needless to say, the poor guy just about soiled his drawers when he saw her.

"How *dare* you come into my garden," said the enchantress, "and steal my rapunzel? You are a thief, and you shall suffer for your trespasses!"

"Wait," the man pleaded. "Please let mercy overcome your wrath! I only did this because I had no choice! My pregnant wife spied your rapunzel from our window, and ever since she has wasted away out of desire for it. I feared she would die if I did not get some for her!"

The fairy enchantress felt sympathy for the man's predicament, and so she did not take his life (she's not a Hexenbiest, after all, but more of a very powerful and rather scary kind of fairy folk). However, actions must have consequences.

"Very well," said the enchantress. "If what you say is true, then I will allow you to take as much of my rapunzel as you wish."

"Oh, thank you for your kindness and mercy," the man replied.

And, for just a moment, it seemed as if everything was going to be okay.

"But there is one condition," the enchantress continued.

So close!

"What condition?"

"Your wife will soon bring a child into the world," she explained. "You must give it to me once it's born. I will treat the child well, and she will want for nothing. I will love and care for her like a mother. Agree to these terms, or die where you stand."

Scared out of his mind, and apparently preferring childlessness to being dead, the man agreed. He was allowed to live, as well as to take all the rapunzel his wife wanted from the enchantress's garden.

On the day of the child's birth, the enchantress appeared almost as soon as the baby was born. She demanded the child as she'd been promised, and the parents reluctantly handed her over. The enchantress took the child away and named the girl Rapunzel (a fitting name, considering her mother had eaten a bunch of the stuff while she was pregnant with her).

Over the next twelve years, under the enchantress's care, Rapunzel grew into the most beautiful girl anyone had ever seen (of course, no one but the enchantress had ever actually *seen* her). On her twelfth birthday, the enchantress took her to a tall tower and locked her away in it. The tower was deep in the forest and had neither a door nor stairs that might allow entrance. The only way in was through a window at the top of the tower.

When the enchantress would visit Rapunzel, as she did almost every day, she would call up to the girl: "Rapunzel, Rapunzel, let down your hair to me."

Rapunzel, you see, had never cut her hair. As a result, her fine golden locks had grown incredibly long. She kept her hair combed and braided, allowing the enchantress to use it as a makeshift rope. She would fasten it to a hook next to the high window, then let the rest of it fall to the ground, a full twenty ells down. The enchantress would then use the hair-rope to climb up the tower.

GRIMM WORDS

Ells: An outdated unit of measurement. As with many older forms of measure that used body parts, one ell was equal to roughly six hand widths. Since people have different hand sizes, it wasn't all that accurate. In modern terms, one ell equals about 45 inches, or 1.14 meters. So 20 ells, or the distance from the tower window to the ground in "Rapunzel," would be about 900 inches (25 yards or 22.8 meters).

About two years after Rapunzel was first locked in the tower (so she would be roughly fourteen years old at this point) a young prince came riding through the forest and discovered the tower. He heard the voice of a girl singing, and it was the most beautiful sound to ever grace his ears. It was the voice of Rapunzel, who often passed her lonely days in the tower by singing to herself.

The prince wanted nothing more than to enter the tower and find the girl, whose beauty must have surely matched that of her voice. However, he could find no door by which to enter the tower. He finally returned home, but he came back to the tower every day to sit below and listen to Rapunzel sing.

Soon there came a day when, as the prince was lounging behind a tree as he listened to Rapunzel sing, the enchantress came for a visit. She called up to Rapunzel in the usual way: "Rapunzel, Rapunzel, let down your hair to me."

The prince remained hidden behind the tree and witnessed Rapunzel lower her hair-rope down to the enchantress. He watched the old fairy godmother climb up, and he realized this must be the only way into the tower.

Tasty Morsels

Frau Göthel, or Mother Göthel, is a regularly occurring name in many stories. It is often used as a name for female enchantresses and fairy godmothers in various fairy tales from Germany and other parts of Northern Europe.

"If that is the ladder to get into the tower," he said to himself. "Then tomorrow I too shall try it."

The next evening, the prince returned to the tower. He stood at the base of it and called up to Rapunzel: "Rapunzel, Rapunzel, let down your hair to me."

Almost right away, a rope of braided golden locks descended to him, and he began to climb as fast as he could. Up the tower he went until he reached the window and came inside the tower.

When Rapunzel saw the prince, to put it bluntly, she had a freak-out to end all freak-outs.

She'd never even *seen* a man before, or *anyone* besides the enchantress for that matter. The prince might as well have been an alien, as far as Rapunzel was concerned.

He spoke to her kindly and explained to her how his heart had been moved by her singing and that he'd had not a moment of rest since he first heard it. After that, Rapunzel chilled out a bit. And, of course, the prince immediately asked her to marry him.

Wow . . . that certainly escalated quickly, didn't it?

Seeing that the prince was young, as well as pretty easy on the eyes, Rapunzel thought to herself: *This prince will love me more than Frau Göthel ever has.*

At least she wouldn't have to worry about him locking her up in a tower.

GRIMM WORDS

Skein: As the word is used here, refers to a length of thread or yarn wound up in a loose coil.

"Come away with me," said the prince.

"I would love to," said Rapunzel. "But I have no way to get down from here. You will have to bring me a skein of silk every day when you visit me. I'll weave a rope ladder out of the silk. Once it is ready, I can escape with you, and we can ride away from here on your horse."

It seems it never occurred to them to just *cut off* her hair and use *that* as a rope to escape.

The couple then agreed to a plan. The prince would come to her with the requested silk every evening. The enchantress, you see, always visited Rapunzel only during the daytime. By sticking to this schedule, they were able to keep their love a secret from the enchantress for some time.

Then Rapunzel just had to go and open her fool mouth. One day, as Frau Göthel was combing her hair, Rapunzel asked her, "Mother Göthel, why are you so much heavier than the prince? When he visits, he always climbs up here in a flash."

Yeah . . . bet he does.

"What did you just say?" asked Frau Göthel. "What evil have you done, you wretched child? I've done everything in my power to keep you safe from the outside world, and this is the thanks I get? You just stab me in the back the first time a cute boy comes across your path?"

Overcome by rage, Frau Göthel snatched Rapunzel by her long locks and with her free hand took up a pair of scissors. Frau

Tasty Morsels

In the original folktale, Rapunzel's affair is revealed when she asks Frau Göthel why her clothing no longer fits. You see, her clothes were getting tighter because she was *pregnant*. However, Wilhelm Grimm felt that discussing anything related to sex or pregnancy was inappropriate for children (especially since there was no way Rapunzel and the prince could have been properly married), so he changed this part. While the change may have reflected the moral standards of the time, it causes the rest of the story to become more than a little confusing.

Göthel then wrapped the golden hair twice around her forearm, pulling it tight. Next, she came at Rapunzel with the scissors and, *snip, snip*, cut off her long tresses. The braids, shining like spun gold, fell in a heap to the floor.

This wasn't the end of Frau Göthel's wrath, however. After that, she took Rapunzel from the tower and left her to live alone deep in the woods. This was a very tough life for a girl who had always had all of her needs provided for her. Rapunzel's days soon went from carefree to being filled with hardship and grief.

On the evening of Rapunzel's banishment from the tower, the prince came to visit with a skein of silk. He stood at the base of the tower and, as usual, called up: "Rapunzel, Rapunzel, let down your hair to me."

Frau Göthel, however, had kept the braided rope of Rapunzel's hair and was waiting in the tower for him. Hearing the prince, she fastened one end to the hook and lowered the rest down. The prince climbed up . . . but instead of finding his beloved Rapunzel, he was confronted by Frau Göthel. The powerful fairy enchantress stared down the prince, her eyes like daggers.

"So! You thought you'd come to fetch your beloved," she snarled. "But your pretty bird has flown the coop. One might say a cat got her, and that same cat is about to scratch out your eyes! Rapunzel is lost to you forever, and never again shall your eyes see her."

What happens next, similar to the pregnancy change, is a bit of an issue. Some versions claim Frau Göthel used her powers to curse the prince with blindness and that he felt his way to the window and jumped out of the tower. Other versions, such as that of Brothers Grimm, claim that he threw himself out the window to escape the wrath of Frau Göthel but landed in a thorn bush, the thorns of which stabbed out his eyes. The first scenario sounds more believable, if not more likely . . . but you can take your pick.

One way or another, the poor prince was stricken blind and left to wander in the woods alone. Unable to find his way back to his horse, let alone his way back home, the prince just trudged on. He ate nothing but roots and berries, and he did nothing but weep for the loss of Rapunzel, whom he refers to as his dearest wife (which is odd, since the two *still* couldn't be properly married).

The prince went on living miserably in this way for a number of years. One day, however, his blind wandering brought him to the place in the woods where Rapunzel had been living all this time. Since her banishment from the tower, Rapunzel had given birth to twins—a boy and a girl.

Rapunzel and the twins had been living in wretched poverty for years, all alone in the woods. When the prince came upon the ramshackle home where they lived, however, he heard the all-too-familiar voice of his beloved. He stumbled in the direction of the voice and, soon enough, Rapunzel saw him coming to her. She ran to her long-lost prince and threw her arms around him. The prince collapsed into her arms, and she held him close.

When she saw what had become of him, she wept tears over his face. Two of the tears fell, one into each of his blinded eyes . . . and suddenly his sight came back to him.

His eyesight returned and, reunited with his beloved Rapunzel, the prince took them all to his father's kingdom. They lived there happily for many, many years and wanted for nothing the rest of their days.

Lost and Found: A *Grimm* Comparison

I have good news. We found Holly alive.
> —Hank Griffin, "Let Your Hair Down" (1-07)

In addition to the fact that both the Rapunzel of the story and the character Holly Clark from *Grimm* had ridiculously long hair, there are a number of other overlapping elements between "Rapunzel" and the *Grimm* episode "Let Your Hair Down" (1-07). One of the first and most notable similarities between the two is that both involve a woman who wishes for nothing more than to have a child, only to have that child taken away. However, the roles get switched around between the fairy tale and *Grimm*. In "Rapunzel," her biological mother loses her to the adoptive fairy godmother Frau Göthel. In the *Grimm* episode, Holly Clark had already been removed from the home of her biological mother (who, the show explains, was a drug addict) and adopted by a loving family when she goes missing. Though Rapunzel was taken from her parents because her father trespassed in the garden of Frau Göthel (her adoptive mother, of a sort), Holly Clark was kidnapped by a man who trespassed into her adoptive mother's backyard.

Another comparable overlap between the two is the location to which both girls are taken after they are snatched from their mothers (Rapunzel from her birth mother and Holly from her adoptive one). Rapunzel, of course, is taken away to her cozy little tower in the woods, where she grows up. Holly Clark is also forced to grow up in a "tower" of sorts, and she raises herself like a wild child in a hunter's tree blind by stealing supplies from campers and hikers. Of course, one has to admit that Rapunzel's experience of living in a tower while Frau Göthel saw to her every need was probably far preferable to the nine years Holly Clark spent living like an animal in a tree blind.

The last point of comparison between the fairy tale and the *Grimm* episode is that of a hurtful separation followed by a joyful reunion. Rapunzel is separated from the man she loves when Frau Göthel learns of him. She is kicked out of the tower and left to fend for herself in the woods, while her prince wanders around blind. In *Grimm*, Holly Clark is taken from her adopted mother and also left to take care of herself in the woods. Both girls get to experience reunions at the end of their stories—Rapunzel with her prince and Holly Clark with her adoptive mother—and the bonds that were for a time broken are mended.

The Wild World of Feral Children: Reality or Hoax?

In *Grimm*, Holly Clark is lucky enough to have her abilities as a Blutbad to help her survive during her years in the wild. However, occurrences of children who survived alone in the wild are not unheard of. In fact, there have been over a hundred reported cases of these so-called "feral children" (such children are often said to have Mowgli Syndrome, a reference to the character Mowgli in Rudyard

Kipling's *The Jungle Book*). Unfortunately, the facts surrounding many of these reports are difficult to substantiate at best, and some are now believed to have simply been hoaxes or misunderstandings of mental conditions such as autism or schizophrenia. One of these cases occurred in the early twentieth century and involved two girls found in Bengal, India—Kamala and Amala.

Despite it being perhaps the most well-known case of feral children throughout history, the validity of this case has long been a point of controversy. This is mostly due to the fact that the only available account of the two girls comes from one man—Joseph Amrito Lal Singh—an Anglican missionary who ran a local orphanage and first took charge of the girls in October 1920. He later published an account of his experience in a 1926 issue of the Indian English-language newspaper the *Statesman*.

In his original account, Singh wrote of how he'd been guided to the two girls by a man who lived in the jungle village of Godamuri, west of Calcutta, where he found them living in a cage near the man's house. In his personal diary, Singh contradicts himself by claiming that he rescued the girls from a wolf den. No matter how Singh found the girls, he brought them to his orphanage sometime between October 9 and 17, 1920. Some of his journal entries are dated, while others are not, which makes pinpointing the exact day difficult. In fact, the validity of his journal was recently debunked in a 2007 study published by French surgeon Serge Aroles, *L'Enigme des enfants-loup* (Enigma of the Wolf-Children).

According to Singh, the girls did not assimilate well to life at the orphanage. He named them Kamala (then estimated as having been about eight years old) and Amala (estimated at eighteen months old). When staff members tried to dress them in clothes, they bit and scratched. They often walked on all fours, growled when angry, and howled when unhappy. They refused to eat cooked food or to do so sitting at a table, and so the girls had to be fed raw meat in bowls left on the floor. Amala, still only a toddler, died less than a year later from a kidney infection. Kamala, in similar fashion, died of kidney failure in 1929 at roughly seventeen years of age.

Interestingly enough, the first case of a feral child to receive widespread fame was that of "Wild Peter," which occurred in Hanover, Germany, in 1724. A boy estimated to be twelve years of age was captured near Helpensen in Hanover and, according to accounts from the time, was naked and covered all over in hair, though this was likely an embellishment. It was said that he was especially apt at tree climbing and preferred eating such things as plants, roots, and even tree bark to offerings of bread. Luckily, after a while he developed a taste for fruits and vegetables. He was also incapable of grasping the human language, suggesting he entered the wild before learning the skill. Eventually, he found himself taken before the royal court in Hanover and handed over to George I of England. The king had the boy taken back to England in order to be studied by his best scholars. Despite the fact that "Wild Peter" spent a total of sixty-eight years among civilized humans, he never learned to speak (though he did learn to say two things—"King George" and "Peter").

Were these wild children truly feral? Or were they just abandoned and/or misunderstood? That is up to you. It is, however, safe to say that none of them ever got a "happy ending," unlike the characters of fairy tales and *Grimm*, where everybody gets a chance at a "happily ever after." Well . . . almost everybody. Frau Göthel loses her beloved Rapunzel, and James Addison, the man who kidnapped Holly Clark all those years ago (and then abandoned her in the woods when she "fanged out" and tore up his leg in full-on Blutbad woge mode), gets to spend the rest of his days in prison for being the pedophile kidnapper he is.

Seriously . . . the guy is almost as bad as an ogre . . . almost.

[9]

GIANTS, OGRES,
AND GIANT OGRES

MONROE: *Siegbarste ... Your basic ogre. You're saying you saw one here in Portland?*

NICK BURKHARDT: *Yeah.*

MONROE: *Aw, man. I just got a knot in my stomach. Siegbarste are the worst. I mean, fortunately, they're very rare, but if you ever run across one ... well, I guess you have.*

NICK: *You've dealt with one before?*

MONROE: *Yeah. When I was a kid. I mean, I didn't deal with him directly. He came after a neighbor of mine, two doors down. Their son Freddy was a buddy of mine. This guy beat Freddy's dad to death in his own garage and then used his power tools to ... you know. Trust me. You're lucky to be alive.*

—"Game Ogre" (1-08)

When Portland judge Logan Patterson's dead body is found in his home, with his own gavel shoved down his throat, Nick Burkhardt finds himself on the trail of perhaps the most deadly (not to mention hard to kill) Wesen he has yet to encounter—a Siegbarste. Some viewers were initially baffled when the opening line "fee-fi-fo-fum," from

"Jack and the Beanstalk," was used for the episode "Game Ogre" (1-08). This was likely due to the misconception that Jack faced *giants* in the tale. This is a common point of confusion when it comes to the "Jack" tales, mainly because there are various versions of these stories. Two of the most well-known stories from the "Jack" tradition—"Jack and the Beanstalk" and "Jack the Giant Killer"—are often mixed up (in fact, these two stories were integrated to create the 2013 film *Jack the Giant Slayer*). In the original "Jack and the Beanstalk" tale, as it was written down by Joseph Jacobs in his 1890 work *English Fairy Tales*, the young hero Jack climbs his famous beanstalk three times to face off with a human-eating ogre. As you'll see in the following retelling, based on Jacobs's version, Jack chooses to risk life and limb in order to secure a future for himself and his mother when their prized milk cow stops producing.

Jack and the Beanstalk: A Retelling

Oleg Stark was a contract killer . . . But this time, it was personal. Jack Lambert was a business associate of Stark's who knew that Stark demanded to be paid in gold. Apparently, Jack found out where Stark stashed his gold and stole it. It was a revenge killing. —Hank Griffin, "Game Ogre" (1-08)

Once upon a time, a poor old widow lived out in the country with her only son, Jack. Their one source of sustenance and income was their prized cow named Milky-White (a fitting name for a cow, one must admit). For years, Jack and his mother had their fill of milk and then took the rest to sell at the town market. That is until the morning came when Milky-White's udders ran dry.

"What shall we do?" said the widow to her son.

"Don't fear, Mother," said Jack. "I'll go into town and find work."

"We tried that once before, remember? It didn't work out so well," his mother replied. "No one would take you." (Jack, it seems, wasn't thought of too highly by the men in town.)

"Then what do you suggest?" he asked.

"Well, I guess we have no choice but to sell Milky-White. With the money we get for her, we can find some new kind of way to earn our living. Maybe we can set up a shop or something like that."

"Very well," agreed young Jack. "It's still morning, and today is market day in town. I'll take Milky-White and sell her for as much as I can get. After that, we'll figure out what to do next."

Jack took the cow by its halter and led it off down the path to town. He wasn't yet halfway to his destination when he suddenly encountered a peculiar old man along the way.

"Good morning, Jack," the old man said.

"A good morning to you as well, sir," Jack replied, very curious that this old man knew his name, since he'd never seen him before in all his life.

"Where are you off to on such a fine morning?" the old man said.

"I'm off to the town market to sell poor old Milky-White, here."

"Indeed? Well, you certainly have the look of a proper cow salesman," said the old man. "But I wonder if you know *how many beans make five?*"

"Of course I do," replied Jack. "Two beans in each hand and one in my mouth. That adds up to five beans."

"You are correct, indeed, young sir," said the old man. "And I just happen to have those very beans right here in my pocket."

Tasty Morsels

"How many beans make five" was an old British turn of phrase. To say someone "knows how many beans make five" is sort of like saying that person "knows his/her business." It means the person is skillful or knowledgeable in a certain vocation or endeavor. The original saying came from the days when merchants and/or scholars used an abacus, an ancient counting device that used beads (or "beans") slid across a series of bars. So the original usage of this phrase just referred to someone who was skilled with numbers. The fact that Jack answers the old man as he does illustrates, more or less, that he is not such a bright guy. The storytellers were making a bit of a joke in this part.

The strange-looking old man then produced from his pockets a handful of equally strange-looking beans.

"Seeing as how you are obviously such a bright young lad," the old man continued, "I'm willing to offer you a good trade—these incredible beans for that old cow you've got there. What do you say?"

"Walker!" laughs Jack. "I bet you *would* like me to make such a silly trade with you!"

"Oh, my dear boy! I understand your hesitation. But what you do not realize is how special these beans truly are," the old man explained. "Plant them in the evening, and by morning you'll have a beanstalk that's grown all the way to the sky!"

"You don't say?" replied Jack.

"I promise it's true," swore the old man. "And if what I say turns out to be untrue, then I'll even give you the cow back."

"Very well," said Jack. He handed over Milky-White, took the beans from the old man, and put them in his pocket. Then he

GRIMM WORDS

Walker: The short form of an old slang term from nineteenth-century England, it was meant as an expression of comical disbelief. Saying "walker" to someone more or less meant that the speaker was calling BS on that person, claiming either that his/her story wasn't true or that what the person said would never happen. The original full/proper usage of this term was "Hooky Walker!"

headed home . . . for what might be the last time once his mother found out what he'd done. Since he hadn't needed to travel all the way to town, he got back earlier than his mother expected.

"Are you back already, Jack?" called his mother when she saw him. "Well, you don't have Milky-White with you, so you must've sold her. How much money did she go for?"

"You'll never guess what I got for her," Jack said . . . and boy, was he right about that!

"You don't say? Well, what a pleasant surprise! And here I was worried you'd muck it all up. How much did you get? Ten pounds? Fifteen?"

Jack just shook his head.

"No! Don't tell me you got *twenty* for her?!"

"See? I told you that you'd never guess it! Check out these beans I got. They're magical, you see, and if we plant them this evening, they'll grow into a beanstalk that reaches up to the sky by morning."

"Excuse me?" his mother replied. "I don't think I heard you right . . . because it sounded to me like you just said you've sold our cow, Milky-White, who's been the best milker in this parish for years, not to mention a specimen of prime beef, for a handful of *beans*!"

"Well . . . yes," Jack said. "You see, they are magic, and if we plant them this evening then—"

Thwack!

At this point, Jack's mother beat the ever-loving snot out of the boy then snatched the beans from his hand and tossed them out the window. After a few more well-aimed smacks across the back of Jack's head, she sent him to bed without dinner. Jack retreated to his tiny room in the attic and curled up on his bed, feeling very sorry for himself. After a while, however, he somehow drifted off to sleep.

When Jack woke up the next morning, something about his room seemed unusual. The sun was only shining into one half of his room through the open window. The other half was darkened by a shadow that had never been there before. Curious to see what'd happened, Jack got up, dressed, and poked his head out the window.

What he saw, to put it simply . . . blew . . . his . . . freaking . . . mind!

Overnight, just as the old man promised, the beans that his mother had tossed out the window had sprouted into a giant beanstalk that had grown all the way up to the sky. The stalk shot up right past Jack's attic bedroom window. Seeing this, he jumped out, right onto the beanstalk.

So Jack climbed . . .

And he climbed . . .

And he climbed . . . When Jack finally reached the top of the beanstalk, he found that he'd come to the start of a long and wide road.

So Jack walked . . .

And walked . . .

And walked . . .

He didn't stop walking until he came upon a giant house at the end of the road. On the front porch of the large house was a fittingly large woman—a giantess, if you will. Jack, rather haphazardly, immediately decided to strike up a conversation with her.

"Good morning, madam," said Jack. "Would you mind sparing a poor soul, such as I, a little breakfast? I'm awful hungry."

What Jack said to the giantess was true, of course, since he'd been beaten within an inch of his life then sent off to bed without supper the night before. By this point Jack's tummy was likely growling like a cornered pit bull.

"Breakfast?" replied the giantess. "You best get stepping, little man, or you're gonna *be* breakfast! My hubby is an ogre and young boy broiled on toast is his favorite meal. He'll be here any minute, so I highly suggest you start running."

But Jack persisted, testing the patience of a giantess . . . married to a boy-eating ogre (not an advisable thing to do).

"Please, good madam. I haven't eaten anything since yesterday," Jack said to her. "I may as well just wait here to be eaten, seeing as how I'm just going to die of hunger soon anyway."

The ogre's giantess of a wife turned out to have a heart big enough to match her size. Being a kindhearted gal (as giantesses go), she brought Jack into her enormous kitchen and gave him a hunk of bread and cheese, along with a big glass of milk to wash it all down. Ravenous as he was, Jack started chowing down on the food. Then suddenly, like a scene right out of *Jurassic Park*, the ground began to quake from impact tremors.

Thump! Thump! THUMP!

The ogre was on his way home.

"Oh, no! It's my hubby," exclaimed the giantess. "He'll be here any second! What do I do with you? I know! Quick, get in the oven!"

Now, normally (like in "Hansel and Gretel") getting into an oven on the advice of a female monster would not be an advisable course of action for a character in a fairy tale like this one. Jack's case, however, is an exception to this rule. Getting into the oven actually saved Jack's life. Just as the oven door shut, the ogre stepped into the house.

This ogre was an especially large fellow, even by ogre standards. On his belt hung three calves, strung there by their rear hooves. The ogre took them from his belt and tossed them onto their enormous kitchen table.

"Here you are, woman," he said. "Broil these up for my breakfast. And . . . *sniff, sniff* . . . wait . . . I know that smell."

Fee-Fi-Fo-Fum,

I smell the blood of an Englishman.

Be he alive, or be he dead,

I'll have his bones to make my bread.

"What rubbish," said his wife. "You're imagining things. I'll bet you smell the leftovers from that boy you had for dinner last night. Why don't you go wash up, and I'll have your breakfast ready when you get back."

The ogre thought better of it and went to the washroom. Jack, seeing his opportunity, was about to jump out of the oven when the giantess told him to stay put.

"He may see you," she warned. "He always naps after he's had breakfast. Just wait until he's asleep."

The ogre had his breakfast, snuggled up with a few of his favorite bags full of gold, and drifted off to sleep. While the ogre snored away, Jack snuck out of the oven and started to make his escape. As he passed the ogre, however, he decided to help himself to one of the bags of gold just before he made a run for it. When he reached the beanstalk, Jack tossed the bag down, and it landed in his mother's garden. After some downward climbing, he got back home and showed his mother the gold.

"See? The beans really were magic, after all," he told her, quite proud of himself.

Despite the fact that the bag of gold was far more money than Jack or his mother had ever seen, not to mention it was far more than they ever would have gotten for selling Milky-White, the pair do not seem to have done much of anything with it to ensure a future source of income for themselves. They just lived extravagantly on the gold until, eventually, it ran out. And so Jack decided to venture up the beanstalk once again, in search of even greater treasures.

After lots of climbing and walking, he reached the same giant house with the same giant woman working on the same front porch.

"Good morning, dear madam," he said. "Spare a little something to eat?"

"You best get on out of here, little man, before my husband comes home and eats you," she replied. "Wait a second! You're that boy who came here before! My hubby found a bag of his gold missing after you left, I'll have you know."

"How odd," said Jack. "I might know where it is, but right now I'm just too hungry to think of it."

Hoping to retrieve her husband's bag of gold, the giantess brought him into her kitchen and fed him as she had before. And, once again, the ground began to quake beneath them with the pounding footfalls of the approaching ogre. Things pretty much went the same way they did the last time. Jack got in the oven, broiled livestock for the ogre's breakfast, fee-fi-fo-fum, etc., etc., etc.

This time, however, instead of snuggling up with bags of gold after his meal, the ogre ordered his wife, "Bring me the hen that lays the golden eggs!" The giantess did as she was told and brought the hen to him. The ogre looked at the hen and said "Lay!" Then, lo and behold, the hen laid an egg of solid gold. The giant nuzzled up with his newly laid golden egg and drifted peacefully to sleep. Apparently, gold is like the ogre version of Ambien. Hearing the loud snores of the ogre, Jack snuck from the oven and headed for the door. As he passed by the giant, he snatched up the hen, causing the animal to let out a *Cluck!*, which woke the ogre.

"Woman," bellowed the ogre upon noticing that his prized pet had gone missing, "what'd you do with my golden hen?"

"Why do you ask, hubby?" she replied.

That's the last thing Jack heard as he made a hasty exit with the hen. He shimmied back down the beanstalk and returned home, where he presented the hen to his mother.

As one would expect, having a hen that laid a solid-gold egg every time they told it to "Lay!" came in pretty handy. The animal kept Jack and his mother well taken care of for quite some time. However, this still didn't seem enough for greedy old Jack. After a while, he decided to risk one last trip up the beanstalk.

So Jack ventured out early one morning.

He climbed a bunch.

He walked a bunch.

This time, however, Jack stopped before he reached the front porch of the giant house. He knew full well that he'd receive no

GRIMM WORDS

Copper: As it is used in this story, a large kettle specifically used for either boiling water or doing laundry. More or less, this meant it was set aside so that it was *not* used for cooking. After all, who wants to eat soup that's been boiled in the same pot that's used for washing everyone's underwear? That's just gross.

welcome from the giantess, now that he'd stolen from her husband twice. Instead of convincing her to let him inside, he hid behind a nearby bush. A short time passed before the ground again quaked upon the ogre's arrival with yet *another* belt full of livestock for his breakfast. As the giantess fetched water for cooking the ogre's breakfast, Jack stole into the house and hid in the copper.

The ogre, however, started sniffing at the air again.

"Fee-fi-fo-fum, I smell the blood of an Englishman. I smell him, wife! I smell him!"

"You do, hubby?" she replied. "Well, if it's that little thief who came before, then I'll bet he's hiding in the oven!"

The both of them went to the oven and threw open the door. They didn't find Jack or squat—or Jack squatting.

"Here you go again, with all your 'fee-fi-fo-fum' nonsense!" the giantess said, scolding her ogre husband. "It's probably just what's left of that boy you ate last night. You should be ashamed of yourself, not being able to tell the difference between a live one and a dead one!"

The ogre washed up and had his breakfast. While he ate, he'd stop every now and then and sniff the air with a confused expression on his face as he grumbled to himself, "I swear I can smell—"

Then he'd go running around the house, looking here and there. However, he never thought to check the copper.

After the ogre finished eating, he called to his wife, "Bring my golden harp!" She did as he said. Then the ogre told the harp, "Sing!" And the harp made the most beautiful sounds ever heard. As it sang its beautiful song, the ogre fell asleep. Hearing the snores, Jack came out from the copper. He immediately snatched the harp and hightailed it out of there.

The harp, however, seemed to have liked its current home. The enchanted instrument called out loudly, "Master! Master, wake up! Thief!" The ogre awoke and saw Jack making off with his golden harp. With the ogre hot on his heels, Jack ran like hell until he reached the beanstalk and started his way back down. Being as big as he was, the ogre hesitated when he came to the beanstalk because he was uncertain that it was strong enough to hold him. This, luckily, gave Jack a nice head start. As Jack disappeared from view, passing below the clouds, the ogre finally decided to risk it and began climbing down after him. The beanstalk trembled under the ogre's weight, but it held. All the while, the ogre could hear the harp calling out to him, "Master! Master, save me! Thief!"

As Jack neared the bottom of the beanstalk, he called out to his mother, "Axe! Axe! I need an axe! Hurry!" His mother came running out of the house with the requested axe, just in time to look up and see the ogre climbing down. Stricken by panic and awe, she froze up. Jack jumped down the last couple of yards, grabbed the axe from his suddenly catatonic mother, and started going all Paul Bunyan on the beanstalk. He chopped away until the beanstalk gave way and finally snapped under the ogre's immense weight. The ginormous piece of vegetation fell to the side, the ogre along with it. Unfortunately for the ogre, the fall shattered his skull . . . and that was that for him.

Once she recovered from the shock of seeing a real-life ogre, Jack presented his mother with the golden harp. Between having a hen that laid golden eggs and an enchanted golden harp to show in town (charging admission, of course), Jack and his mother grew very wealthy. Eventually, Jack married a princess, and together they lived happily ever after.

When a Siegbarste Goes Medieval: A *Grimm* Comparison

Convict displays signs of congenital analgesia, a rare genetic disorder, which deadens the nerve endings, making it difficult to process pain. In addition, Stark's bone structure appears abnormally dense.

—Excerpt from the medical records of Oleg Stark,
"Game Ogre" (1-08)

To be honest, finding points of comparison between Jacobs's "Jack and the Beanstalk" and the *Grimm* episode "Game Ogre" (1-08) was not an easy task. After all, Jack doesn't pop a Nitro Express cap in the ogre with a Siegbarste Gewehr; nor does Oleg Stark die from falling down a beanstalk after Nick Burkhardt takes an axe to it. However, there are at least a few things they have in common (though even these similarities require a little reaching).

In "Game Ogre" (1-08), we learn that Oleg Stark was originally a hit man who always insisted on being paid in gold. This is certainly comparable to the gold-centered hoarding of the ogre in "Jack and the Beanstalk." In fact, the first thing the Jack in the original story steals from the ogre is a bag of gold. It is also Jack's thefts that cause the ogre to begin chasing him, hell-bent on twisting off his tiny head, broiling what's left, and eating him on toast. A theft is also what originally sparked Oleg Stark's violent rampage of revenge. After learning that Stark demands to be paid in gold, a man name Jack Lambert steals the hit man's hard-earned hoard. During an outing for medical evaluation, Stark makes his escape from prison while serving time for kidnapping and torturing Jack Lambert's wife and child, and begins killing all those who put him behind bars.

In the end, both in *Grimm* and in Jacobs's story, the ogre is defeated. Of course, the manner of his defeat differs greatly from the show to the story. The Jack of the story chops down the beanstalk, resulting in the ogre taking a fatal fall. In *Grimm*, Monroe saves the day (and Hank's life) by filling Stark full of Siegbarste Gift–laced ammo from a BFG (see Chapter 2). Apparently, this is one of the only known methods for killing a Siegbarste. You have to admit, it sounds a lot easier then chopping down a giant beanstalk with an axe and counting on gravity to do the rest.

Luckily, taking out a troublesome Hexenbiest—both in *Grimm* and in the story covered in the next chapter—is just a tad bit easier, as long as one has the proper tools. Grimm blood helps, but sometimes kicking the chick into an oven can be just as effective.

[10]

BREAD CRUMBS AND PEOPLE EATERS

CAPTAIN RENARD: *No matter how you look at it, it's cannibalism.*
SERGEANT WU: *I think it's pronounced "capitalism."*

—"Organ Grinder" (1-10)

When it comes to Grimm tales, the story of "Hansel and Gretel" is definitely one of the more widely known. Much like "Little Red-Cap/ Riding Hood," it remains an iconic example of a children's cautionary tale. However, it's so much more than that. This story is an incredibly elaborate and potent metaphor for some of the most deep-seated anxieties and terrifying phobias that exist within a child's psyche—parental abandonment, sustenance deprivation, death by starvation, being lost, and even being cannibalized by adults or eaten alive by wild beasts.

While the retelling that follows is primarily based on the original Brothers Grimm version, I've done a little cherry-picking this time. The original version of the story written down by the Brothers Grimm was *significantly* changed by them over the years. For example, Hansel and Gretel were originally abandoned by their father and *biological* mother. However, by the fourth volume of their *Kinder- und Hausmärchen* the Brothers Grimm had changed the character to be

GRIMM WORDS

Geier: The German word for "vulture." In the *Grimm* universe, it is used to refer to vulture-type Wesen.

Hexenbiest: Despite most translations, this does not mean "witch beast." *Hex*, in German, means "spell" or "curse." Therefore, a more accurate translation might be "cursing/hexing beast" or "spell-casting beast."

their *stepmother*. Likewise, the evil, child-eating woman Hansel and Gretel meet in the woods was not originally called a "witch." This may explain why the writers of *Grimm* chose to portray the cannibalistic Wesen in "Organ Grinder" (1-10) as Geiers (a vulture-type Wesen) instead of Hexenbiests.

If you wish to read some of the various root versions of the "Hansel and Gretel" tale, please refer to the Further Reading section at the back of the book. For now, however, sit back, grab some bread crumbs or croutons, and enjoy the following retelling.

Hansel and Gretel: A Retelling

MONROE: *This might be a little awkward but, for example, you probably didn't know that your testicles—I mean, not your testicles specifically—but that part of the human male anatomy has a kind of Viagra-like effect on certain species. Not that I ever had the need to . . . I mean, everything works great.*

NICK BURKHARDT: *Oh, no . . . that wasn't awkward at all.*

—"Organ Grinder" (1-10)

Tasty Morsels

There has been a widely circulating email in recent decades that claims the origin of the phrase "dirt poor" comes from the Middle Ages and refers to how only the rich could afford proper flooring in their homes. The poor, this email claims, had only dirt floors and were, therefore, "dirt poor." But the fact is that there is absolutely no evidence to support the claim that this phrase was in use prior to the twentieth century. Theorized to have possibly originated in the American Dust Bowl, some believe it referred to the poverty and dirty living conditions caused by the drought and dust storms that marked this period. However, there is still no direct evidence to conclusively prove this theory either.

Once upon a time, there was a tiny ramshackle cottage that sat on the outskirts of a vast and deep forest. This was the humble abode of a dirt-poor woodcutter, who lived there along with his two children and his wife. The woodcutter's children were a boy and girl named Hansel and Gretel.

When the entire region in which they lived was stricken by a terrible famine, the woodcutter realized he was no longer earning enough to put food on the table for everyone. The stress of it all kept the poor guy up at night. He tossed and turned in bed, trying to find a solution to their plight. When he was unable to come up with anything useful, he rolled over and said to his wife, "What'll become of our family? How can we possibly feed the kids when we don't even have enough to feed ourselves? What can we do?"

"I'll tell you what we can do," she told him. "Tomorrow, at daybreak, we'll take Hansel and Gretel deep into the forest. We can go about our daily work cutting wood while they rest by a fire with a crust of bread for each of them to eat. Then, when the day

Tasty Morsels

The problem with famine has always been an issue of supply and demand. In times past, for those who didn't grow their own food (such as the woodcutter in this story), famine was an even more serious problem because the scarceness quickly sent food prices soaring. For the poor who had nonagricultural occupations, this soon made even staples such as bread nearly unaffordable. This is why the woodcutter is unable to provide for his family, despite living near a large forest where wood is (assumedly) plentiful.

ends, we'll just come back home and leave them in the woods. They'll never find their way back here. So we'll be rid of them. See? Problem solved."

"Great *saints*, woman! You are EVIL!" . . . is what the woodcutter should have said. Instead, he asked, "How could I abandon my children to the forest? It would break my heart to do such a thing. They'd surely be torn apart and devoured by wild beasts."

"You're a fool, then," spat his wife. "You've doomed us all to death by starvation. You might as well start to plane the boards for our coffins!"

Unfortunately, this was not the end of their conversation. The wife kept on nagging and harassing her husband, day in and day out, so that he knew no peace until he finally agreed to her plans of abandoning Hansel and Gretel to a grisly fate alone in the forest.

"I'll do it," the woodcutter finally told his wife as they lay together in bed one night. "But I do feel bad for the children."

As anyone who's ever gone to bed with an empty belly will tell you, sleep doesn't come easy when you're hungry. So Hansel and Gretel were awake this entire time. It was a tiny cottage, after all, and voices carry (at least, that's what the band Til Tuesday would have us believe). The siblings had been eavesdropping on the whole conversation between their father and stepmother, and they were horrified to hear what their parents planned to do with them.

Gretel appears to have been a "cup half empty" type of gal. She burst into tears, whispering to her brother Hansel, "That's it . . . We're doomed!"

Luckily for Gretel, her brother Hansel was more of a "take charge" kind of guy.

"Quiet yourself, Gretel," Hansel said. "Don't worry your little head. I'll figure a way out of this for both of us."

Once Hansel heard the snores of his father and stepmother, he crept out of bed and got dressed. He opened the bottom half of the Dutch door and stepped out into the night.

The moon shone brightly in the night sky, casting a reflection upon certain shiny white pebbles in front of the cottage. The light reflected so brightly on the stones that Hansel realized they'd be easy to see at night. He filled his pockets with as many pebbles as would fit. Once he was satisfied he had enough of them, he slipped back into the house and got in bed.

"Nothing to worry about, little sister," he told Gretel. "Go back to sleep. God will show us the way. We are not forsaken."

The next morning, Hansel and Gretel were awakened by their stepmother.

"Get out of bed, you lazy good-for-nothings. We are going into the forest to chop wood, and the two of you are coming along," she snarled, handing each of them a hard crust of bread. "This is your lunch. If you eat it now, you'll be sorry, because you're not getting anything else."

Gretel took Hansel's crust and put it in the pocket of her apron along with her own, since Hansel's pockets were full of the

GRIMM WORDS

Dutch door: Also known as a stable door or half door, this is a style of door cut horizontally across the middle, into two halves. This way, the top and bottom halves can be opened independently. This is, more or less, an early version of the modern baby gate. The closed bottom half was meant to prevent small children from getting out of the house as well as animals from getting in, while allowing the top half to be opened to allow light and air to come in. Such doors were common in sixteenth-century northern Europe, and can still be seen in Amish and Mennonite communities. Since Hansel exits through the bottom half, this shows that he's still only a small boy, likely no older than eight or nine.

shiny pebbles he'd collected the night before. The siblings then started into the forest behind their parents. As they traveled, Hansel stopped every few paces in order to toss one of the pebbles from his pocket. This eventually caused him to lag behind, and their father noticed the boy wasn't keeping up.

"What are you doing, Hansel? Stop falling behind and remember what your legs are for!" their father scolded.

"I'm just trying to get one last look at my white kitten, Father," said Hansel. "He is perched on the roof, telling me good-bye."

In reality, of course, Hansel wasn't looking back at his cat. As already stated, he was really just stopping to throw pebbles down to mark the way back home.

Once they were deep in the forest, their father said to them, "Go gather some fallen wood to build a fire. We don't want the two of you getting cold."

Hansel and Gretel, ever the obedient children, did as their father said and gathered as much fallen brushwood as they could.

Soon, a roaring fire was before them, and their parents headed off into the woods. When lunchtime rolled around, Hansel and Gretel ate their bread crusts. They could still hear what sounded like their father's axe chopping wood. Believing he was nearby, they fell asleep next to the warm fire. However, the sound they heard was *not* their father's axe. It was a branch he'd tied to a dying tree. As the wind blew, the wood knocked together to mimic the sound of an axe. When the siblings woke up, it was the middle of the night.

Gretel, in simple terms, freaked the hell out.

"We're really in trouble now," she fretted. "How will we ever get out of this forest on our own?"

"Just hang on," Hansel told her. "Once the moon comes out, we'll be able to find our way home."

When the moon rose, it shone down on the ground, and its light reflected off the pebbles Hansel had strewn along the way. Hansel and Gretel walked through the night, hand in hand, until they found their way back home. They arrived just as the sun broke over the horizon. They knocked at the door, which was answered by their stepmother.

Though the arrival of Hansel and Gretel likely startled the living bejeezus out of their mean-as-hell stepmother, she did her best to mask her surprise.

"Where have you two layabouts been?" she said. "We'd begun to think you were going to spend the rest of your lives sleeping in the woods! We were wondering if you'd ever come back."

Meanwhile, their father had been completely heartbroken by what he'd done to his own flesh and blood. So, unlike his evil wife, the woodcutter was delighted when he saw that his children had found their way home to him. He embraced them both and shed tears of joy.

The famine eventually passed. However, bad things tend to have a way of coming back around. Soon enough, an even worse famine hit the area. It didn't take long for Hansel and Gretel's stepmother to return to her original plan. She again started nagging the woodcutter without end, especially at night once the children were in bed.

"We're out of food again," she said to the woodcutter. "The cupboard has nothing but half a loaf of bread in it. Once that's eaten, we'll all starve. Those kids of yours have got to go! This time, we'll lead them so far into the forest that they'll never find their way out. If we don't do it, we'll all die."

The woodcutter's heart was torn as to what he should do.

"It would be better," he said, "if we all shared the last crust of bread together."

However, the woodcutter was now "in for a penny, in for a pound." Since he had given in to his wife's demands the first time, he also buckled this time.

Just as before, Hansel and Gretel were eavesdropping on the conversation. Hansel again waited until the adults were asleep. Then he got dressed and tried to sneak out as he had before. This time, however, the Dutch door had been barred shut, and he was unable to get out. When Hansel came back to bed, Gretel was in a fit of tears.

"Don't cry sister," he told her. "The Lord will protect us. Just go back to sleep."

As the sky turned from dark to light the next morning, the stepmother woke Hansel and Gretel. She again gave both of them a crust of bread, though these were even smaller than the ones they were given the last time. Hansel, clever boy that he was, crushed his bread crust into crumbs once it was in his pocket, hoping to use them in the same way he'd used the shiny pebbles.

They all set out into the forest yet again. As before, Hansel stopped now and again, this time to scatter crumbs behind him. And, as before, he started to lag behind as a result.

"Hansel, what are you doing?" said his father. "Stop falling behind and get moving."

"I'm trying to get a last look at my little pet dove," Hansel replied. "It's on the roof trying to say good-bye to me."

"You stupid little thing," scolded the woodcutter's wicked-hearted wife. "That's not your dove. That's the sun reflecting off the chimney."

As they traveled, Hansel kept throwing crumbs from his pocket. But they continued to go ever deeper and deeper into the forest, until they reached a place the children had never been. They built a fire, as before, and the stepmother told them to stick close to it.

When lunchtime came, Gretel shared her bread crust with Hansel since he'd used his crust to mark the way back. With even such a tiny bit of food in their bellies, the siblings fell asleep next to the soothing warmth of the fire. As the sun set and darkness fell, no one came to get them.

Again they woke up in total darkness, and again Gretel had a full-blown panic attack. Hansel did what he could to comfort his sister.

"The moon will come out as before," he told her. "Then we'll be able to get back home by following the bread crumbs I scattered. They'll show us the way."

Apparently, Hansel had never gone on a trip to feed ducks. When the moon came out, not a crumb was left. Poor kid might as well have just eaten the crust, for all the good it did. Every crumb he'd tossed upon the ground had been eaten by birds.

Gretel, true to form, freaked out even worse than before.

"Don't worry," Hansel told her. "We'll find our way home, somehow."

Unfortunately . . . they *didn't*. In fact, they got so lost that they soon had not a clue as to even what direction they should travel. They walked from sunrise to sunset that day with no luck.

Their second day in the forest didn't go any better. They still couldn't find a path out of the woods. With nothing to eat but the occasional wild berry, their stomachs grumbled, and they could barely sleep at night from the hunger pangs.

By the third day, the brother and sister were so tired they couldn't walk any farther. Side by side, they lay down under the shade of a tree and fell asleep.

At midday the children awoke to see a beautiful white bird, the likes of which they'd never seen before, perched upon the branch of a tree. The sounds it made were so lovely they could not help but listen. After a few moments, the bird quit singing and took to flight. The children followed it until they came to a small house in the middle of the woods. The strange bird landed on the roof, as if leading them to it. As Hansel and Gretel came closer, they realized the house was made of bread. Its roof was made of cake, and the windows were hardened sugar. This place was like a diabetic's worst nightmare.

"Let's have a bite or two," said Hansel. "May the Lord bless this meal we are about to receive. I'll take a piece of the roof. Gretel, take one of those sweet-looking windows."

The children each grabbed a piece of the house and got to eating. That's when a voice suddenly called out to them from somewhere inside, "Nibble, nibble, gnaws the mouse. Who is nibbling at my little house?"

To which Hansel and Gretel replied, "The wind, the wind. The Heaven-born wind."

Or, in some translations they are written as having said, "The wind so mild. The heaven-born child."

Then the pair got right back to the business of gorging themselves on pieces of the sugary house. Hansel appears to have enjoyed the taste of "roof cake," and he tore down another giant chunk of it. Gretel, likewise, had found her first nibble of "sugar glass" to be delicious. So she pushed out an entire pane of it, sat down, and went back to filling her belly.

As Hansel and Gretel sat down and began working their way into a sugar-fueled frenzy, the door of the house opened and out stepped an old woman. How old, you ask? "As old as the hills." That sounds pretty old. She leaned on a crutch, and her movements appeared slow and feeble. At first, Hansel and Gretel were scared to death of the old hag and dropped their sweets just in case they needed to make a break for it. The old woman, however, spoke kindly to them.

"You poor little dears," she said. "How did you come to be alone so deep in the woods? Please come inside and stay here with me. I promise no harm will come to you in my house."

The old woman led the children by the hand into her sugary abode, where she presented them with a hearty breakfast of milk and pancakes topped with powdered sugar, apple slices, nuts, and cream. Once their bellies were full, she showed them to a pair of cozy little beds. The exhausted siblings snuggled in and crashed . . . which is impressive, considering how much sugar they'd just consumed. As they fell asleep, Hansel and Gretel believed their troubles were finally at an end.

Unfortunately for them, their problems had only just begun. The old woman was in fact a cannibal (or, to put it in *Grimm* terms, a Hexenbiest) who used her enchanted bird and house of sugary delights to trap lost kiddies.

Seriously . . . How often did children get abandoned in the woods by their parents back then?

Once the old woman got a child into her home, she would kill it, cook it, and eat it . . . after she'd fattened it up if it was too scrawny, of course. The hag had red eyes and could not see very well, but she had a very keen sense of smell, which allowed her to sniff out any nearby humans.

Early the next morning, as Hansel and Gretel slept, the old hag arose from her bed and stared creepily at the slumbering children. They were sleeping so soundly and peacefully that the old hag thought to herself: *Maybe I shouldn't eat them.*

Just kidding. She still totally planned on eating them.

These two will make a tasty pair of morsels, was what the old hag really thought.

The old hag snatched up Hansel by the arm, led him out to a little shed, and locked him inside. Gretel, presumably still exhausted from her ordeal, didn't even move until the old hag came back and roused her from sleep, shaking the poor girl until she woke up.

"Get out of bed, you lazy good-for-nothing," the old hag said. "Fetch some water, and cook some good food for your brother. He'll stay locked up in my shed until he's not so skinny. Once he's fattened up, I can eat him."

Gretel, as per her usual response to such things, started crying, but did as the hag ordered. All the good food she cooked was fed to Hansel, while Gretel got nothing but crab shells.

Every morning the old hag hobbled out to the shed so she could see (or *not see*, since she had those useless red eyes of hers) if Hansel had gained any weight. Ever the clever boy, Hansel took a bone from his meal each day and held it out for the ill-sighted witch to grasp. Thinking the bone was Hansel's finger, she wasn't happy with his progress. However, the old hag's patience for child steaks appears to have had a limit.

When a month had passed and Hansel didn't seem to be growing any fatter, despite being constantly fed every day, the old hag was no longer willing to wait. She decided she was going to eat that boy now, whether fat or skinny.

"Gretel," the old hag snarled. "Fat or thin, I'm going to butcher your brother like a pig in the morning. Then I'll cook him for my supper."

And what did Gretel do? Gretel started bawling her eyes out.

"God help us," she cried. "It would've been better if we'd been torn apart and eaten by wild beasts in the forest. At least then we would have died together."

Yeah, Gretel was definitely a "glass half empty" type of gal.

"Shut your cake hole," scolded the old hag. "Prayers can't save you now. Your brother dies in the morning."

The old hag got up early the next day, happy with anticipation of the meal to come. She woke Gretel and made her fetch water then light the fire beneath the kettle.

"The oven should be warm, and I've kneaded the dough," the old hag told Gretel when these tasks were done. "Now it's time to do some baking."

The old hag shoved Gretel toward the red-hot oven, flames dancing from its open door, and told her, "Crawl in there and let me know if it's hot enough to put in the bread."

In her first wise move since this story began, Gretel realized the old hag was going to push her into the oven once she peeked in. Demonstrating uncharacteristic gumption, she played dumb.

"How does a person get into an oven? I don't know how to do that," Gretel told the old hag.

"You silly little goose," the old hag chuckled. "There's plenty of room in that door for a skinny thing like you. Just watch. I'll show you that even I can fit."

The old woman went over to the oven and poked her head inside. Seeing her opportunity, Gretel kicked that hag as hard as she could into the blazing furnace. Then the young girl slammed shut the oven door. The old hag let forth an ear-piercing wail as she burned to death, cooked alive in her own oven. It was an ugly way to go.

Gretel wasted no time getting to her brother and immediately ran out to the shed.

"We are free, Hansel," she told him as she unlocked the door.

Since the old hag was most certainly a crispy critter at this point, Hansel and Gretel decided it was time to loot her house. They discovered the place was full of chests that overflowed with jewels, pearls, and coins.

"These treasures," noted Hansel, "are even better than the shiny pebbles I once found."

"I'll take some too," said Gretel.

So Hansel filled his pockets with treasure, and Gretel did likewise with her apron.

"We should get going soon," said Hansel. "We need to get clear of this old hag's forest."

So the children fled from the home that had been their prison for a month, their pockets full of loot. After a few hours of traveling, they came upon a lake. The newly resilient Gretel didn't freak-out this time (thank heavens!). Hansel, however, chose this exact moment to break down. Can you say, "role reversal"?

"We'll never make it across," Hansel said. "And I don't see a bridge anywhere."

"No boats around either," Gretel agreed, which probably wasn't too comforting to her brother. "However, I see a duck over there. She'll aid our crossing, if I ask properly."

Gretel now called out to the duck, perhaps magically, and said:

Little duck, little duck, dost thou see?
Hansel and Gretel are waiting for thee.
There's not a plank or bridge in sight,
Carry us over on thy back so white.

Hearing these words, the duck paddled over to them. Hansel got on the duck's back and told Gretel to join him.

"Not yet," Gretel replied. "The two of us are too much weight for such a little duck. We'll cross over one at a time."

And all happened just as Gretel said. The duck took both siblings across, one then the other. Once they reached the other side, they started walking. Soon, the woods began to seem more familiar. Eventually, they spied their home in the distance and began to run to it.

Their father was in the house and, in a turn of good luck, his wife had died while the children were imprisoned by the cannibalistic hag. The woodcutter had become a completely broken man ever since the day he'd joined his wife in abandoning Hansel and Gretel. Seeing each other, the father and his children embraced and shed tears of joy at being reunited.

At this point, Gretel emptied the treasures she'd stored in her apron. Hansel likewise emptied his pockets of treasure.

It was more money than they would ever need.

Their worries now truly at an end, the family lived happily ever after.

And the Grimm brothers end the tale with this weird little ditty:

Sing everyone,

Our mystery is done,

And look! Round the house,

There runs a mouse.

He who catches it, gets to make a fur hat out of it.

When Geiers Attack . . . and Then Sell Your Organs: A *Grimm* Comparison

Geiers are the most vile of all. They harvest human organs while the victim is still alive, seeming to take pleasure in the savage pain they cause.
　　　　—Nick Burkhardt, reading from the Grimm Journals,
　　　　　　　　　　　　　　　　　　"Organ Grinder" (1-10)

When it comes to eating children or, at least, harvesting their organs . . . Geiers are the usual suspects. In the episode "Organ Grinder" (1-10), young runaways are the preferred prey of Geiers— who take delight in tearing apart their prey while they're still alive. So perhaps it should be no surprise that Gracie and Hanson end up on their table, just shy of getting their vital organs surgically removed by the local Geiers at the Folter Clinic.

When comparing the original Brothers Grimm story of "Hansel and Gretel" to the events of the "Organ Grinder" (1-10) episode of *Grimm*, there are plenty of things to discuss. First and foremost, there's the most obvious thing: both have a brother and sister with names that start with *H* and *G*—Hansel and Gretel in the story, Hanson and Gracie in the *Grimm* episode.

Tasty Morsels

Remember the Folter Clinic where the runaways of Portland go for medical treatment? Well, maybe they should have paid more attention to the clinic's name. In German, the word *Folter* means "torture." So . . . yeah . . . not exactly the kind of place you'd want to go for a sore throat.

The next comparable element of both stories is that of parental abandonment. Like Hansel and Gretel, who were abandoned in the forest by their parents, Hanson and Gracie have been left to their own devices in the "urban jungle" of Portland. They are just kids, abandoned and left with no choice but to fend for themselves in a scary and dangerous place. And, just as in the world of Hansel and Gretel, there are predators lurking under the guise of saviors. When Hansel and Gretel meet an old woman in the forest, they believe their problems are at an end and that she wants nothing more than to help them. When Hanson and Gracie go to the free Folter Clinic in Portland when they are sick, they believe these are people who only wish to help them. In both stories, the children are wrong.

This brings us to the next overlapping element between the two portrayals—starvation. In the "Hansel and Gretel" story, they find themselves starving in the woods, and this leads them to fall into the "sweet house" trap of the old hag. In *Grimm*, however, it is not the evil Geiers who satiate the hunger of Hanson and Gracie—it's a Grimm. Nick Burkhardt and Juliette Silverton are the only people who care enough to feed these wayward teens. Even after Nick pays a rather high price for one of Gracie's necklaces, he still treats her and her brother to a hot meal (which, judging from how they wolf it down, they haven't had in a long time). Gracie's necklace, actually, brings us to our next comparison—marking the way to salvation.

Hansel used objects to mark his way home on two occasions— once with stones and again with bread crumbs. Hanson, on the other hand, marks his path with shells from his sister's necklaces. Instead of leading the way home, the shells are meant to lead anyone who comes looking—namely, Nick Burkhardt—to where he and Gracie have been taken.

Abandoned Children in Fairy Tales

While the tale of Hansel and Gretel is unique in some ways, the theme of child abandonment is an oddly common occurrence in folktales across the globe. Sometimes a lone adolescent is left to wander in a story, while in other tales (such as "Hansel and Gretel") multiple children or siblings are abandoned by their parents. Their abandonments are for a number of various reasons, often unique to the situational experiences of the culture groups that created the stories. For example, in some stories a child may be driven out from a tribe or village due to a superstitious belief that they are evil, possessed, or bear some mark considered to be an ill omen. Other times, the child is kicked out or left behind for being ungrateful, disobedient, or just plain dumb. Lastly, there are economic reasons—such as Hansel and Gretel's parents leaving them in the woods when they are no longer able to feed the entire household. In fact, extreme poverty and/or lack of food are the most common motivations.

In the real world situations like these would likely lead to tragic results for the child; however, such is not usually the case in the fairy-tale world—quite the opposite, actually. The forsaken children in fairy tales do quite well for themselves, more often than not, finding inner strength they never knew they had and using it to overcome obstacles or to defeat the monsters who wish to devour them. Sometimes, as with Hansel and Gretel, the children even find their way back home to a remorseful parent and live happily ever after . . . as long as they remember to use stones instead of bread crumbs, of course.

While a trail of shells may have led the way to salvation for Hanson and Gracie . . . the Coins of Zakynthos often lead the way to ruin for those who dare to possess them.

[11]

COINS OF BLESSING,
COINS OF CURSE

Eighth century BC, gold was being mined on the island of Zakynthos in ancient Greece. Now certain coins that were struck from that mine were stamped with a swastika on one side, signifying good fortune, and a lion's head on the other, symbolizing wealth and power . . . And, it would seem, those who held the coins possessed a kind of charismatic influence over other men.

—Farley Kolt, "Three Coins in a Fuchsbau" (1-13)

Ever since the Coins of Zakynthos first turned up in the belly of a dead shop owner in the episode "Three Coins in a Fuchsbau" (1-13), they've been causing all sorts of problems for Nick Burkhardt. In fact, considering that his mother had to fake her own death back when Nick was still only a boy to avoid Verrat assassins while she was guarding the coins, one could say they've been causing him trouble his entire life.

The idea of coins, gold, and/or treasure that have adverse affects on the hearts of humans is nothing new. Mythology is full of such tales, and many works from modern literature and pop culture—such as the One Ring from J. R. R. Tolkien's *The Lord of the Rings* trilogy and

Tasty Morsels

Napoleon is one of the men, according to the mythos of the *Grimm* universe, who once possessed the Coins of Zakynthos. These coins, of course, are said to contain poisonous levels of arsenic. For many years a theory persisted that Napoleon died from arsenic poisoning, and not stomach cancer as previously believed, either due to deliberate poisoning by his British captors or from environmental factors. However, a 2008 study conducted by scientists from Italy's National Institute of Nuclear Physics debunked this theory and claimed the levels of arsenic found in Napoleon's hair were no higher than those found in other bodies from the same period, including those of his wife and son.

the horcrux in the Harry Potter series—have been influenced by them. When it comes to the Brothers Grimm tale "The Master Thief" and the plot of the episode in which it is mentioned, strangely enough, the two have almost nothing in common. However, let's take a look at the Grimm story anyway . . . just to be thorough. The following is a retelling of "The Master Thief," from the Brothers Grimm work of 1812, *Kinder- und Hausmärchen*.

The Master Thief: A Retelling

One day, as an old country couple sat together on the porch of their ramshackle cottage, a beautifully adorned carriage suddenly approached. Covered in gold and silver, and drawn by magnificent horses, they were certain it belonged to some great lord or other wealthy nobleman. When the carriage stopped in front of their humble home, the old countryman stood up to ask if he could be of service. A finely dressed stranger emerged from the carriage and extended his hand as he stepped out.

"Good sir," the stranger said, "I would like nothing more than to be served a dish of traditional country food. If I could join you for dinner this evening, I'd be most grateful."

"It's obvious to me you are a count or a prince or at least of noble birth," the old man replied. "You rich folks have these odd little fancies, now and again. We don't have much, but we'd be delighted to share our table with you."

The old countryman's wife went to the kitchen and began preparing the potatoes—washing them, rubbing them, and forming them into little balls as was the custom of country folk in those times. As she worked, her husband spoke to their unusual guest.

"You can join me in the garden, if you like, while my wife readies dinner," the old man told the stranger. "I still have some work to finish before the day is done."

The old man led the stranger to an area in the garden where several small holes had already been dug. He grabbed a young tree and began to plant it in one of the holes. The stranger could see it was difficult work for such an elderly man.

"Have you no children," asked the stranger, "perhaps a young son who could do this work for you?"

"No," the old man replied. Then he thought for a moment and continued. "Well, to be honest, I once had a son. But he left us long ago. He was a bit of a problem child, it saddens me to say—plenty smart enough and sharp of wit, to be sure. However, he never listened to a word I said and often caused trouble with his tricks and scams. One day, he ran away from us, and we never saw him again."

The old man took another young tree and placed it in a hole. This one was not growing straight, so he took some ropes and bound its still-flexible trunk to a sturdy pole.

"Why are you doing that?" said the stranger.

"So it will grow straight."

"Then why not do it to that older tree over there, which is so crooked?"

"Good sir, you speak as one who is not familiar with gardening," replied the old man. "That tree there is old and far too crooked. Nothing will make it straight now. Trees must be conditioned while they are still young and flexible."

"I would imagine that's how things went with your son, didn't they?" the stranger said. "Had he been properly conditioned when he was young, he might not have run away. By now, he must have grown old and crooked . . . just like that tree."

"It's been many years since he left. I'm sure he's changed a lot."

"Do you think you'd recognize him if you saw him now?" said the stranger.

"I probably would not know his face," the old man admitted. "However, he had a bean-shaped birthmark on his shoulder. I'd always recognize that, sure enough."

The stranger then removed his tunic and bared his shoulder, on which could be seen that very same bean-shaped birthmark!

"God in heaven," cried the old man. "You are my lost son! But how can this be? You are obviously a man of great wealth! How have you, the lowborn son of a gardener, come to be a lord?"

"I'm no lord, Father," said the son. "I am like that tree, bound to no post in my youth, and so I have grown to be a crook. All that I have I've earned because I am a thief. Please do not be worried, however. I am a *master* thief. Locks and doors pose no obsta-

GRIMM WORDS

Halter: This term usually refers to a harness or rope used to lead or tether a domesticated animal. However, it is used in this story as a reference to a hangman's noose.

cles to me. And do not think I just steal indiscriminately. I only take the unneeded items and frivolous trappings of the very wealthy. I would never rob from the poor! In fact, I often give a large portion of my take to the less fortunate. I also never steal anything that's easily taken—if it's not a challenge, then I don't even bother with it."

"I cannot say I'm pleased to hear this, my son," said the father. "A master thief is still a thief . . . and thieves often earn their final reward on the gallows."

The father took his newly returned son to the kitchen to see his mother. When she saw he was indeed her son, she hugged him and wept tears of joy. When he told her he'd become a master thief, however, she wept even harder for sorrow. After a time, though, she pulled herself together.

"Whether he is a thief or not," she said, "he is still our son. I am just so glad I'm able to see him with my own eyes once more."

The reunited family sat together at the dinner table to eat. The master thief was so glad to be dining with his parents again that he didn't even mind the taste of the terrible country food, which he hadn't eaten in so many years.

"If the lord count, who still lives up there in his castle, learns what you are," said the father as they ate, "he won't pick you up and hug you, like he did when you were a baby. Instead, he'll have you swinging from a halter."

"Don't worry yourself, Father," said the master thief. "He will not hang me. I know my trade well, perhaps better than any. In fact, I plan to visit my godfather the lord count this very day."

As evening approached, the master thief boarded his carriage and rode up to the lord count's castle. He was received cordially since, upon seeing his fine carriage and expensive clothes, the lord count assumed he was either a fellow nobleman or, at least, a man of some distinction. However, the master thief immediately told the lord count who he was . . . as well as what trade he now practiced (if one can really call stealing other people's stuff a "trade"). When the lord count heard this, he turned white as a sheet and said nothing for a very long time.

"You are still my godson," the lord count finally said. "And for that reason only, I shall allow mercy to take the place of justice. I shall give you some leniency, but do not think you're getting off scot-free. Since you claim to be a master thief, I am going to put your skills to the test. If you fail, your bride shall be the rope maker's daughter, and the caws of the ravens shall be your wedding song."

FYI—in case it isn't obvious, the above was just the lord count's fancy way of saying the master thief would be hanged if he failed. It's just a morbid metaphor . . . no one is getting married here.

"Dearest Lord Count," said the master thief, "think up three of the most difficult tests your mind can conjure. If I fail even one of them, you may do to me what you will."

The lord count took some time to think carefully on how best to challenge his delinquent godson. Once he felt he had come up with three tests of appropriate difficulty, the lord count spoke.

"First, you must steal my personal riding horse from the castle stables without being seen. Second, you must steal the bed-

GRIMM WORDS

Parson: A permanently appointed member of the clergy, such as a vicar or rector.

Clerk: This is a lay clergy position, commonly a record keeper tasked with tracking church finances, as well as recording the births, deaths, and marriages of the local congregation.

sheets from my chambers while my wife and I are still sleeping on them, as well as the wedding ring from my wife's finger, all without being discovered. Lastly, you must steal both the parson and the clerk from the church. Please understand the gravity of your situation. Though I love you as a godson, I do not make idle threats. Fail at any one of these tasks, and you will hang from my gallows like any other common thief."

The master thief accepted these challenges and, without another word, rode his carriage to the nearest town. Once there, he bought clothes like those of an old poor woman. Next, he used leather stain to dye his face and hands brown. He then sharpened a piece of charcoal to draw wrinkles on his cheeks. By the time he was done, his own mother wouldn't have known him (then again, she hadn't recognized him when he *wasn't* disguised in "poor old lady" drag . . . so, perhaps that's not the best comparison). Lastly, he bought a skin cask of old Hungary wine and mixed it with a powerful sleeping potion.

The master thief placed the wine cask in a basket he'd strapped to his back. Stepping slowly and feebly, so as to match his elderly disguise, he passed through the front gates of the lord count's castle. When he reached the courtyard, the master thief sat down on a stone in front of the stable and began to fake a

> ### *GRIMM* WORDS
>
> *Hungary wine*: By the early 1800s, Hungary had a long-standing and well-developed winemaking tradition. Hungary wine was often viewed as especially strong compared to other vintages. Louis XIV of France once referred to a type of Hungarian wine from Tokaj in northern Hungary as "Vinum Regum, Rex Vinorum" (Wine of Kings, King of Wines).

coughing fit so he'd appear to any passersby like an asthmatic old woman. He rubbed his hands and shivered, as if the cold weather made his arthritic hands hurt.

As the master thief went on this way, some of the lord count's soldiers were in the nearby stables tending to the horses. One of them saw the "poor old woman" and felt sorry for her (men often see any old woman and are reminded of their grandmothers, after all). Some of the soldiers had just finished their work and were lounging near a fire.

"Old woman," the one soldier called. "You should come over here and join us by the fire. Some warming up would do you good."

The "old woman" groaned as she stood up and hobbled over to them, ever so slowly. When she drew near, the "old woman" asked the soldier if he'd be so kind as to help her get the basket off her back. The soldier kindly did so, and she joined them by the fire. As the soldier put down the basket, he noticed the wine cask.

"What have you got in this wine cask, old woman?" he asked.

"A very tasty and strong Hungarian wine," she told them. "If you'd like a glass, I'm willing to trade with you. For a few coins and some polite conversation, I'd be happy to share my wine with all of you."

The soldiers all took out a coin each and gave them to the "old woman." It was a fair price for such a nice vintage of Hungary wine.

"Now, let's see if your wine is worth the price we paid," one of them joked, and swallowed a mouthful. The others joined him, passing around the cask and filling their cups.

"I must say, that *is* a good wine," another soldier said. "And when the wine is good, I always enjoy a second glass. I think I'll have another."

The soldiers passed the cask around a second time and again drank down their cups.

"My friends," one of them called out to several other soldiers who were still at work inside the stables. "There is an incredibly generous old woman out here with some wine that, I swear, must be as well aged as she is! Try some! It'll warm your bellies!"

"Please," the "old woman" said. "Allow me to bring it to them."

The "old woman" got up and took the cask into the stables to serve it to the other soldiers, who just so happened to be attending to and guarding the lord count's personal riding horse (you didn't think he was just going to leave it unprotected, did you?). One soldier was mounted on the saddled horse, a fine destrier. A second soldier held the horse's bridle. The third soldier, for reasons that aren't made entirely clear in the original story, was holding on to the horse's tail (perhaps he thought this would prevent it from being stolen?).

The "old woman" let them all drink as much of the wine as they desired. Apparently, they desired quite a bit, because they drank the entire cask dry (which, as you will remember, was spiked with a sleeping potion). Soon enough, the first soldier had fallen asleep in the saddle. The second soldier dropped the bridle, and the third let go of the horse's tail. They all began snoring

GRIMM WORDS

Destrier: A breed of medieval warhorse, commonly used by European knights and nobility.

away. The "old woman" checked on the soldiers outside and found they were also having a bit of a nap.

Unfortunately, the one soldier remained in the saddle when he drifted off to sleep, which now presented a problem. If the master thief pushed him down, he might wake up. So, instead, the master thief suspended the saddle by some ropes that he attached to wall rings and unbuckled it from the horse. He then hoisted up the saddle a bit, resecured the ropes to the wall rings so it remained held in the air, and led the horse right out from under it. The master thief then gathered up some old rags and used them to pad the horse's hooves. Otherwise, someone might have heard it clopping along on the paving stones as it trotted out the castle gate. Moving stealthily, he led the horse out of the stables. He removed the rags once they were past the castle gate, mounted the horse, and took off at a full gallop.

At dawn the next day, the master thief (no longer in old lady drag) rode the horse back to the front of the castle gate. The lord count, who'd just awoken to the cock's crow, got out of bed and looked out the window to see the master thief waiting just outside the castle gate . . . mounted on the lord's personal riding horse.

"Good morning, Lord Count," called the master thief. "I think you'll find you are missing a horse! Your guards are likely still asleep! If you check your stables, however, I believe you'll find at least one of them is still in the saddle!"

The master thief laughed, and the lord count could not help but laugh along with him. It was an impressive feat, after all. And he was likely grateful he wouldn't have to hang his godson . . . for another day, at least. This was only the first of three tasks, after all.

"Very well," the lord count said to the master thief when he came down to retrieve his horse. "That's one task down. Two still remain. Fail at either, and I shall deal with you as a thief."

That night, the master thief had to steal the bedsheets from the lord count's bed while he and his wife slept. Not to mention he also had to find a way to steal the countess's wedding ring in the process. And the lord count wasn't about to make things easy on him. As he and his wife went to bed that night, the lord count instructed his wife the countess to clench her left hand into a fist so that her ring could not be easily slipped from her finger.

"I have securely barred all the doors," he told her. "I shall not sleep but will stand watch all night with my pistol. The thief will have to come through the window. When he does, godson or not, I will have no choice but to shoot him."

That night, under cover of darkness, the master thief went to the gallows and cut down the body of a dead thief who'd been left hanging there from a noose. He then took the corpse to the castle. He placed a ladder under the lord count's bedchamber window, hoisted the dead body onto his shoulders, piggyback style, and climbed up. The master thief stopped just as the head and shoulders of the dead thief reached the open window. The lord count, upon seeing the intruder, aimed his pistol and fired a shot right into its face. When the master thief heard the shot, he let go of the corpse and let it fall to the ground below. Using the smoke of the black powder from the pistol shot to mask his movements, the master thief snuck into the window and hid himself in the shadows. From his hiding spot, he watched as the lord count crawled out the window and climbed down the ladder. The master thief watched from the window as the lord count dragged the body to the garden and began digging a grave.

This is my chance, thought the master thief. He snuck up to the sleeping countess (apparently, that lady could sleep through just about anything if *gunfire* wasn't enough to wake her) and spoke to her, mimicking the voice of the lord count.

"My dearest wife," he said. "I've killed the thief. However, he is still my godson. I refuse to shame him openly, as I would any other common thief. I also cannot help but feel grief for his parents. I'm going to bury him in the garden before sunrise approaches. However, I need the sheets to wrap up his body."

And the countess handed over the sheets.

"I feel so terrible about this," he continued, once he had the sheets. "Please let me have your wedding ring. My godson did risk his life, after all, and lost it, trying to gain that ring. He deserves to be buried with it."

Since the countess would never have dared refuse the lord count, she handed over her ring after just a brief moment of hesitation. She then, presumably, went back to sleep in her sheetless bed. The master thief gathered up his loot and made it back home before the lord count returned from . . . well . . . "burying him" in the garden. Thinking the matter was now settled, the lord count climbed back up the ladder and went to sleep (though, one would imagine, he slept a bit restlessly considering he thought he'd just shot his own godson in the face).

When the lord count awoke the next day at dawn, he went pale as a ghost when he looked out the window and saw the master thief standing just in front of the castle gate. In one hand he held the bedsheets, and in the other hand he held up the shiny wedding ring. The lord count dressed quickly and rushed down to the gate, unsure how all this could be possible.

"Are you a wizard or something?" the lord count said as he approached the master thief. "I shot you! You *died*! How can you be standing here, when I buried you in the garden with my own two hands?"

"Simple . . . You did not bury *me*," the master thief answered. "You did bury a thief, though, to be sure . . . one of the men you recently hanged on the gallows."

The master thief then explained to the lord count how the entire caper had gone down. His nobleman godfather had no choice but to admit that his godson was indeed the most cunning and crafty thief he'd ever encountered.

"The third task still remains," the lord count reminded his godson. "This isn't over yet. If you fail at this last challenge, these first two victories will mean nothing. You will hang, unless you succeed at the very end."

The master thief said nothing. He just smiled and walked away. If he'd been holding a microphone (they didn't exist yet, of course) . . . he probably would've held it up and dropped it.

Now the master thief had come to the third and perhaps most difficult task, which was the whole business of stealing the parson and the clerk from the village church. Stealing objects is one thing. Stealing people, obviously, would be a bit more challenging than making off with horses and bedsheets.

The master thief spent the day acquiring the items he needed to pull off this last task—a long sack he could wear on his back (which he filled with a large number of live crabs . . . just don't ask where he got them) and a bundle sack (in which he packed a bunch of wax candles, a fake gray beard, and a long black robe).

One would hope he didn't buy all of these items in the same place, as the merchant probably would have driven himself insane trying to figure out what he planned to do with it all.

The master thief waited until nightfall and set out for the church. When he reached the churchyard, he took out one crab and one candle. He then stuck the candle to the crab's back, lit the wick, and turned the little creature loose to run about. He then repeated this with a second crab, and a third, and so on until all the crabs were running around with lit candles on their backs.

The master thief took out the long black robe (which was, presumably, hooded and similar to a monk's cowl) and put it on. He donned the fake beard next, which made him completely unrecognizable. He then grabbed the long sack (which was now empty of crabs), entered the church, and went up to the pulpit.

Just then, the church's clock tower struck midnight—*bwong! bwong! bwong!* The master thief then raised his arms to the heavens and cried out in a bellowing voice, "Hear me, you poor sinners! The time of Armageddon has come! The end is nigh! This is the end of times! Hear me! Oh, hear me! For I am Saint Peter, and I alone have been given the authority to open the gates of heaven! Let those who wish entrance into heaven climb into this holy sack! Behold! Outside this church, the dead are rising from their graves! They run about, collecting their bones! Let those who believe come unto me and take refuge in this holy sack! But hurry, true believers! For the world shall soon be destroyed!"

The master thief spoke so loudly that the parson and clerk, who shared a house in the churchyard, could hear him quite well. They'd already awoken, in fact, roused by all the flickering lights moving about outside (the "candle crabs"). They had been listening for a while, when the clerk finally gave the parson a nudge with his elbow.

"It might look bad if we both go running in there at the same time," said the clerk. "It'll look like we're scrambling for an easy way to heaven."

"I was just thinking that same thing," replied the parson. "So let us go separately."

"I agree," said the clerk. "Since you are the pastor of this church, though, you should have priority. Therefore, I should go second. I'll be right behind you."

So the parson ran into the church first. He entered and approached the robed figure at the pulpit. The master thief opened the long sack, and the panicked clergyman gladly stepped into it. The clerk showed up next, only a moment later, and did the same. Now that both men had been kind enough to get into a sack *voluntarily*, the master thief wasted no time. He tied the opening shut and began dragging the heavy sack along behind him—*thump! thump!*—down the pulpit steps. The two morons in the sack cried out and complained of bumping their heads.

"We are crossing over the mountains, true believers," the master thief told them. "Otherwise, we will not be able to reach heaven."

The master thief kept dragging the sack that held the two men right on through the village. As he dragged them through a puddle, the sack and its occupants got a good soaking. This time, he spoke to them quickly so they wouldn't cry out again.

"Do not be worried, ye true men of God," the master thief told them. "We are just passing through some wet clouds. Heaven awaits us on the other side."

When the master thief reached the steps to the castle tower, he had no choice but to drag the sack up behind him—*thump! thump!*—one by painful one.

"Do not be alarmed, ye chosen two," he told them. "We have reached the steps to the heavenly gates. Soon, we shall be in the courtyard of paradise."

The master thief finally got them to the top of the castle tower, and once there, he shoved them into the lord count's pigeon coop. The pigeons, disturbed, fluttered about and flapped their wings.

"Behold how the angels flap their wings," the master thief told them. "How glad the hosts of heaven must be to have two holy men such as you in their company!"

The master thief then barred the pigeon coop door, trapping the parson and clerk inside (still in the sack, mind you). Then he just walked away calmly, like an action hero during an explosion.

At dawn the next morning, the master thief met the lord count at the castle gate. He told his godfather that he'd passed the final test and that both the parson and clerk were no longer in the church. The lord count had the entire church grounds searched, but there was no sign of either man (but, oddly enough, there *were* quite a few crabs found with wax all over their backs).

"Okay, they are indeed gone from the church," the lord count conceded. "And just *where*, if you don't mind me asking, can they be found?"

"They are safe and sound at the top of the castle tower," the master thief explained. "They're bundled up together in a sack and locked up in your pigeon coop. However, I imagine they probably still believe they are in heaven."

Before finally letting his godson off the hook, the lord count made the master thief accompany him up the tower to retrieve the parson and clerk. Sure enough, there they were . . . still in the sack . . . surrounded by pigeons and covered in bird poop. The lord count and master thief both had a good laugh before they finally let the two fools loose.

"You are indeed a master of thieves," the lord count later said to his godson. "You have passed all three of my tests. As I am a man of my word, you are forgiven and free to leave. This time, you managed to escape my noose. I cannot allow a thief to live in my lands, however—especially one as skilled as you. Therefore, I order you to leave my lands—today—and if I ever see you in my domain again, I *will* hang you. I give you my word. If that happens, there will be no games to save you from my judgment. All you will find here, should you return, is death."

The master thief knew when to leave well enough alone. He bid a loving farewell to his godfather the lord count and went home to see his parents one last time. He hugged them both, said his good-byes, and ventured back out into the world. No one ever saw him in that part of the world ever again.

This isn't exactly one of those tales with a "moral." However, it does offer a lesson of sorts—any challenge, no matter how difficult, may be overcome if one only has the wits and resourcefulness to figure out how.

While this story really has nothing whatsoever to do with the Coins of Zakynthos, it is mentioned in the *Grimm* episode "Three Coins in a Fuchsbau" (1-13). Therefore, it seemed worthy of inclusion in this chapter. And, besides, "The Master Thief" is just a plain old fun story to read (and one that rarely receives the kind of attention given to other stories recorded by the Brothers Grimm).

Coins and Rings That Stain the Soul: A *Grimm* Comparison

I know what these guys want. The Coins of Zakynthos. At this very moment, I'm on my way to destroy them. And as with any mystical or arcane nonsense, you can't just toss them in the recycling. What a pain in the ass.

—Kelly Burkhardt, *Grimm* comic adaptation (Issue 0, Free Comic Book Day Edition)

SPOILER ALERT: If you have not read the first five issues of the *Grimm* comic book adaptation, you may want to skip the next paragraph.

The Coins of Zakynthos disappear from the *Grimm* television show when Kelly Burkhardt leaves Portland with them on her quest to see the accursed things destroyed. This part of the *Grimm* storyline is not seen on the show and was expanded only in the comic books. Nick, Hank, and Monroe travel to Europe after finding a cryptic message from Kelly Burkhardt, Nick's mother and fellow Grimm, who has gone missing while traveling to the island of Zakynthos—the only place where one can destroy the coins. During the trip, Nick meets a fellow Grimm named Maya. Unfortunately, and unbeknownst to Nick, she is only pretending to assist him and secretly works for the Verrat. Maya intends to obtain the cursed

Tasty Morsels

While the Coins of Zakynthos may only be a fictional creation of the writers of *Grimm*, the island of Zakynthos is a very real place. Known as Zante in Venetian, Zakynthos is a Greek island in the Ionian Sea (located between the Mediterranean and Adriatic seas) and is the third largest of the Ionian Islands (also known as the Seven Islands).

coins for her employers. Nick and the others finally catch up with Kelly Burkhardt, and they make it to Zakynthos to destroy the coins. Of course, there is a snag—Maya switches the real coins with fake ones, and it is these that are destroyed. The turncoat Grimm-for-hire then takes the genuine Coins of Zakynthos to Cairo, Egypt. As of the end of season 2 of *Grimm*, the true fate of the Coins of Zakynthos remains unknown.

Before we go any further with our comparison, let's first take a look at the attributes of the Coins of Zakynthos:

They give the possessor charismatic influence over other humans, giving the person nearly irresistible powers of leadership.

Those who come into physical contact with the coins often become possessive of them.

The coins also poison those who possess them. The toxic levels of arsenic and mercury poison the body, while the power-maddening grip of the coins poisons the mind and soul.

The power of the coins is only temporary, and their possessors are eventually brought to nasty ends—Alexander the Great died of a mysterious illness, Julius Caesar was assassinated by a pack of Roman senators, Marcus Antonius (or Marc Antony, who is said to have taken the coins from Caesar) fell on his own sword when he mistakenly believed his beloved Cleopatra had committed suicide, Napoleon Bonaparte died in exile of stomach cancer, and Adolph Hitler committed suicide by shooting himself (after biting into a cyanide capsule, by some accounts).

There is an object in mythology that has also come to be portrayed in modern literature and movies, which could be referred to as "the ring of power." Many modern readers and moviegoers have come to know it as the One Ring of J. R. R. Tolkien's works—such as *The Hobbit* and *The Lord of the Rings* trilogy. By comparison, there are definitely some parallels between this object and the Coins of Zakynthos:

Tolkien's One Ring does not give the user any true power. However, it makes the possessor at least *feel* powerful.

Those who come into contact with the ring become extremely possessive of it. The ring can drive even those who look upon it to homicidal madness. Tolkien's character Gollum originally killed a friend over the ring back when he was known as Sméagol, long before the ring deformed him.

The ring, over time, soils the body, mind, and soul of whoever possesses it for too long. Gollum is an extreme example, but even Frodo Baggins felt himself changed by the ring's influence as he traveled to destroy it in *The Lord of the Rings* trilogy (as did his predecessor, Bilbo Baggins, who first obtained the ring during *The Hobbit*).

The ring will eventually destroy the one who possesses it, as it only serves one master—Sauron—and the forces of evil in general.

Interestingly enough, Tolkien's tale of such a ring takes its origin from a much older story in Teutonic (Scandinavian) mythology about Siegfried (also written Sigurd or Sigmund, depending on what language the tale comes from) and Fafnir the Dragon. This tale appears in the epic saga *Nibelungenlied* (Song of the Nibelungs) and the *Völsungasaga* (Saga of the Volsungs), among other works. The *Nibelungenlied*, originally an epic poem written in Middle High German, chronicles the life and, later, the murder of a dragon-slaying hero named Siegfried as well as how his wife, Kriemhild, took revenge for his death. One of the most well-known, and equally tragic, parts of Siegfried's heroic life is his battle against the dragon Fafnir and the events that follow soon after.

Things began when the dwarf king, Hreithmar, lost his son Ótr (who apparently enjoyed transforming himself into an otter while swimming) because of a careless stone throw by the trickster god Loki. The god killed and skinned the boy, thinking him to be just a giant otter. As compensation for the death, Hreithmar demanded that Odin (chief god of the Aesir) give him a hoard of gold large enough to fill the giant otter skin (some versions have him demand a pile of gold so high that he will be unable to see the goddess Freya standing behind it). Loki got the gold by robbing a wealthy dwarf named Andvari. Among his take was a cursed ring called Andvarinaut, which could make gold but would drive whoever possessed it to madness and ruin.

Long story short, the gold was cursed . . . right along with the ring, which, like the one in Tolkien's story, soiled the mind and soul of whoever possessed it. Shortly after the gold hoard came to Hreithmar, two of his other sons—Fafnir and Regin—asked to be given a share of it. After all, Ótr had been their brother. When Hreithmar refused, Fafnir (presumably overcome by madness at seeing the ring) flew into a rage and murdered his own father with his sword (some versions have him killing his brother). He then took the gold hoard and fled. Meanwhile, Regin did his best to figure out how to make right what his brother had done. As the years passed, the cursed hoard transformed Fafnir into a fearsome dragon as he lived in solitude in the barren mountain lands of Gnitaheith. Things were made even worse by the fact that he possessed the Fear Helm, an enchanted object that struck terror into the hearts of all living things.

Siegfried was but a very young boy when all this happened. Therefore, when the fatherless lad sought out Regin—a dwarf and master of blacksmithing—the son of Hreithmar agreed to become Siegfried's master and tutor. Regin educated and raised the boy as his own. He also told Siegfried of Fafnir, and of the evil he had done. As would be expected, Siegfried grew up to be a fearsome warrior . . . with plans for avenging the wrong that was done to the father of his foster father. Regin forged an unbreakable sword for Siegfried (after he broke a number of initial attempts) called Balmung out of the shattered pieces of his father's sword, Nothung, and put the fledgling hero through a number of trials and tests as preparation for his battle with Fafnir.

It is important to note that there are varying versions of this tale, and from this point the version you read may differ from others.

Now might be a good time to mention that, back when Fafnir killed Hreithmar, Regin also got a pretty good look at that cursed ring. Though he'd also felt a great urge to possess it, he'd been able to control himself at the time. While he hadn't been immediately affected by madness, as Fafnir had been, over the years his lust for the ring grew nearly unbearable. He wanted the ring for himself and saw his incredibly strong and brave student Siegfried as his ticket to finally attaining it. Regin asked Siegfried, more and more frequently and urgently as time passed, to finally begin his quest to kill Fafnir and take the gold hoard for his own. Finally of age and ready, Siegfried eventually agreed.

Tasty Morsels

Two of the Norse god Odin's most powerful tools are his ravens—Hugin and Munin. They perch on the Aesir's shoulders and whisper into his ear. Hugin (truth/thought) always tells Odin the truth of things. Munin (memory) gives Odin access to every memory in existence, even those that are not his own.

Again, for the sake of brevity, we won't get too heavy with the details. In short, Siegfried managed to kill Fafnir (with a little guidance from the god Odin) while Regin cowered from a safe distance and waited to see what happened. Once the dragon was defeated, however, Regin decided to come near. Before the dwarf blacksmith reached him, however, two ravens came to Siegfried—most versions say these are the ravens of Odin, Hugin (truth/thought) and Munin (memory)—and warned him that Regin planned to kill him and take the ring and gold hoard for himself.

Regin finally arrived and, to put it simply, started losing his freaking mind. The dwarf began yelling "The hoard is mine!" and shouting accusations at Siegfried like "You've killed my brother, Fafnir!" and "Murderer!"

At this point, one must assume Siegfried was thinking, *Mo-fo . . . Isn't that what you've been telling me to do my whole life?*

Regin rushed at Siegfried, finally overcome by the madness of the ring. In his careless advance, however, Regin fell upon the blade of Balmung. The dwarf was dead before he hit the ground. Siegfried saw how the ring and gold hoard brought the only father he'd ever known, the man who'd raised and educated him, to such madness. His heart was broken. However, he also found himself with a choice to make— take the gold hoard and ring for his own or seek glory in a different way and abandon it all. Remember, this hoard is said to have contained more wealth than any man in the world possessed.

Siegfried chose the high road, much like Nick Burkhardt and the other Grimms of his family with the Coins of Zakynthos, and refused to even look upon the ring or the gold hoard. He simply mounted his horse and rode away—on to the next adventure. He chose wisdom over wealth, and for this reason he came to be known as one of the greatest heroes of his time.

So, Siegfried is a hero who chooses a good and just path over the easy path to power offered by a cursed object. And Frodo Baggins from Tolkien's *The Lord of the Rings* trilogy also manages to dispose of the One Ring (though perhaps not as voluntarily). One must admit that these characters bear a lot in common with the Burkhardt Grimms who choose to attempt to destroy the Coins of Zakynthos instead of desiring to use their influential power for themselves.

And, since we've already discussed one dragon . . . why not discuss Dämonfeuers, while we're at it? These Wesen are big on hoarding too, after all . . . though it seems they prefer copper to gold, these days.

[12]

AND NOW ... DRAGONS! OR ... DÄMONFEUERS

NICK BURKHARDT: *I thought dragons were only a myth.*
MONROE: *Dragons are ... Dämonfeuers aren't.*

—"Plumed Serpent" (1-14)

When it comes to monsters of the mythical tradition, few beasts can hold a candle to dragons ... or to Dämonfeuers (dragon-type Wesen). Actually, holding a candle anywhere near a Dämonfeuer is probably ill advised. When Nick Burkhardt begins seeking out a fallen Dämonfeuer named Fred Eberhart while investigating the discovery of two charred bodies on a commercial site that's regularly robbed for copper, the unknowing Grimm instead ends up dealing with Eberhart's daughter Ariel (who is on the *way* wrong end of the crazy-to-hot scale). Unfortunately for Nick, the situation escalates into a full-blown "hero's quest" scenario of warrior vs. dragon, with Juliette forced to play the part of damsel in distress.

While dragons show up a lot in world mythology, they are, believe it or not, a bit of a rarity in the Brothers Grimm fairy-tale tradition. This may explain why, in the *Grimm* universe, Dämonfeuers are said to be nearly extinct. In fact, only two stories penned by the Brothers

---

Tasty Morsels

The title of this episode, "Plumed Serpent," gets its origin from a figure in Mesoamerican mythology. Alternately referred to in the English-speaking world as the "plumed serpent" or "feathered serpent," this feather-covered snake deity was known to the Aztecs as Quetzalcoatl. The oldest surviving artistic representations of this figure date as far back as roughly 1400–400 BCE.

Grimm in their original 1812 work *Kinder- und Hausmärchen* involve men doing battle with dragons. And, interestingly enough, both of these tales involve brothers—"The Four Skillful Brothers" and "The Two Brothers." Let's look at one of them here.

The Four Skillful Brothers: A Retelling

Dämonfeuer. Really don't know much about them. There's not many of them around anymore. They're kind of a throwback to the days of yore, you know? Knights in shining armor. From my understanding, they come from a dragon-like lineage.

—Monroe, "Plumed Serpent" (1-14)

There was once a poor man who had four sons.

"My sons," he said to them one day. "I have no inheritance to give any of you. Therefore, all I can do is send you out into the world to seek your own fortunes in life as best you can. It would be best for each of you to find a trade or skill to learn, so that you may earn livings for yourselves."

So the four brothers grabbed their walking sticks, packed what little they had, and said good-bye to their father. They hit the road together until they came to a four-way crossroads, each road going in a different direction and leading to a different country.

"From here, we should go our separate ways," said the oldest brother. "However, let's all meet back at this very spot four years from now. Until then, let's do our best to make lives for ourselves as Father intended."

So each brother chose a direction, and they journeyed from one another into unknown futures. As the oldest brother traveled, he soon encountered a man on the road who asked where he was headed.

"I'm off to seek my fortune in the world," the oldest brother replied. "I'm hoping to find some trade or skill that I might learn and use to support myself."

"Then you are in luck, young lad," said the man. "Come with me, and I'll teach you to be the most skilled thief in the world."

"That doesn't sound like an honest way to make a living," the brother said. "I'm afraid all I'd earn from that is a trip to the hangman's gallows."

"A true thief need not fear the gallows," the man told him. "I'll teach you not only *how* to steal but *what* to steal. I only take that which will not be missed and do so in such a way that the owner rarely even knows it's been taken. That's why no one ever comes after me . . . or, at least, they don't know *who* to come after."

The oldest brother thought it over for a moment and then finally agreed to learn the thief's trade. Over the next few years, he grew to become one of the most skilled and cunning thieves in the world. Once he'd decided to steal an item, nothing and no one could keep him from it.

The second brother also met a man on the road as he traveled. The two began a conversation, and the man finally asked the brother what trade he thought he might pursue.

"I'm not sure yet," answered the second brother.

"Then follow me, and I shall teach you to be a stargazer," said the man. "Nothing is unknown to a man who understands the stars."

The second brother agreed, and soon began to learn the tools and methods of a stargazer (most people these days would probably call this trade "astrology"). In only a few years, he'd learned all that his master had to teach. When, after four years, the second brother asked to be released from his apprenticeship, the master stargazer gifted him with a fine telescope.

"With this," his master told him, "you will be able to see all that is passing in heaven and earth. Nothing will be hidden from your sight."

The third brother met a huntsman and chose to learn that trade. In only four years, this brother became very skilled and knowledgeable in the ways of hunting and living off the land. When it was time for his apprenticeship to end, the master huntsman gifted him with the finest bow he'd ever seen.

"Whatever you shoot at with this bow," his master told him, "you are sure to hit."

The youngest brother met a tailor and chose to learn the profession (talk about getting the boring end of the stick). By the time his apprenticeship was nearing its end, this brother was able to pass a needle through almost any material without harming it. When it was time for him to leave, his master gifted him with a special needle.

"You will be able to sew anything with this needle," his master told him. "Whether it is as soft as an egg or as hard as iron, your stitches will be so fine that your seams will appear nearly invisible."

When the agreed upon period of four years had passed, the four brothers met back at the crossroads. They rejoiced and greeted one another, then set off together to see their father. When they arrived at the house in which they been raised, all of the brothers reported to their father which vocations they had learned.

"I think I'd like to see what each of you can do," their father said to them. So they all walked out to a tall tree that grew in front of the house. Their father challenged the stargazer brother first. "Can you tell me how many eggs are in the finch's nest at the top of this tree?"

The stargazer brother took out his telescope and looked through it until he spied out the finch's nest.

"There are five eggs, Father."

The father next challenged the thief brother.

"I want you to take all five eggs without the mother bird noticing you or even realizing they are gone."

So the thief brother climbed the tree as stealthily as a cat. He took the five eggs so swiftly and gently that he didn't even disturb the mother bird, though she was sitting on them. He brought the eggs down to his father, who then took the eggs inside the house. He set one on each corner of the table and then placed the fifth egg in the center. He then gave a challenge to the third brother, the huntsman.

"Break all five of these eggs in half by loosing only one arrow from your bow."

The huntsman brother took out his bow and nocked an arrow. He aimed, drew a slow and steady breath, and loosed the arrow which (in what must've been one *hell* of a shot) broke all five eggs. Now it was time for the father to challenge the youngest brother, who'd become a tailor.

"My young son," the father said, "sew these eggs back together, as well as the unborn chicks within them, so perfectly that it will be as if they were never shot by your brother's arrow." (Try not to think about this part too much.)

The tailor brother threaded his needle and went to work. Soon, both the eggs and the chicks were as good as new. Next, the thief brother returned all five eggs to their nest . . . and again the mother bird was none the wiser. A few days later, the chicks hatched and the baby birds had only a few tiny red marks on their necks from where the tailor brother had stitched them back together.

"Amazing," said the father. "You've all made good use of your time, indeed. Now I can only hope fate will offer you all a chance to gain great fame or fortune from your impressive skills."

Shortly thereafter, news began to spread throughout the land that a powerful and enormous dragon had kidnapped the daughter of the king. The ruler of the country now offered her hand in marriage to any man capable of rescuing her and returning her safely to him. The brothers decided this was their chance to prove their worth to the world, and they all agreed they'd work together to save her.

"I'll soon figure out where she is," said the stargazer brother, who began scanning the area with his telescope. "I see her! She's sitting on a giant rock out at sea. I can see the dragon as well. It is standing guard nearby."

The brothers went to the king to request a ship with which to launch their rescue mission. They were granted a fast ship and set sail for the dragon's rock. They soon approached it and found the princess there with the sleeping dragon's head resting on her lap. The huntsman brother drew his bow, hoping to kill the dragon in one shot, but then thought better of it.

"I can't get a clear shot," he said. "I might hit the princess."

"Let me give it a try," said the thief brother.

The thief brother used his skills to steal away the princess, just as he'd done with the eggs, so swiftly and quietly that he did not even disturb the slumbering dragon. The brothers got the princess into the boat and immediately set sail back to shore. Before they got safely back to land, however, the dragon awoke to find the princess had been taken.

And, as you can probably imagine, the only thing more dangerous than a dragon . . . is an angry dragon that's just realized someone has stolen its stuff.

The scaly creature roared terribly as it flew into the air, and soon began to circle above the boat. The beast was just about to swoop down at them when the huntsman brother drew his bow and loosed an arrow straight at the dragon's heart. The arrow hit its mark, and the enormous dragon plummeted into the sea . . . right next to the boat. The dragon collided with the surface of the water, throwing up waves that smashed the ship to pieces and tossed all those on board into the sea. Everyone quickly grabbed hold of the floating planks. The tailor brother threaded his needle and sewed everyone's planks into a raft. They used it to paddle around, picking up pieces of the boat as they went. Soon, the tailor brother had sewn the entire ship back together so well that one could barely tell it had ever been damaged.

They sailed into the king's harbor and returned the princess safely to her father. However, they now had a new problem. The king, you remember, had promised his daughter's hand in marriage as a reward . . . but, obviously, she couldn't marry all *four* of them. So the brothers began arguing over which of their skills had been the most instrumental in the princess's rescue. In all honesty, each had played an equally crucial role. It seemed as if things were about to get ugly between the brothers when the king finally intervened.

"Since *all* of you cannot have her," he told them, "perhaps it's best if *none* of you marry her. Besides, there's another man she has loved for many years and long wished to marry. However, please accept my counteroffer—I will give each of you, as reward for your deeds, an equal portion of my kingdom."

The four brothers agreed that the king's proposal was a much better solution than quarreling with each other about who deserved the princess more. Besides, none of them wished to marry a woman who was already in love with another man. The king divvied up his kingdom into four portions and gave one to each, as promised. The brothers lived peacefully and happily for many years and were able to take excellent care of their aging father.

So the princess was free to marry the man she truly loved, and never again got kidnapped by dragons or argued over by a quartet of skillful brothers.

So remember . . . learn a trade so you'll be able to kill dragons and gain a kingdom.

When Dämonfeuers Light Up: A *Grimm* Comparison

NICK BURKHARDT: *Well . . . so they can breathe fire?*

MONROE: *Well, in an obtuse way, I guess they can. Yeah. I mean, from my understanding—and I'm telling you, I'm not an expert on this— it's a kind of ketonic . . . What's the word for it? Vomit . . . Highly*

explosive and kind of disgusting . . . unless, of course, you're dancing
half-naked on a stage.

—"Plumed Serpent" (1-14)

In mythology, folklore, and fairy tales of the Western world, dragons
(or, in the *Grimm* universe, Dämonfeuers) have a pretty specific skill
set—kidnapping maidens, hoarding gold/treasure, and killing or getting killed by heroes. That's about it. And it would seem that these
three things—if their portrayal on *Grimm* is any indication—are the primary motivating factors in the lives of Dämonfeuers. They hoard things
of value, first and foremost, and then protect them with their lives against
any would-be dragon-slaying heroes. If they get to kidnap a damsel and
put her in distress every now and then, that's just a bonus. These are a
few of their favorite things. Deal with it. This is not *The Sound of Music*.

As you read in the previous chapter, the dragon Fafnir hoarded
gold in much the same way that modern Dämonfeuers hoard copper
in the *Grimm* universe. Ariel's home and her father's abandoned mine
are both covered in all sorts of copper. Why copper, you may wonder?
Well, it's far more readily available than gold these days (when was
the last time you saw a bunch of gold that wasn't guarded in some
fashion?). Even a Dämonfeuer would probably attract way too much
unwanted attention if he or she was to go after enough gold to make
a hoard of any respectable size. And, besides that, the value of copper
has steadily increased in recent decades due to its widespread use in
wiring and electronics. This is why construction and commercial
sites (such as the one depicted in the *Grimm* episode) have come to be
plagued by copper thefts (such as wall wiring and plumbing fixtures),
often carried out by thieves who turn around and sell to corrupt
scrap-metal salvagers. Therefore, it stands to reason that copper
would make a perfect substitute for gold in the eyes of Dämonfeuers.

If Dämonfeuers are anything like the dragons of Western mythology, they don't actually *use* the copper for any constructive purpose or to gain personal wealth. The mythical dragons of old often hoarded gold and fiercely guarded it, but they never spent any of it. Nor did they seem to gain anything from it, aside from the satisfaction of having it. However, these hoards frequently attracted brazen young warriors looking for wealth or fame. Perhaps the gold served only as a type of lure. You've got to admit, however, that sleeping alone in a cave with a bunch of gold probably gets boring after a while. And, if the dragon's gold didn't bring all the boys to the yard, they could always kidnap some wealthy young princess or beautiful maiden. The reward and betrothal that her kingly father offered were usually enough to bring the fellas running. Whether it was for gold, love, or glory—some young knight, prince, or warrior would eventually come to call.

Nick Burkhardt, obviously, doesn't want anything to do with the Eberharts' copper. When Ariel snatches Juliette and puts her in the mine/lair with the half-mad Eberhart, however, it gets Nick's attention. With a makeshift lance and shield of copper scrap, Nick manages to slay the Dämonfeuer Fred Eberhart. Seeing her father has been killed, and finally satisfied he's been given a dignified death after failing to protect his wife many years ago (at the hands of a Grimm, one could assume), Ariel starts spewing flammable liquid all over and incinerates the entire place. It is presumed she commits suicide. At the episode's end, however, viewers are shown that Ariel has survived. Perhaps one day she will return to create more headaches for Nick Burkhardt. Only time will tell.

Dragons: East vs. West

As already stated, dragons can be found across the board when it comes to world mythology. Though their appearance may change here and there, nearly all dragons have at least *some* reptilian or serpentine anatomical features. However, their behaviors, motivations, and roles often differ from one culture group to another. This is especially the case when one compares dragons of Western myths with those of Eastern/Asian myths.

In the Western mythical tradition, dragons are almost exclusively associated with evil. They are a terrible hindrance so powerful that only a great hero can destroy them. They steal princesses, despite having no need for them, and hoard riches they have no intention of using. Even in the pre-Christian times of Europe, dragons were portrayed as a common threat to all—burning fields and raining down indiscriminate destruction upon both the highborn and peasantry alike. Dragons were something to be destroyed and conquered, an enemy to all mankind. After the spread of Christianity throughout Europe, dragons were integrated into the new religious imagery and associated with the devil. This is likely due to the common association of serpents with evil in Judeo-Christian writings. In fact, in the apocalyptic verses of Revelation 12:9 and 20:2, King James version, the following is written:

"And the great dragon was cast out, that old serpent, called the devil and Satan, which deceiveth the whole world: he was cast out into the earth, and his angels were cast out with him" (12:9).

"And he laid hold on the dragon, that old serpent, which is the devil and Satan, and bound him a thousand years" (20:2).

Needless to say, whether it was before or after the arrival of Christianity, you'd be hard-pressed to find a dragon in the Western tradition being portrayed as a "good guy." If you look to myths from farther east, however, you will find a far different depiction of these very ancient beasts—especially in the myths of China.

In Chinese mythology, dragons are often more helpful than hurtful in their relationships with humans. Of course, when wronged by humans, they are more than capable of opening up a gargantuan can of epic whoop ass. So in Asian stories it often behooves a hero to be nice when in the company of dragons, lest they get a curse where they hoped for a blessing. The philosophical view of a Chinese dragon can be summed up pretty simply—treat me with respect, and I will treat you in kind . . . do otherwise, and I will *end* you.

That sounds fair enough, doesn't it?

Chinese dragons often have a role similar to cultural heroes in Western myths in that they regularly bring technology and knowledge to humans. Around roughly 3000 BCE, a dragon is credited in the Chinese mythical tradition with showing the current emperor the truth of the *bagua* (sometimes known in English as the "eight mystic trigrams") used in the spiritual practice of Taoism. By around 1110 CE, dragons were finally categorized into the following groups by the imperial scholars of the Chou dynasty:

Blue Spirit Dragons: rulers of compassion
Yellow Spirit Dragons: favorably receive vows given sincerely
Red Spirit Dragons: rulers of lakes
White Spirit Dragons: rulers of virtue
Black Spirit Dragons: rulers of the unknown (or mysterious) lakes
Spirit Dragons: capable of traveling between heaven and earth
Earthly Dragons: It is written one could see their heads, as these are what men call "mountains." These dragons live within the earth and often protect hoards of treasure. (Again . . . this sounds a lot like a Dämonfeuer.)

Whether from the myths of the East or West, it would seem that dragons are associated with treasure hoards. From the *Grimm* point of view, perhaps this is because both cultures encountered Dämonfeuers at one time or another? Who's to say? As long as they weren't as mental as Ariel Eberhart, the Chinese might have perceived them as fairly nice folks to have around.

Speaking of crazy women who cause headaches for Nick Burkhardt, Ariel was nothing more than a minor nuisance in comparison to the spell-casting tricks of one very troublesome Hexenbiest—Adalind Schade. In the next chapter, we will take a look at how the Hexenbiests' use of food to create curses and/or enchantments stems from certain stories in the Brothers Grimm tradition.

[13]

CABBAGES AND COOKIES, DONKEYS AND LOVE SPELLS

JULIETTE SILVERTON: *So how long has this been going on between you and Adalind?*

HANK GRIFFIN: *Not long. It's the weirdest thing. It's like I woke up one day and I couldn't stop thinking about her.*

—"Love Sick" (1-17)

Nick's partner, Hank, starts to get a little weird when the Hexenbiest Adalind Schade puts something more in his cookies than chocolate chips (not to mention what it does to poor Sergeant Wu). With a little luck, and a lot of help from Rosalee's apothecary expertise, Nick is able to put Hank (and Wu) right again. And, with a little Grimm blood from Nick's cut lip, he is able to put an end to Adalind's troublemaking by robbing her of her magical powers . . . for a time, at least. However, when it comes to stories of love, betrayal, and funky food that does crazy stuff to people (though even in the old tales, it's hard to find something crazier than Wu chowing down on his couch stuffing like it's cotton candy), the Brothers Grimm had the perfect story—"Donkey Cabbages." Yes . . . it's a weird title. Funny thing, though, this title makes perfect sense once you're familiar with the story. The following retelling, based on the original tale from the 1812 *Kinder- und Hausmärchen*, should help you to do just that.

Donkey Cabbages: A Retelling

Don't go giving those away. I made them just for you.
— Adalind Schade, "Island of Dreams" (1-15)

A young huntsman went into the forest one day, planning to lie in wait for some game to pass by. As he looked around for signs that might tell him what animals had recently passed through, an ugly old crone approached him.

"Good day, Huntsman," she said. "You seem happy and healthy. Alas, I am starving and thirsty. Would you be so kind as to give an old woman a little charity?"

The huntsman took pity on the poor old woman. He reached into his pocket and, at first, gave her only as many coins as he could afford. Then he figured he could stand to give her a little bit more and reached back into his pocket. The crone, however, stopped him.

"You've given me quite enough," she said. "And now let me give you something in return. If you do as I'm about to say, your kindness will be paid back a hundredfold. Go walking deeper into the forest, and you will come to a tree where nine ravens are holding a cloak in their talons. Fire your weapon, and they'll scatter, dropping down the cloak. However, you will also end up killing one of the ravens with your shot. Pick up both the bird and the cloak, which is a wishing cloak. When worn, all you have to do is wish to be somewhere, and there you'll be. Next, you must take out the

Tasty Morsels

A person eating the heart and/or liver of a special bird and being blessed with a gold piece under his or her pillow each morning can also be found in another Grimm fairy tale called "The Two Brothers."

heart of the raven and swallow it whole. If you do this, every morning you will wake up to find a gold piece under your pillow."

The huntsman thanked the old crone and went about his merry way.

What she said sounds all well and good, he thought as he walked. *But what are the odds that her words are even true?*

If an old homeless woman told most of us to swallow a bird's heart, we'd probably think she was just crazy.

As the huntsman walked on, he came to a tree that (just as the old crone had foretold) had nine ravens in its branches. In their talons, they all clutched at a cloak and quarreled over it. The huntsman was, needless to say, more than just a little astonished when he saw this.

"Wow! This is great," he said. "It's just as the old woman said!"

He shouldered his weapon, took aim, and fired a single shot. The ravens scattered in a flurry of black feathers. However, one bird didn't escape and fell dead to the ground along with the cloak.

The huntsman did as the old crone had instructed. He cut open the raven and removed its heart. Taking it between his fingers, he popped it into his mouth and swallowed it whole. Anxious to get home, he grabbed up the cloak and began the walk back.

You read that right . . . he *walked*, instead of using his amazing Technicolor wishing cloak. Either the huntsman wasn't the brightest of guys, or he just really wanted to stay in shape.

When the huntsman awoke the next morning, he immediately checked under his pillow. Sure enough, there was a shiny gold piece waiting for him, like a gift from the world's creepiest tooth fairy. In fact, there was a gold piece under his pillow *every* morning from that day forward. Within a few weeks, he had already gathered together a nice little fortune.

"What good is having all this gold if all I do is just sit here at home?" he said to himself. "I shall travel the world and see all its wonders."

So the huntsman packed his things and went out to see the world. As he walked through a great forest one day, he came upon a magnificent castle (*Again* with the walking? What good is that wishing cloak if he never *uses* it?). Looking down at him from one of the windows, he saw a beautiful maiden and an old woman. Unfortunately for the huntsman, the old woman was actually a "witch" (or Hexenbiest), and the maiden was her daughter.

"That man down there," said the old woman to the maiden, "has a great treasure within his body. We must steal it for our own, my daughter. We would make better use of it than him, anyway. That bird's heart within him places a gold piece under his pillow each day."

Then the mean old Hexenbiest spoke to the maiden and explained her plan for stealing the huntsman's golden gift.

"And if you do not do as I've told you," the Hexenbiest threatened, "your fate will be even worse than his."

Still standing in front of the castle, the huntsman called up to the maiden. He was weary from traveling and figured this would be a nice place to rest for a night or two. He could certainly *afford* it, after all. Besides that, he really wanted to get a better look at the maiden. She was hot.

The huntsman was welcomed into the castle and treated like an honored guest. He stayed there for many days and soon enough had fallen in love with the maiden, who was herself a young spell worker. He loved her so much, in fact, that there was nothing in the world he wouldn't have done for her.

"Now is our chance to steal the bird heart," the old hag told the maiden. "He will never even know it is gone until it's too late."

The evil spell caster concocted a zaubertrank (potion) and gave it to the maiden, instructing her to get the huntsman to drink it. The maiden had grown fond of the huntsman, but she feared her mother's wrath so much that she did as she was told and took it to him.

"Drink this, my love," she said to him. "Drink to me."

Anxious to encourage the maiden's affections, the huntsman guzzled down every last drop. As he swallowed the last bit, he suddenly puked . . . and out came the bird heart. The poor guy was probably mortified. Perhaps this is why he didn't notice it when the maiden grabbed up the vomit-covered bird heart and quickly swallowed it herself (which is just gross . . . did she even wipe it off?) just as her mother had ordered.

After that day, the huntsman no longer found gold pieces under his pillow each morning. The gold instead appeared under the maiden's pillow and was quickly snatched up by her cruel mother. The huntsman was so in love with the maiden that he didn't even care about the gold anymore. All he could think about was spending time with her. Likewise, the maiden's fondness for him was beginning to grow into love.

"We've taken the bird heart," the mother said to the maiden one day. "Now we must take his wishing cloak as well."

To be honest, they might as well have just taken the cloak. It doesn't seem the huntsman ever really used the thing. However, the maiden protested this time.

"No!" she replied. "We will leave him that one thing! We have already taken the source of all his wealth."

"Do you have any idea how rare it is to find a wishing cloak? I want it! I must have it! I *will* have it! And here's what you get for your defiance!"

The cruel mother gave the maiden a thorough beating and threatened that, if she didn't obey, she'd suffer a fate even worse than death. So the maiden agreed to do as she was told. She went to a window in one of the castle halls, stared into the sky, and wept. Soon the huntsman passed by and was concerned to see her looking so upset.

"Why do you look so sad?" he asked.

"Oh, my love," she told him, "I'm looking at Garnet Mountain over there in the distance, where there are so many precious stones. I want them so much, but I could never get to them. Only birds can reach such a place. No person can ever get there."

"Is that all?" said the huntsman. "Well, I can fix that for you right now."

The huntsman pulled out his cloak (finally!), threw it over the both of them, and wished to be at Garnet Mountain. He and the maiden were immediately transported there and found themselves surrounded by the glittering precious stones. They rejoiced and worked together to gather the very best ones to take back. However, at that same moment, the cruel old mother was working a spell that suddenly made the huntsman very sleepy.

"I think I need to rest a bit," he said. "I am so tired all of a sudden, that I feel as if I can barely stand."

The huntsman sat on a rock beside the maiden, rested his head in her lap, and passed out like a Jägerbomb-saturated frat-boy on spring break. As he slept, the maiden took his wishing cloak. She gathered up all the precious stones they'd collected, threw the cloak over her shoulders, and wished herself back to the castle . . . leaving the huntsman stranded on the impassable mountain.

Eventually, the mother's spell wore off, and the huntsman finally woke up. When he looked around and saw the maiden was gone, along with his wishing cloak, he realized what had happened and was heartbroken. The maiden had betrayed him. To make things even worse, she had left him stranded to die alone on the mountain.

"Oh, what true evil there is in this world!" wailed the huntsman.

It should be noted that Garnet Mountain was inhabited by giants, which made it a pretty dangerous place for humans. These grumpy behemoths often didn't take too kindly to trespassers. The huntsman soon saw three giants coming his way. Unsure of what else to do, he just lay back down and pretended to still be asleep.

"What is this little worm thing, here?" said one of the giants when he saw the huntsman.

"Who cares? Just step on it and kill it," said the second giant.

"Why bother," said the third giant. "Just let the thing alone. It's not like it can *stay* here. If it climbs any higher, it'll hit the clouds, and they'll carry it off."

So the giants decided to just move on and, fortunately for the huntsman, chose not to crush him underfoot. Luckily, he'd also been listening to what the third giant said. Once they were gone, he climbed a bit higher up the mountain until he was near the summit. Then he just took a seat until a cloud came along and carried him away (try not to think too hard about some of this stuff). He traveled on the cloud for a time. Eventually, however, the cloud sank down and landed in a vast cabbage garden surrounded by walls. The leafy vegetables were enough to soften his landing, allowing him to come safely back down to earth.

"Man, am I hungry," said the huntsman. "If only I had some apples or pears. But all I see around here are cabbages. I don't really like cabbages, but I guess it's better than starving to death. At least they'll tide me over until I can find something better to eat."

The huntsman picked out a fresh head of cabbage, peeled off the outer layers, and began to eat. After just a few bites, however, he began to feel a bit . . . peculiar. His arms suddenly turned into hairy, skinny legs. His face grew long, and his ears grew even longer. He realized with horror that he was turning into an ass (the animal . . . not the other thing). However, with each bite of cabbage his hunger for it increased. Since donkeys love cabbages, he just kept on eating away. Eventually, he grazed his way to a new flowerbed in which a different kind of cabbage was growing. He began eating it and soon found himself restored to his human form.

And now you know why this story has the title "Donkey Cabbages."

Worn out from this whole donkey ordeal, the huntsman decided to lie down and take a nap. When he awoke the next morning, he was inspired with a plan for getting back at the maiden and her evil mother. He took one of the cabbages that had made him a donkey, as well as one of the cabbages that had made him human again.

Tasty Morsels

Walled, enchanted gardens in which plants and herbs with magical properties grow are a common element in many fairy tales. They are depicted as being the property of enchantresses and/or fairies in some stories (such as "Rapunzel," as seen in Chapter 8). In "Donkey Cabbages," however, the garden's owner is never revealed, and he or she does not play a role in the story.

"With these," he said, "I may have some vengeance on those who wronged me."

He climbed over the garden wall and started seeking out the castle where he'd met the Hexenbiest and the maiden. After a few days of wandering, he managed to find his way back to it. He disguised his face by dyeing his skin brown and approached the castle, pretending to be a weary traveler.

"I am so exhausted," he called out to the castle. "Please take me in! I do not think I can take another step!"

"Who are you, traveler?" called back the wicked mother from inside the castle. "State your business."

"I'm a messenger for the king," he replied. "I was ordered to discover the most delicious salad in all the world . . . and I have found just the cabbage for it! I carry it with me. However, this terrible heat is causing the cabbage to wilt and whither. And I am so tired that I don't think I can carry it much longer without some rest."

When the wicked mother heard this, she was overwhelmed by her own greedy nature and wanted the salad for herself.

"My good man," she told him. "I would be delighted to give you shelter, if you'd only let me taste this wonderful salad."

"You've got a deal," the disguised huntsman replied. "It'd be my pleasure. I brought two heads of it, and I'd be more than happy to give one to you in reward for your kindness."

He was given entry into the castle and handed over the cabbage that turned people into donkeys to the wicked mother. She suspected nothing and immediately took the cabbage to her kitchen and made a salad of it. Before she had reached the dining table, she had already eaten a few mouthfuls. Before she knew what was happening, she'd transformed into a donkey, and she ran out into the courtyard.

As this happened, the castle maidservant walked into the kitchen and saw the bowl of salad. She figured it must be for the maiden and went to carry it to her. However, as was her habit, she sampled a few bites for herself along the way. Before she got halfway to the maiden's room, she turned into a donkey and ran out to the courtyard as well.

By this time, the huntsman was seated at the dining table alongside the maiden (who did not recognize him because he was still disguised as a dark-skinned messenger). She had heard about the arrival of this delicious salad and was anxious to try some for herself. However, quite a long time passed, and the salad still hadn't been brought to the table.

"I wonder what's taking the salad so long," said the maiden.

The cabbage must have already had its effect on the others, the huntsman thought to himself.

"I'll go to the kitchen and figure out what is causing the delay," he told her, excusing himself from the table. He found the partially eaten bowl of salad as well as the two donkeys wandering around in the courtyard. He took up the bowl and brought it to the dining table, where the maiden sat waiting.

"Is that the special salad?" the maiden said.

"Indeed," he replied. "I have brought it to you personally, so that you will not have to wait one moment longer."

The maiden began to eat the salad and, soon enough, was transformed into a donkey. She ran into the courtyard and joined the others. The huntsman, knowing the targets of his vengeance were incapacitated for the moment, took time to wash his face. After all, he wanted them to *know* who had done this to them. Looking like himself once again, he returned to the courtyard.

"Now you will get what you deserve," he told the donkey-women. "You'll pay for your treachery!"

The huntsman tied the three of them together with a rope and led them to a nearby mill. He knocked at the door and the miller answered.

"What can I do for you?" the miller said.

"I have three beasts here that I just cannot manage," he replied. "I want you to work them at your millstone for a time. Will you take them, care for them, work them hard, and treat them exactly as I instruct you to? If so, I'll pay you whatever price you ask."

"Fine," said the miller. "But how do you want them treated?"

"The old donkey (who was actually the wicked mother) should get three beatings and only one meal each day. The younger donkey (the maidservant) should get one beating and three meals each day. As for the youngest donkey (the maiden), as she is the best behaved of the bunch, she should get three meals a day . . . but no beatings for her. Understood?"

What in the heck did the *maidservant* ever do to this guy to deserve being subjected to daily beatings? The poor woman hadn't even been mentioned until she ate that salad!

Leaving the trio of donkey-women in the care of the miller, the huntsman went back to the castle and spent a few days just taking it easy. Meanwhile, the three donkey-women were being worked hard, beaten (except the maiden, of course), and fed according to what the huntsman felt they deserved (except the maidservant, of course, whose only apparent crime was sneaking a few bites of salad). After he'd enjoyed a few days of leisure, he went to the miller for a report on their condition.

"I hate to tell you this," said the miller, "but that old donkey—you know, the one you told me to feed once and beat three times each day? Well, she died this morning. As for the other two, I'm still treating them exactly as you instructed. To be honest with you, though, I don't think they're gonna last much longer."

The huntsman, who was a fairly kindhearted guy, took pity on the maiden and maidservant. He decided justice was served, paid the miller as promised, and took the two remaining donkey-women back to the castle. Once there, he fed them both the cabbage that undid the spell, and they were restored to their human forms. The maiden fell to her knees before him, her eyes full of tears.

"Forgive me, my love," she implored. "Forgive me for the wrongs I've done. My mother made me do it, under threat of pain or death. It was all forced on me against my will. I love you! Truly, I do! Your wishing cloak is hung in the cupboard, and I know how to make a potion that'll cause me to vomit up the bird heart we took from you."

"You keep them," the huntsman said after thinking it over for a moment. "What does it matter? After all, I would rather have you for my wife. Despite all that has happened, I still love you and ask that we be married."

The huntsman and the maiden were married shortly thereafter. Their wedding was a fine occasion, with much celebration and joy. And so, the huntsman and his young wife lived together happily for the rest of their lives.

One could also assume that, one day years later, the maidservant suddenly cornered the huntsman in a castle corridor and said, "What the *heck*, man? Why did *I* get beaten? I didn't do anything to you!"

Maybe It Was Something You Ate?: A *Grimm* Comparison

NICK BURKHARDT: *Hey, you okay?*

SERGEANT WU: *I don't know . . . I've been having some stomach problems lately.*

NICK: *Well, maybe it's something you ate?*

WU: *No, I've been eating pretty good lately. Although, I have gained some weight . . . Hey Nick, you know what?*

NICK: *What?*

WU: *I think I'm gonna pass out.*

—"Love Sick" (1-17)

The first and most obvious parallel between "Donkey Cabbages" and "Love Sick" is the presence of "magic food"—the cabbages in the story and Adalind Schade's cursed cookies on the show. The most interesting thing to note about this "magic food" element is that its usage and results are polar opposites between the story and the show. In *Grimm* it is the cursed cookies that cause all the problems and force Hank to begin having obsessive and amorous feelings for Adalind Schade, whereas in the story it is the cabbages that provide the huntsman with the tools he needs to serve justice upon the mother-daughter team of Hexenbiests who have wronged him.

Both the fairy tale and the episode involve a man who falls in love with a Hexenbiest. However, the nature of this relationship is again turned around. Hank doesn't truly love Adalind but is only feeling the effects of the cursed cookies. Unlike Hank's magically fabricated feelings for Adalind, the huntsman's love for the maiden in the story seems to be genuine (until she leaves him stranded on a mountain full of murderous giants and steals all his stuff, of course). Unfortunately for Hank, he falls in love with a *bad* Hexenbiest, whereas the maiden loved by the huntsman is somewhat good of heart and only wrongs him because she fears the threats of her *wicked* Hexenbiest mother. This brings us to the last parallel between the story and the show—the defeat of the *wicked* Hexenbiest.

In the story, the wicked mother Hexenbiest dies under the strain of working for (and being frequently beaten by) the miller. With her evil mother out of the picture, the maiden is free to love the huntsman and be a good person as she wishes. In *Grimm*, the wicked Hexenbiest Adalind Schade is stripped of her powers (but not killed, sadly, leaving her free to keep on causing problems) when Nick Burkhardt passes some of his Grimm blood into her mouth from his cut lip. Apparently, Grimm blood is like kryptonite to Hexenbiests. However, the effects are more permanent—well, sort of. Ms. Schade eventually finds a way to regain her powers, using her unborn royal-blooded child (which she conceived with Renard) as a bartering chip. Now that she's regained her powers, Adalind Schade is back and will likely be causing all sorts of new problems in the life of Nick Burkhardt.

Supernatural Snacks:
The Mythology of Enchanted Food

The concept of food with supernatural or magical properties has been around for a very long time and can be found in myths that date as far back as ancient times. Eventually, this ancient motif found its way into fairy tales. Perhaps the oldest example of magic food is the taboo food of the underworld or taboo food in the land of the dead. The idea behind this scenario is simple—if a (living) person is in the underworld (or land of the dead), he or she must not eat or drink anything while there. If the person consumes so much as a tiny morsel or drop of fluid while in that dark realm, he or she risks becoming stuck there for eternity.

The most well-known example of this mythological scenario is probably the ancient Greek story of Persephone. This daughter of Zeus and Demeter, the goddess of fertility, nature, and agriculture, finds herself in quite a pickle when she is abducted by Hades, lord of the underworld, and taken to his realm to be his bride. She declines any food or drink Hades offers her. However, hunger eventually gets the best of her and she eats some seeds from a pomegranate. When Zeus arrives to retrieve his kidnapped daughter, he is unable to liberate her completely due to the fact that she's eaten roughly half the seeds. Because of this, Persephone must remain in the underworld with Hades for half the year (this is fall/winter, caused by Demeter's sadness at her daughter's absence) but is allowed to return to the realm of the living for the other half (this is spring/summer, when Demeter rejoices at her daughter's return). Similar myths, such as the ancient Sumerian tale of the goddess Inanna, can be found all the way back to the cradle of civilization.

In the nineteenth-century compilation of Karelian and Finnish epic poetry known as *Kalevala*, the hero shaman Väinämöinen journeys into Tuonela—the underworld realm of the dead—in his quest to obtain special magic words. While there, he is offered a bubbling tankard of delicious ice-cold beer. Luckily, Väinämöinen is a pretty wise fellow, and he refuses the drink. By doing so, he secures his ability to return to the land of the living.

As you can see, supernatural foods have been giving mythological heroes and heroines headaches since the dawn of the written word. And the same is true for Nick Burkhardt and his crew. Of course, their Hexenbiest-laden troubles don't end with cursed cookies. Adalind Schade curses Juliette with a *cat*, causing her to enter a coma that wipes away her memories of Nick. Speaking of which, perhaps it's time for us to talk about more chicks in comas.

[14]

CHICKS IN COMAS

CATHERINE SCHADE: *The person who wakes her has to be pure of heart. It's challenging finding someone like that nowadays, so we have to do it chemically. The more pure of heart you are, the less painful the process.*

CAPTAIN SEAN RENARD: *What are these lumps?*

CATHERINE: *It's better you don't know.*

—"The Kiss" (2-02)

The idea of pretty princesses (or, in *Grimm*, girlfriends) who end up in comas due to dark magic is a common element in the fairy-tale tradition. From the fairy curse of Charles Perrault's "The Sleeping Beauty in the Wood" to the Grimm Brothers' "Snow White," it seems that the lovely ladies of most fairy tales just can't keep their eyes open when evil magic is involved. And, as the mythos of the *Grimm* universe supports, it takes a kiss from a prince who is pure of heart to liberate these drowsy damsels from their enchanted slumbers. The following retelling is based on the previously mentioned story from Perrault.

The Sleeping Beauty in the Wood: A Retelling

Once there lived a king and queen who had long wished for a child. Their inability to conceive a child made the couple sad beyond words. They made pilgrimages to a number of sacred places said to have magical properties or to promote fertility. None of it worked. After years of praying and trying, however, the queen finally became pregnant.

Soon after the birth of their long-awaited child, a daughter, the king and queen held the grandest christening anyone had ever seen. Nobles and friends from throughout the country were invited to the event. The king also invited all the fairies that could be found in the land, wishing to appoint them all as god-mothers to the newborn princess. In his search, only seven fairies could be found.

As was the custom of fairies in those days, of which the king was well aware, each of the seven would bestow a magical gift on the princess. Fairies did not give mere objects as gifts, but instead gave special or exceptional traits or abilities to the child ... which, one must admit, sounds way more useful.

After all the business and ceremony of the christening had ended, everyone gathered in the palace's dining hall for a feast. The seven fairies were treated as guests of honor. Once the fairies were seated at the table of honor, the king presented each with a beautiful embroidered blanket as well as a special case made from solid gold. Inside each case was a spoon, knife, and fork, all of solid gold and inlaid with diamonds and rubies. It was a jubilant occasion.

Tasty Morsels

It is possible that the mention of the old fairy having left a "tower" here is a reference to "Rapunzel." This may have been intended as a hint that the rather grumpy old fairy in "Sleeping Beauty" is the same one as in "Rapunzel."

As everyone sat down to enjoy the feast, however, an unexpected visitor showed up and quickly killed everyone's buzz.

Into the dining hall stepped a very old fairy. One problem—she hadn't been invited. The king and queen hadn't meant to snub this fairy intentionally. No one had seen her in over half a century, not since she'd left a certain tower. It had long been assumed that she was either dead or trapped by some unknown enchantment.

The king was wise enough to know it was a bad idea to insult a fairy, purposely or not. So he had a fine blanket, just like those he had given to the other seven fairies, brought to her immediately. The chest and utensils of solid gold, however (definitely finer gifts), had required time to be made. The king had only commissioned seven of them. As a result, he did not have another to give. The cranky old fairy felt she'd been shortchanged and grumbled under her breath about it.

Luckily, one of the younger fairies was paying attention and overheard the old fairy's quiet bellyaching. The young fairy feared her grumpy elder might attempt some mischief out of spite, perhaps giving the princess a terrible gift (and receiving a terrible gift from a fairy can be a *very* bad thing . . . it's not like you just get a pair of socks). So, when all the fairies stood up from the table to bestow their gifts upon the infant princess, the young fairy hid behind some curtains so she'd be the last called upon to speak her gift. That way, if the grumpy old fairy tried to do something harmful, she would be able to counter it with her own gift.

The first fairy gave the princess the gift of beauty; she would grow to be the most beautiful girl in the world.

The second fairy gave her the wit of an angel.

The third fairy gave her the gift of poise and grace in all her endeavors.

The fourth fairy gave her the ability to dance with perfection.

The fifth fairy gave her the ability to sing as beautifully as a nightingale.

The sixth fairy gave her the talent to play all kinds of music perfectly.

Now came the grumpy old fairy's turn to speak. Shaking with rage, she declared that the princess would one day prick her finger on a spindle from a spinning wheel and die from the wound.

This malicious gift sent everyone present into fits of panic and sorrow when they heard it, especially the king and queen. In a world where spinning was a part of everyday life, this "gift" was a death sentence. However, the young fairy now stepped out from behind the curtains and spoke.

"Calm yourselves, oh, King and Queen," she told them. "Your daughter shall not die from my evil elder's terrible gift. Unfortunately, I do not have the power to completely undo what she has done. However, I can soften the result. If the princess is ever cut by a spindle, she will not die. Instead, she'll fall into an enchanted sleep for a hundred years. After this time has passed, the brave son of a king shall come to her. When he arrives, she will awaken, and the enchantment shall be broken."

Tasty Morsels

"Spinning," as the term is used in this story, refers to the use of a spinning wheel to transform certain materials into yarn. Spinning materials could include animal hair, such as sheep's wool, or plant fibers, such as straw.

The king, however, still wasn't too keen on the idea of having his only daughter stricken comatose for a century. So he did the only thing he could think to do. He outlawed spindles and spinning wheels, under penalty of death. Even the act of spinning or possession of a spindle could get one sent to the executioner.

Fifteen or sixteen years later, thanks to the gifts of the fairies (well, the first six of them anyway), the princess had grown into a beautiful young maiden, full of talent and grace. One day, however, the king and queen took a brief trip away from the palace for a little alone time at one of their pleasure houses. In their absence, the princess became bored, so she started running all around the palace looking for something of interest.

After a bit of wandering, the princess came to a little room at the top of one of the palace towers. Inside, she found a little old woman spinning with a spindle. It appears the woman was new to the palace and wasn't aware it was outlawed. She had no intention of doing the princess harm, as she was a kind old woman. She was just in the wrong place at the wrong time. The princess saw the spindle and spinning wheel, and was overwhelmed with curiosity about this contraption she'd never seen before.

"What are you doing with that, good woman?" the princess asked.

GRIMM WORDS

Pleasure house: Pretty much what it sounds like. It's a place where people would go to get away from their everyday responsibilities and have some fun, enjoy a bit of relaxation, and get in a little "private time." In some cases, this could refer to a place where royals or nobles kept mistresses or prostitutes.

"I'm only spinning, dear child," the old woman answered, not aware of who the girl was or the fairy's curse. "How is it a girl your age has never seen a spindle?"

"How wonderful," the princess said. "What a beautiful thing! How does it work? Please let me try it."

And with that, the princess reached out for the spindle. As soon as she touched it, her finger was pricked—perhaps from her carelessness, perhaps from her ignorance about spindles, or perhaps just because of the fairy's curse—and immediately collapsed to the floor as if dead.

Not knowing what to do, the old woman started screaming for help. Everyone in the palace soon came running to the room when they heard the commotion. They tried everything they could think of to revive the fallen princess—splashing her face with water, unlacing her corset, and even rubbing her temples with Hungary water. None of it worked, of course.

The king and queen soon returned to the palace. Upon seeing what'd happened to the princess, the king realized the fairy's curse had been fulfilled. He ordered his beloved daughter be carried to the finest bedchamber in the palace, wherein there was a beautiful bed with embroidered blankets and a frame of silver and gold.

GRIMM WORDS

Hungary water: Sometimes called "the Queen of Hungary's Water," this was an alcohol-based perfume that's believed to have been used in the seventeenth century. A legend was spread about the perfume that claimed it was created in the fourteenth century at the command of Queen Elisabeth of Hungary. No one knows for sure when it was invented, as the truth has been lost to history, and there are some who believe the legends of its royal origins were spread in order to make the perfume more appealing to the wealthy. The earliest known Hungary water consisted of rosemary and/or thyme mixed with a potent type of brandy.

Some people in the palace wondered, at first, if perhaps the princess was actually dead. However, her complexion remained normal, and she was found to still be breathing, though very softly. She was only sleeping. The king announced a new proclamation that his daughter's sleep was not to be disturbed. He wished her to be allowed to slumber in peace until the set time of her awakening . . . in a hundred years.

While all this was going on, the young fairy who'd saved the princess from death was twelve thousand leagues away in the Kingdom of Matakin. However, the news was brought to her by a dwarf who wore "boots of seven leagues," meaning they allowed him to travel seven leagues with every step. So, roughly 1,715 steps later, the dwarf arrived to tell her the spell had begun.

Luckily, the fairy had an even better mode of travel than a pair of seven-league boots. She had a chariot of fire . . . drawn by dragons! This method of transportation was way faster (not to mention awesome as hell). It only took the fairy an hour to reach

GRIMM WORDS

League: A somewhat outdated unit of measurement used for distance, equal to roughly three miles (or 4.83 kilometers).

the comatose princess. The fairy was a very welcome sight to the king, who immediately welcomed her into his palace.

The fairy was glad to see the king had left the girl to sleep in peace. However, in her wisdom, she knew the princess shouldn't wake up all alone in an empty palace (not to mention a hundred years in the future), as she would not know what to do. You can't really argue with her logic on that one.

The fairy started running around the palace, tapping everyone and everything she came across with her magic wand— servants, governesses, minstrels, maids of honor, cooks, guards, pages, bedchamber maids, soldiers, and even the beefeaters. The princess's dog, a spaniel named Mopsey, also got a wand tap on the head.

As soon as they were touched by her wand, all fell into the same enchanted hundred-year-long sleep as the princess. This way, they would all still be around to serve her when she woke up.

The only people who did not join the princess in her sleep were the king and queen. They now had to leave their daughter in the hands of Fate. They gave the princess one last kiss on the forehead, packed up their things, and left the palace forever. The king, as he seemed fond of doing, proclaimed that no person could enter the palace for a hundred years.

Of course, fairy magic is a lot more effective at deterring people than royal proclamations.

GRIMM WORDS

Beefeater: Originally a derogatory word for a well-fed servant. However, by the seventeenth century the word had come to mean a tower/castle guard.

The fairy put an enchantment on the palace, and soon the entire palace was so surrounded by vegetation that it was nearly invisible—trees, thorny bushes, and brambles sprouted up everywhere to create a natural barrier against any would-be intruders. Not even the forest animals could get through. Only the very tip-tops of the palace's highest towers were visible.

If history tells us anything, it's that time never stops. The foretold century of the princess's sleep came and went, as centuries tend to do, and on the day of its passing the son of the king who then reigned came riding through the woods while hunting (the story makes a point of explaining the prince is of a different family, so he is of no relation to the sleeping princess). During his hunting trip, he noticed what looked like the tops of palace towers. When he returned to his own palace, he began asking around about them.

"What are those towers in the thick woods?" he said to a number of people.

Everyone seemed to tell him something different.

"It's a cursed old castle, haunted by demons and evil spirits."

"It's a place where those who practice dark magic meet at night to hold their black Sabbaths."

"It's the home of an ogre who loves to catch and eat little children. He's the only creature the thick woods will allow to pass, which is why no one is able to follow after him."

With such a variety of insane stories to choose from, the prince wasn't sure what to believe. He was just about to give up on the whole thing when a very old countryman, who had over-heard the prince's inquiries, approached the young lord.

"Your Highness," the old man said. "It's been nearly half a century since my father told me the story of that place, told to him by his father. He told me that one hundred years ago, the most beautiful princess ever beheld by human eyes was put to sleep there by some fairy enchantment. According to the story, this spell is to last for one hundred years until the son of a king awakens her and breaks the enchantment. She is said to still be sleeping there, awaiting the prince with whom she is destined to fall in love."

The old man's words lit a fire in the prince's heart. Right away, he was certain that he was the only one who could break the princess's enchantment. It'd already been one hundred years, after all . . . and he *was* a prince. So, it only made sense to give it a go. Inspired by love and honor (with just a dash of youthful arro-gance), he decided to attempt to pass through the thick woods to discover if there might be any truth to the old man's tale.

The prince rode out and, as soon as he approached the thick woods, the wall of trees, bushes, and brambles moved out of his way. The century-old barrier of pointy thorns and vegetation, which had kept the castle separated from the outside world, yielded to his approach and opened a path by which the prince could enter. When a group of royal guards attempted to follow their prince in, however, the plants and trees quickly closed up behind him. Apparently, only the "chosen one" could pass.

Being separated from his guards did not deter the prince. He continued forward, pushed on by the kind of youthful curiosity and thoughts of eternal love that often make young men brave in the face of danger. He entered the palace courtyard and found something rather strange. The ground was littered with people and animals, strewn about as if dead. It was a sight that would've scared off most men. However, the prince was sharp-witted. When he observed their ruddy complexions and heard their faint breathing, he knew they were simply sleeping.

The prince crossed the courtyard and dismounted from his horse to enter the palace. He stepped into the main court, and from there he found a staircase. He ascended it until he reached the chamber of the royal guards, all asleep (but, interestingly enough, still lined up in military formation—rank and file). He continued exploring, finding room after room of slumbering people. Some were on the ground. Some had fallen asleep sitting in chairs. Some were even sleeping where they stood (these poor folks must have had some seriously stiff and sore legs when they woke up).

Finally, the prince went up the tower in which the princess slept. At the top, he discovered a grand bedchamber with a bed that had a frame of solid gold and silver. Asleep upon the plush mattress was the most beautiful girl he had ever seen. Overcome with adoration, the prince fell to his knees at her bedside.

And that was all it took . . . that's right . . . *NO KISS* (if that's what you were expecting). Disney made up that whole "awoken by a prince's kiss" thing. The approach of the brave son of a king was enough to break the enchantment, just as the young fairy had foretold.

The princess opened her eyes and, upon seeing the prince, spoke, "Is it really you, my prince? I've been waiting for you for so very long."

The prince fell in love with her on the spot (he appears to have had a bit of an impulse control problem). The two began to converse, though the prince had a lot less to say than she did.

There's actually an explanation for this. You see, the princess had been provided with more time to consider what she would say. The story tells us that "very probably" the fairy had occupied the princess's mind with dreams during her hundred-year slumber, dreams that told her of the prince who would come to wake her. They spent more than four hours in conversation. Anyone who's ever been in love knows what this is like . . . that blissful time when it feels like you could spend eternity just talking. However, by this point, everyone else in the palace had also woken up . . . and they were *really* hungry and growing impatient, waiting for them to come down. They didn't have love to keep their bellies from grumbling, after all . . . and none of them had eaten in a hundred years. So this is kind of understandable.

The chief lady of honor was perhaps the most famished of them all and decided to end everyone's wait for the love-struck pair to come down from the tower. She went up the tower and, rather curtly, announced to them that dinner was served. The princess was already fully dressed, as she'd been left to slumber in her favorite dress. (No mention of the fact she hadn't *showered* in a hundred years. Just saying.)

The prince was a kindhearted young man, and so he did not tell the princess that her clothes reminded him of something his grandmother would have worn. Despite her antiquated wardrobe, the prince still thought she looked perfect as he helped her to her feet and they descended the tower together.

Dinner was served in the Great Hall of Looking Glasses, which one can only assume was a banquet hall with wall-to-wall mirrors. Served by the newly awakened kitchen crew and dining staff, the pair of young lovers feasted together while the minstrels played songs that had long ago passed into obscurity. The prince noticed he hadn't heard any of these songs since his early

GRIMM WORDS

Chief Lady of Honor: A title similar to that of a "lady in waiting." It was a nonspecific court title, often bestowed upon women who were from nonroyal noble lineages (such as certain duchesses or baronesses). The primary duty of a lady of honor was to attend to the needs of queens, princesses, and/or noblewomen of especially high rank, kind of like the medieval version of a personal assistant.

childhood. Again, however, he was kind enough not to make a joke of it. And, besides that, the minstrels played the songs quite beautifully.

After dinner, the lord almoner was summoned to the palace chapel. The prince and princess were properly married before all present. They then retired to the bedchamber to consummate the union. The chief lady of honor led them to their wedding bed (a "witness" was customary in those times) and drew the curtains to give them some privacy.

Neither the prince nor princess did much sleeping that night. Having been gone from his palace overnight, the prince left the next morning and returned home to his worried parents. He explained to his father (the king) and mother (the queen) that he'd become lost in the woods while hunting and had to spend the night at a woodsman's cottage.

The king was a pretty laid-back guy and didn't see any need to question the prince further. He was just happy to have his son safely home. The queen, on the other hand, did not quite buy her son's story. She became more suspicious when the prince began taking frequent hunting trips, staying at the "woodman's cot-

GRIMM WORDS

Lord Almoner: A religious official of a royal court, commonly in charge of collecting alms (such as charity donations, holy offerings, and church tithes). Since this position was often occupied by a member of the church clergy, this explains why a lord almoner was summoned to perform the marriage of the prince and princess in the story.

tage" for days on end and rarely if ever coming back with any game. The queen became convinced her son had taken a lover, especially when his regular hunting trips continued for two full years. All that time, of course, the prince was actually going to his wife the princess at the palace in the thick woods.

The queen discussed the matter with her son on a number of occasions, explaining that such pleasures were often indulged in by princes, in the hopes he would open up to her about it. However, the prince did not dare to reveal his secret to the queen. And there was a very good reason—though the prince loved his mother, he was smart enough to fear her as well.

The queen, you see, was descended from a race of ogres. The only reason his father had married her was for the incredibly large dowry that came with the deal. Throughout the kingdom, it was rumored she still had the savage urges that came with the ogre blood flowing through her veins, and that she had obvious difficulty restraining herself when children were around . . . as if she wanted to attack and devour them.

In those couple of years, the princess gave birth to two children—a girl named Aurora (in this usage, her name would mean something like "the dawn" or "daybreak") and a boy named

GRIMM WORDS

Queen Mother: A royal title for the mother of a reigning king. For example, if Queen Elizabeth II (the current ruling Queen of England) were to step down from the throne, she would become Queen Mother and her son, Prince Charles, would become the reigning king of England.

Day, since his fair and handsome face was said to shine even more beautifully than his older sister's. Fearing that his ogre-blooded mother might do harm to his wife and children, the prince had no choice but to keep his mouth shut about his secret family.

A few more years went by, and sadly, the king passed away. The death of his father meant the prince was now king of the realm, which also meant he'd be expected to take a queen almost immediately. This left him no choice but to reveal his marriage and bring the princess, along with their children, to the palace. Their entry into the capital city was like a grand parade, at the head of which was the princess (the new queen, which meant the prince's mother would now be the Queen Mother), riding between her two lovely children. Many commented on what a beautiful sight the three made.

The family settled into their new home. However, a day came when the king (formerly known as "the prince") was forced to leave. The ruler of a neighboring country, Emperor Cantalabutte, was causing problems for his subjects and was in need of a good, old-fashioned butt whooping. So the king rode off to war, kissing his wife and children good-bye. Most believed that the war would last an entire summer, which meant the king wasn't likely to return for many months. In his absence, he left the kingdom's affairs in the hands of the Queen Mother. He also charged her with taking care of his wife and children, trusting her to keep them safe until his return. Since their arrival in the capital, his mother had given no indication that she meant any harm to the children or queen.

As soon as her son was gone, the Queen Mother sent her daughter-in-law, along with Aurora and Day, to stay in one of their country estates under the pretense that they'd have a more enjoyable time there and it'd make the days pass more quickly. However, her real motivation was far more horrid. The Queen Mother intended to satisfy her ogreish urges once she had them away from the capital, by making a meal of them, one by one.

After the queen and her kids had been staying at the country estate for a few days, the Queen Mother went there herself. Upon arrival, she went straight to the chief cook.

"I'll be dining on little Aurora tomorrow evening," she told him.

"No, Your Highness! Please," begged the chief cook.

"You will do as I command," the Queen Mother replied, using the frightening tone of voice common for an ogress. "And I want her served up with a Sauce Robert."

The chief cook knew better than to get on the bad side of an ogress, not to mention one that was also the Queen Mother. So he took a butchering knife and went to Aurora's bedchamber, where he found the four-year-old little girl playing happily. When Aurora saw the chief cook, she ran to him laughing, gave him a big hug, and asked if he had any candy. It broke the poor guy's heart to think he'd even considered carrying out the Queen Mother's commands. He dropped the knife, held the little girl, and wept. Realizing she was in danger, he whisked her away to his own house. Once he'd left the girl in the care of his wife, he

GRIMM WORDS

Sauce Robert (sauce RO-behr): A French sauce consisting of shredded onions sautéed in butter then mixed with vinegar, salt, mustard, and wine. There are a number of variations to this recipe, of course.

went out and butchered a young lamb. He served it up, nice and tender with Sauce Robert, to the Queen Mother. She claimed it was the most delicious meal she'd ever had.

Unfortunately, her urges were not yet satiated. A week later, she returned to the chief cook with another savage command.

"Tonight, I believe I shall feast on Day. If he's half as tasty as he is handsome, he should make a delicious meal," she told him.

This time, the chief cook offered no protest. Hoping to fool the ogress once again, he did everything as he had before. He found three-year-old little Day outside in the courtyard . . . fencing with a monkey.

Because apparently that was a thing back then . . . little boys fencing with monkeys.

The chief cook snatched the boy in his arms and, as he had with Aurora, hid the child with his wife. He then went out and butchered a newborn goat, dressed it with the same Sauce Robert, and served it to the Queen Mother at dinner. Once again, she complimented him on making such a fine dish. However, her desire for human flesh was now even greater.

Not long after this, she came to the chief cook a third time.

"I shall eat my daughter-in-law, the queen, tonight," she commanded. "Oh, and please do serve her with the same sauce you used with the children."

The chief cook now found himself in quite a pickle. He worried he couldn't fool the Queen Mother a third time. Substituting the tender flesh of the children was easy enough. The queen may have looked like a woman in her twenties, but she'd actually been alive for well over a century. As a result, her flesh would be incredibly firm and hard to find a convincing substitute for. Finally, he decided he had no choice but to actually kill and cook her. Otherwise, the Queen Mother would learn of his deception with the children and have him killed. He took up his butchering knife and went to the queen's bedchamber, creeping up from behind. However, he couldn't bring himself to slit her throat in such a dastardly fashion. Instead, as respectfully as he could, he told her the truth of why he'd come . . . that he was under the Queen Mother's orders to kill and cook her.

"Go ahead," the queen replied, to the chief cook's dismay, and lifted her chin to expose her neck. "Do as she commands and kill me. I shall join my children in heaven. I miss them so much that I don't want to live anymore."

"No, Your Highness," the chief cook told her. "You must live if you are to see your children again. They are hidden at my home on the other side of the courtyard, where I have left them in the care of my wife to protect them from the Queen Mother. I have deceived her twice before, my queen, and I shall find a way to do so once more. I shall butcher a hind in your place. That will surely work."

The chief cook led the queen to his home and reunited her with her children. He left them, weeping tears of joy, to butcher a hind as he'd promised. He dressed it as best he could and served it (with the usual Sauce Robert, of course) to the Queen Mother. Apparently, the *idea* of eating human flesh had more impact than the taste of it when it came to the ogress. Once again, she was

GRIMM WORDS

Hind: As it is used here, a female deer that has been alive for more than three years. The older a female deer is, it is said, the more firm the meat becomes.

delighted with the meal. As she had no intention of telling her son the truth when he returned, she had already concocted a story about how a pack of wolves had attacked and eaten his beloved wife and children while they were walking in the woods.

Time passed, and for a while the Queen Mother was none the wiser. Then an evening came when she was out for a walk in the courtyard. As the Queen Mother walked, sniffing at the air and hoping to come upon a fresh young child that might go well with a Sauce Robert, she heard a familiar voice—it was Day, crying because he was about to get a spanking for misbehaving in some way. Then she heard Aurora's voice, trying to come to her brother's aid and begging her mother to forgive Day. Then she heard the voice of her daughter-in-law telling her children that it was all for the best.

Hearing the voices of the family she thought she'd eaten, the Queen Mother flipped out. At sunrise the next morning, she ordered her personal guards to have them all brought into the courtyard—the queen, Aurora, Day, and even the chief cook and his wife and their maidservant. All of them were lined up on their knees with their hands bound behind their backs. In the custom of ogres, the Queen Mother had a tub brought into the courtyard and filled with all sorts of vile creatures—vipers, poisonous toads, venomous serpents, and the like. Her intention was to have them all thrown into her "tub of scaly death," one by one, so she could watch them die excruciatingly painful deaths.

Just as the Queen Mother was about give the kill order to her executioners, however, the king suddenly returned earlier than expected. He'd come straight to the country estate to see his family so they could return to the palace together. Instead, he walked into a nightmarish scene.

"What is the meaning of this barbaric spectacle?" he demanded, aghast at what his mother was doing to those he loved.

The Queen Mother, in a rage (or, perhaps, ashamed of her ogress ways), threw herself headlong into the tub. She was instantly bitten all over her body by fangs dripping with venom. She died a terrible death, being poisoned and devoured by the very creatures she'd had placed there for the suffering of others.

The king mourned the loss. She was his mother, after all . . . a psychotic child killer and cannibal, but his mother nonetheless. However, the king found solace in the knowledge that his family was now safe.

And they all lived happily ever after.

And, according to Perrault, here is the moral of the story:

Many girls have waited long
For a husband brave or strong;
But I'm sure I've never met
Any sort of woman yet
Who could wait a hundred years,
Free from worry, free from fears.
Now, our story seems to show
That about a century ago,

Late or early, matters not;
True love comes by a fairy's lot.
Some old folks will even say
It grows better by delay.
Yet this sound advice, I fear,
Helps us neither here nor there.
Though philosophers may orate
How much wiser it is to wait,
Maids will keep on sighing still—
Young blood must when young blood will!

Narcoleptic Lasses: A *Grimm* Comparison

Nick, this won't wake her up. This will only stop her memory loss.
         —Rosalee Calvert, "The Kiss" (2-02)

Juliette's coma, needless to say, is comparable to (though significantly shorter than) the hundred-year slumber of Sleeping Beauty. However, the events of *Grimm* and those of the original story of "The Sleeping Beauty in the Wood" have far more in common than just the fact that both involve a comatose woman. In fact, the similarities begin long before Juliette even goes to sleep.

The first overlapping element between the show and the story is how the sleeping curse is delivered. In the original fairy tale, Sleeping Beauty falls asleep the moment she pricks her hand/finger on a spinning wheel. A similar wound is placed upon Juliette in *Grimm*, delivered by a scratch from Adalind Schade's psychotic cat. In contrast to Sleeping Beauty, however, Juliette doesn't pass out immediately. The Hexenbiest's curse seems to work more slowly than the fairy curse that befell Sleeping Beauty.

The second point of comparison is found in the fact that, in both *Grimm* and the fairy tale, a good female character intervenes in order to lessen the effects of a curse from an evil female character. In the fairy tale, Sleeping Beauty was initially supposed to die because of the grumpy old fairy's curse. However, the kind younger fairy intervened and altered the curse so the girl will only sleep for a century. The fairy was unable to do away with the curse completely, however, and Rosalee Calvert finds herself in a similar position. The eye-drop potion that Monroe's beloved Fuchsbau, Rosalee, concocts does not have the power to wake up Juliette or undo Adalind's curse completely. It is only meant to stop Juliette from losing any more of her memories while she's in her "curse coma." By the time she finally wakes up, unfortunately, she has lost her memory of Nick. This brings us to our third point of comparison in this chapter—the arrival of a "prince" who is able to finally wake up the "princess."

While Charles Perrault's version of the fairy tale makes no mention of Sleeping Beauty being woken by a kiss from the prince (simply his arrival at her bedside is enough to break the curse), there are plenty of alternate versions of the story where this kiss is included. There are also other stories where a prince's kiss (or arrival) wakes up a cursed sleeping damsel—"Snow White," for example. Considering the fact that a majority of people are familiar with this scenario, it makes sense that the writers of *Grimm* chose to include it. However, in the universe of *Grimm*, only a kiss from a man of royal blood (a "prince") who is pure of heart can save Juliette. There's just one problem with this—Nick Burkhardt may be pure of heart, but he is not of royal blood. As a result, Captain Renard is forced to intervene. He is of royal blood, though definitely not so pure of heart. Renard has to purify himself "chemically," which appears to be rather painful, and this allows him to wake Juliette with a kiss. However, this also opens a whole new can of worms because—just like in many fairy tales—after the kiss, Juliette and Renard become completely infatuated with each other.

The kind of "love at first sight" infatuation displayed by Renard and Juliette is somewhat similar to events that occur in these kinds of fairy tales. The princess wakes up to the prince's kiss, and the two immediately fall in love and stay together for the rest of their lives—no dating, no courtship, and sometimes without even knowing each other's name. Having such intense feelings for a person one doesn't know is not exactly considered "love" by today's standards. In modern times, most people would probably call this "infatuation"—or "stalking," maybe.

Never Anger a Fairy:
The Mythology of Slighted Supernatural Beings

There exists, quite obviously, an impressively large number of tales that involve damsels being forced into magical comas. However, from a mythological point of view, the tale of "Sleeping Beauty" has far more to offer. Aside from its narcoleptic theme, this tale falls into another mythological category—that of the "vengeful supernatural being." While in the Perrault tale it is a fairy who curses the girl for a perceived slight by her parents, in more ancient times it was often gods (or, more frequently, goddesses) doing the smiting for such offenses.

One such tale comes to us from the myths of the ancient Greeks, and it is often referred to as "The Apples of Discord." When the hero Peleus married the beautiful sea nymph Thetis, the newlyweds invited all of the gods to their wedding feast . . . well, almost all of them. They failed to invite only one—Eris, the goddess of chaos and discord. Needless to say, she was most definitely the worst kind of goddess to anger.

Enraged at being snubbed for such a grand occasion, Eris decided to sow a little discord amongst the party. She tossed a golden apple (or a bunch of them) into the soiree, inscribed with the following words: "For the fairest."

You need to understand that every goddess of Olympus was present (except for Eris, of course), and these ladies were nothing if not vain and spiteful. As soon as the apple hit the floor, three goddesses tried to claim it—Hera (wife of Zeus), Aphrodite (goddess of beauty), and Athena (goddess of wisdom, strategy, and warfare). Seeing as how none of them was willing to stand down, they asked Zeus to decide. The Greek god of thunder, however, knew a trap when he saw one (you might call this the origin of what men refer to as a "loaded question"). Zeus wasn't about to do something as dangerous as voice his opinion on the beauty of three goddesses. So he sent them to the prince of Troy, Paris, so he might choose the fairest among the trio.

When the goddesses arrived, they each decided to try a little good old-fashioned bribery. Hera promised the prince power and wealth in exchange for choosing her. Athena offered him eternal victory in battle. Aphrodite, however, offered him the most beautiful woman in the world for his wife. Young stud that he was, Paris chose Aphrodite. While he made an ally of one goddess, there was something else Paris failed to realize—he'd just made lifelong enemies of the other two.

Aphrodite then took Paris to the Greek kingdom of Sparta, ruled by King Menelaus, and introduced the prince to the most beautiful woman in the world . . . Helen . . . Menelaus's wife. That's where things got complicated. You see, back when all the heroes of Greece competed for Helen's hand in marriage, she'd had each and every one of them swear an oath to always defend her and, if necessary, take revenge for her death (we're talking about half-god, badass men such as Odysseus, Ajax, and Achilles). In the end, Helen had chosen Menelaus for her husband. Aphrodite, however, used her powers to persuade Helen to fall in love with Paris. The two fled Greece together and returned to Troy, and thus began what is now known as the Trojan War. Every hero of Greece, having previously sworn an oath to defend Helen, had no choice but to participate. By the end of the war, the great city of Troy had been reduced to ashes.

But look on the bright side . . . at least Helen wasn't stricken comatose. She actually survived the war and returned to Sparta with Menelaus.

While many fairy-tale lasses meet their royal husbands in the romantic "true love's kiss" or "arrival of a handsome prince" fashion . . . others are not so lucky. Take the damsel of the fairy tale in our next chapter, for example. Her kingly husband threatens her life—*twice*—before he finally proposes to her.

[15]

WEIRD LITTLE GUYS WITH FUNNY NAMES

I'm all over this. I've done my fair share of gaming, since my life consists mostly of myself and my cat.

—Sergeant Wu, "Nameless" (2-16)

In the episode "Nameless" (2-16), Nick Burkhardt and Hank Griffin are called out to the scene of a murder that occurred at a local software company during a launch party for their new MMORPG game "Black Forest." Somehow, a young software engineer named Brody Crawford got himself sliced completely in half . . . without a single eyewitness to the crime. The plot thickens when it's discovered that, just moments before his murder, Brody was having a romantic interlude with Jenna Marshall—the software engineer team leader. Things get even weirder when it turns out that Brody's Black Forest avatar was killed in the game—sliced in half—only three hours before he was murdered in the real world in the same way. Nick Burkhardt's investigation into this strange series of events leads him to encounter a goblin type of Wesen known as a Fuchsteufelwild, and he soon finds himself racing against time to save future victims from being killed by a creature with an elusive name.

This *Grimm* episode is a modern take on a tradition of various fairy tales belonging to what is commonly known as the supernatural helper motif. One such tale, "Rumpelstiltskin," was recorded by the Brothers Grimm in their original 1812 printing of *Kinder- und Hausmärchen*, and the following retelling is based on this version.

Rumpelstiltskin: A Retelling

NICK BURKHARDT: *We just found out in the Black Forest game his nom de plume is Nameless.*
SERGEANT WU: *Ah . . . I guess he put a lot of thought into that one.*
—"Nameless" (2-16)

In a country far, far away (though "far, far away" from *where*, the story doesn't say), there was a mighty stream that ran alongside a forest. On the bank of the stream was a mill, and beside it stood the house of the miller. He was rather poor and had only one possession of any real value—his beautiful daughter (whom we'll refer to in this retelling as "the miller's daughter" because, as usual with female characters in such stories, she is never given a name).

In addition to being beautiful, the miller's daughter was also an especially resourceful and quick-witted young lady. And there was little in the world of which the miller was more proud. Pride, however, can sometimes cause even the best of us to do some very stupid things . . . and, in his pride, the miller definitely did something *really* stupid.

The king of the land (whom we'll just call "the king" because, once again, he has no name in the story) was rather fond of taking hunting trips in the forest where the miller lived with his daugh-

Tasty Morsels

The reason the miller's mill/home was beside the river is likely because his mill was powered by a waterwheel. This was a large, horizontally standing, paddle wheel that was constantly turned by the current of the river, which then turned the heavy mill-stone used to grind grain into flour.

ter. Over the years, the king had come to know the miller rather well and would often stop by to visit briefly. Now, it was a well-known fact the king loved only one thing more than hunting—GOLD. So, in an effort to make the king take an interest in the daughter he was so proud of, the miller made a careless boast.

"My daughter is more than just beautiful," he told the king. "She can also spin straw into gold!"

"Now, wouldn't that be a marvelous ability to have," the king replied, somewhat skeptically. "I order you to have her brought to my palace tomorrow, so that I may see this incredible talent for myself."

The king was not a fool, and he was certainly not the sort of guy to accept such an incredulous claim on someone's word alone. Of course, the idea of a person who spins straw into gold would be a pretty hard pill to swallow for anyone.

The miller sent his daughter to the king (the man did not accompany her there, by the way). The ruler planned to put the miller's careless boast to the test . . . and in the most serious way imaginable. The miller's daughter was immediately seized by the king's guards when she arrived. They took her to a chamber of the palace the king had already ordered his men to fill with straw. She was given a spinning wheel, along with a threat from the king.

"I want all this straw spun into gold by dawn," he told her. "Otherwise, you will be executed."

The miller's daughter pleaded with the king, and tried to explain it was nothing more than a ridiculous boast her dimwitted father had made in a moment of haste. She insisted that she couldn't spin straw into gold . . . *no one* could do such a thing! Her words, however, failed to sway the king, who had the door to the room barred. Guards were placed outside to prevent any attempts she might've made to escape.

This king was a real peach, wasn't he?

Seeing no way out of her predicament, the miller's daughter did what most people would likely do in her situation—she found the nearest corner, curled up in the fetal position, and started bawling her eyes out. However, just as all seemed lost, the chamber door opened and in walked a little man . . . *thing.*

"Good day to you, young lady," the little-man-thing said. "What is it that makes you stain that pretty face of yours with tears?"

"I am done for," she replied. "The king is going to have me executed in the morning unless I can spin all of this straw into gold by dawn! I have no idea how to do such a thing! In fact, I don't think it's even possible!"

"And what would I receive in return," asked the strange little-man-thing, "if I was to do it for you?"

"It's not much, but you can have my necklace."

He took the necklace, had a seat at the spinning wheel, and began to whistle and sing:

Round about, round about,
Lo and behold!
Reel on and reel on,
Straw into gold!

The little-man-thing went about his work most happily, not to mention quickly. The wheel spun, faster and faster, until every bit of straw in the room had been transformed into gold . . . and not a moment too soon, as dawn was approaching.

In walked the king that morning, fully expecting he'd have to end the girl's life for the silly words of her father. So he was more than a little bewildered, not to mention absolutely thrilled, when he saw the chamber full of spun gold. However, even this little miracle was not enough to satiate the king's incredible lust for bling. That evening, he had an even larger room filled with straw and shut the miller's daughter inside with a spinning wheel. As he barred the door, the king again threatened the girl.

"Spin all this straw into gold by dawn, or you will lose your life."

The miller's daughter resumed the fetal position in the corner and cried another downpour of tears. After all, what were the odds that she'd again be saved by the miraculous arrival of a weird little-man-thing? Stuff like that usually only happens once in a lifetime, if it happens at all. Luckily for her, this wasn't one of those times. The door opened yet again, and in walked the same odd little fellow.

"I'll do it a second time," he told her, this time getting right to the point. "But what will you give as payment?"

"The ring on my finger," the girl replied.

He took the ring, had a seat at the spinning wheel, and got busy with the spinning and the whistling and the singing:

Round about, round about,
Lo and behold!
Reel on and reel on,
Straw into gold!

The wheel seemed to spin even faster than it had the previous night, as the little-man-thing worked away happily and furiously at his miraculous task. This time, even though there was more straw to be spun, he finished his work sooner than before. It was well before dawn when he spun the last of it, and the entire room glittered with gold.

The king was even more pleased the second time around, and the sight of so much gold made his eyes go wide. However, his desire for gold was still not satisfied. He had a third chamber, this one larger than either of the previous ones, filled to the ceiling with straw. He then locked the miller's daughter inside yet again. As he barred the door this time, however, it was not a threat he uttered but a marriage proposal of sorts (though not the most romantic one, most would agree).

"Spin all this straw into gold by morning," the king told her. "Do it one last time, and I will make you my queen." It's enough to make a girl go all weak in the knees, ain't it?

As the king walked away, he thought to himself, *She may only be a lowborn miller's daughter, but there's not a princess in the world who can offer me a dowry richer than what this girl has already provided.*

Before the miller's daughter even had time to go all fetal-position and become teary eyed, the chamber door opened once again and in walked the little-man-thing.

"You know why I've come for a third time," he said. "But I don't work for free. Payment must be made."

"I have nothing left," she told him. "That ring and necklace were all I had in the world."

"Then we'll have to open a line of credit for you, I suppose," he explained. "Promise me that one day, when you're queen, you'll hand over to me the first child you have by the king."

Who knows, thought the miller's daughter. *It's possible I may never even have a child with the king. But at least I will be alive.*

Seeing no other way to get the job done, the miller's daughter agreed to the deal. The little-man-thing went to work again with the spinning and the whistling and the singing (out of kindness, you won't be subjected to that weird song again). Before she knew it, the miller's daughter was standing in a room full of gold where only straw had been before.

"Remember our deal," said the little-man-thing just before he vanished out the door.

The king nearly had a bling-gasm when he saw the largest chamber in his palace filled from floor to ceiling with gold. Bound by honor, he kept his word and married the miller's daughter. As a result, this girl of non-noble birth found herself a queen. Her luck seemed to have finally taken a turn for the better, and life became a worry-free joy for her.

Until she gave birth to her first child, that is.

Years had passed since the days she'd spent locked in the palace chambers without a hope in the world, and the girl had somehow forgotten the deal she'd made with the strange little-man-thing . . . as one might forget a passing but peculiar dream. One day, as she sat on the floor of the royal bedchamber and played with her precious baby, in walked the odd little-man-thing. Terror struck her heart as she suddenly remembered her promise. With tears streaming down her cheeks, she offered him all the riches in the kingdom if he would only leave the child with her. But the little-man-thing refused to free her from their deal. However, she continued to beg so sincerely that it finally softened his heart a bit.

"Very well," he told her. "I will give you three days. If in that time you are able to call me by my true name, I shall free you from our bargain, and you may keep your child."

And, with that, the little-man-thing vanished again.

That night, the miller's-daughter-turned-queen tossed and turned as she tried to recall all of the unusual names she had ever heard. After all, such an odd little man must've had an equally odd name. At dawn, she sent every messenger in the kingdom riding out in search of new names for her to try.

When the little-man-thing appeared on the morning of the first day, she began by trying out all the names she'd thought of the night before:

"Ichabod?"

"No."

"Benji?"

"No."

"Timothy? Casper? Jeremiah? Balthasar? Methuselah?"

"My good lady," he replied to her every guess, "that is not my name."

That evening, all but one of the messengers returned to tell her of the various weird names they'd discovered for her. On the morning of the second day, the little-man-thing arrived as expected, and she tried out each and every one of them. When she ran out, she still kept guessing for as long as he would let her.

"Cruikshank?"

"No."

"Ribfiend?"

"No."

"Hunchback? Muttonchops? Bandylegs? Spindleshanks? Brown-nose?"

"My good lady," he said to all her attempts, "that is not my name."

All but one of the messengers returned again that evening,

but none of them could ride out far enough to learn of any new names with the little time that was left to them. Before the sun had risen on the third day, the queen was overcome by despair. Suddenly, however, the final messenger (who had been gone since the morning of the first day) returned just before dawn.

"My queen, I traveled out as far as I could in the hope I'd find the right name for you," he told her. "But none seemed any more unusual than another. Forgive me for not riding back sooner, but on my return through the forest, I came upon a strange little house where I found an even stranger little man . . . thing. In front of the house he'd built a fire, around which he danced, hopping on one leg, and sang this odd song:

Merrily a feast I'll make.

Today I brew, tomorrow I bake.

Merrily do I dance and sing,

For tomorrow shall a stranger bring.

Little does my good lady dream,

That RUMPELSTILTSKIN is my name!

Hearing this news, the queen was overjoyed. In fact, she was so delighted that she decided to invite everyone in the entire palace to the throne room so all could witness what was sure to be an entertaining spectacle.

On the morning of the third day, the queen sat upon the throne and acted as if she was distraught. She even had her wet nurse stand next to her, baby in her arms, as if she planned to hand the child over. The little-man-thing's cackles echoed through the throne room as he arrived, happy at the thought of taking the infant to his home in the woods . . . where heaven only knows what horrible things he planned to do.

"This is your last chance, my good lady," he taunted. "What is my name?"

"John?" she replied, choosing common names so as to have a little fun with him before the grand finale.

"No."

"Tom?"

"No."

"Conrad? Jeremy? Harry?"

"My good lady," he said. "That is not my name."

"Hm . . . Well, then . . . Perhaps your name is RUMPEL-STILTSKIN!"

Rumpelstiltskin, upon hearing his true name, threw what might best be described as a full-on-balls-to-the-wall-conniption fit.

"Some witch told you that! Some devil must have told you!" he cried.

Rumpelstiltskin then began stamping his right foot on the ground with such rage and fury that it broke through the floor of the throne room and got stuck. He had to use both hands to pull his foot free (some versions end here and say he tore himself in half while trying to free his foot). Realizing he was defeated, he flew away from the court while everyone—the queen, the king, the nobles present, and even the wet nurse and the baby—had a laugh at his expense.

Adding insult to injury, as he fled from the throne room, they all called after him, "We wish you a very good morning and a very merry feast, our dear Mr. RUMPELSTILTSKIN!"

And the strange little-man-thing called Rumpelstiltskin was never seen in that land ever again.

Say My Name!: A *Grimm* Comparison

Seems like they've been playing games long before there were computers.
—Nick Burkhardt, "Nameless" (2-16)

Even though the worlds of Rumpelstiltskin and the *Grimm* episode "Nameless" (2-16) are separated by centuries, they are the same in many ways. Long before Christianity came along and spawned stories about people who made deals with the devil, there were weird little goblins like Rumpelstiltskin. In fairy tales, these kinds of creatures are known as the "supernatural helper." And it is this classification that bridges the gap between the *Grimm* episode and the story from which it originates.

In both the *Grimm* episode and the story, a supernatural helper appears to a human (or humans, in the show) and offers to complete a difficult or impossible task. However, in both there is a price to be paid that, eventually, becomes something the deal makers will regret—like giving away a firstborn baby. However, both supernatural helpers also offer a way out.

The one-sided deals that are offered by the goblin-like Fuchsteufelwilds come with a difficult price. When the Black Forest software engineers are unable to pay up, they start getting taken out one by one. However, the last of them finds salvation via the same out that Rumpelstiltskin offered to the miller's daughter—to guess and speak his true name. And, just as the miller's daughter sent riders out into the real world to learn of possible names, the characters of *Grimm* travel into the virtual world in order to discover the true name of Chris Murray—Trinket Lipsums. This name, in case you haven't noticed, is an anagram of Rumpelstiltskin. You have to hand it to the writers of *Grimm*, they enjoy hiding little nuggets of weirdness in their work almost as much as a Fuchsteufelwilds enjoy tricking those foolish enough to make deals with them.

Tapai and the Brahman: The Power of a Name in Mythology

As mentioned earlier in this chapter, the motif of the supernatural helper dates back to well before pre-Christian times. The same is true of the "power of a name" concept. In fact, one can find a story that closely parallels "Rumpelstiltskin" in the mythological tradition of the Hindu Dharma religion—"Tapai and the Brahman."

One cold evening, a Brahman was making his way home through the forest. He was starting to fear that he might freeze down to his bones when he spied a fire nearby, which appeared to have a group of people gathered around. The Brahman approached the cozy heat and proclaimed *"Tapai! Tapai!"* (in the Hindi language, this roughly translates as "I'm warmed! I'm warmed!").

As the Brahman came beside the fire, however, he was horrified to find it surrounded by a group of *bhutas* (this word translates as something like "wrathful spirits," though it is often misinterpreted as "demon" or "ghost"). One of the spirits, by strange coincidence, was called Tapai. He and the other wrathful spirits were offended that the Brahman addressed one of them so casually. They were just about to rip him to shreds when the clever Brahman had an epiphany and proclaimed that Tapai's ancestors had been slaves of his family for three generations.

"If that's true," Tapai said, "and you can name ancestors from three generations of my family, I will gladly become your personal slave."

GRIMM WORDS

Brahman: From the caste system of the Hindu Dharma religion. Brahmans are members of the religious/priestly class of this caste system.

"I can't be expected to recall the names from memory," said the Brahman. "I need to go home and look at the family records."

"Very well," said Tapai. "You have three days to return with their names. If you don't show, however, all us bhutas will come to your home and murder you and your entire family."

The Brahman went home, happy to escape with his life but terrified to know in three days he'd likely be killed. On the night before the third day, he fell into despair. He walked into the forest, planning to hang himself from a limb. Along the way, however, he happened upon the home of Tapai; there was a fire roaring outside. He saw Tapai sitting beside it, telling his wife of the Brahman who'd claimed the bhuta's ancestors had been slaves to his family. The bhuta's wife said to him, "Do you even know the names from your family's previous three generations?"

"Of course," said Tapai, while the Brahman eavesdropped. "Haramu, father of Charamu, father of Apai, father of Tapai."

Hearing this, the Brahman knew he had the information he needed. He committed the names to memory and returned home. The next evening, he went to where he'd first met Tapai and the others in the forest. He recited the names, and Tapai had no choice but to become the Brahman's slave as promised. As is often the case in such stories, though, there was a condition: From sunrise to sunset, Tapai would complete any task he was given by the

Brahman. However, he had to keep the spirit constantly occupied. If he could not, then he'd have to release the bhuta from slavery.

At first, this sounded like a pretty sweet deal. For weeks, the Brahman was able to keep the bhuta occupied from dawn to dusk with all sorts of tasks—building a temple to the gods, erecting a grand palace for his family, digging outhouses for everyone in the surrounding villages, and even finding a suitable husband for one of the Brahman's daughters. As the days passed, however, the Brahman found himself running out of jobs for Tapai. Though he was surrounded by wealth and blessed with prosperity, the Brahman was tormented as he constantly tried to come up with new tasks for Tapai to do.

Luckily, the Brahman's wife came to his aid. She plucked a curly hair from his head and told him, "Give this to Tapai and tell him to straighten it."

For once, the enslaved bhuta was faced with a task he could not complete. Try as he might, Tapai could not make the curly hair perfectly straight. When the Brahman saw how vexed Tapai was, however, he took pity on the poor spirit.

As the sun set that evening, the Brahman released Tapai from slavery.

As with Rumpelstiltskin, Tapai found himself at the mercy of a human . . . all because of the power of a name.

Speaking of supernatural beings taking joy in getting one over on humans . . . there are probably even some Fuchsteufelwilds who've found themselves in the debt of the foxy Wesen discussed in the next chapter—Fuchsbau.

[16]

FOXY FUCHSBAU

Haven't seen a Fuchsbau in a Waschbär's age, myself.
                                        —Monroe, "Organ Grinder" (1-10)

Ever since the episode "Organ Grinder" (1-10), Grimmsters have been aware of the existence of the fox-type Wesen called Fuchsbau. And these fox-natured Wesen have come to play an increasingly regular role in the *Grimm* universe. Monroe's love interest, Rosalee Calvert, is a Fuchsbau; the Coins of Zakynthos were found in the belly of a Fuchsbau; and the leader of the Laufer resistance, Ian Harmon, is also a Fuchsbau. Perhaps the reason Fuchsbau show up in *Grimm* more often than almost any other Wesen is due to the fact that fox characters appear in a multitude of Brothers Grimm stories. The retellings that follow are but a sampling of the fox stories to be found in *Kinder- und Hausmärchen* (not to mention in the fairy-tale tradition in general).

The Fox and the Cat: A Retelling

One day, while walking through the forest, the cat happened across the fox and thought to herself: *The fox is a rather clever fel-*

low and has experienced so much. Besides that, he is highly respected throughout the world. So she decided to speak to him, in the hopes she might learn something from him.

"Good day to you, Mr. Fox," she said to him in a friendly and polite manner. "How are you today? Are you faring well in these scarce times?"

The fox, however, was rather arrogant by nature. He looked the cat up and down, and for a long time said nothing because he couldn't decide if she was even worth speaking with. Finally, he broke his silence . . . and spoke to the cat like a proper jerk.

"Oh, you disgusting little cleaner of beards, you silly little fool, you savage little mouse hunter. What could you possibly be thinking, asking one such as *I* how I'm faring? What could *you* possibly know? How many arts have *you* learned?"

"I have learned but one art," the cat replied with a tone of modesty.

"And what art might that be?" scoffed the fox.

"When I find myself being chased by the hounds, I know how to scale a tree to escape them."

"That's all you know how to do?" said the fox. "I have mastered a hundred arts myself and also have cunning by the sackful. I feel sorry for you, honestly. Spend some time with me, and I shall teach you how people get away from hounds."

Just as the fox spoke these words, a hunter showed up with four hounds that were already onto the scent of both the cat and fox. The cat scaled the nearest tree to escape and hid herself among the branches. She looked down to see the hounds falling upon the fox, who just stood there like a fool.

"Mr. Fox! Open one of your sackfuls of cunning!" she called down to him as the hounds pinned him to the ground. "Really, Mr. Fox! You, who are master of a hundred arts, certainly got yourself caught easily enough. If only you'd bothered to let me teach you the one art I know, you'd be safe in the tree like me. Instead, your arrogance will cost you your life!"

And so the cat escaped while the fox was caught, killed, and eaten in a stew, and his fur became a hat for one of the hunter's children.

The moral of this story is quite simple, really: Just because you know more than other people does not mean they have nothing useful to teach you.

The Fox and the Horse: A Retelling

This is a Fuchsbau.   —Rosalee Calvert, "The Waking Dead" (2-21)

Once there was a horse who had served his master, the farmer, faithfully all his life. Eventually, however, the horse grew too old and weak to work. Because of this, the farmer stopped feeding him one day.

"Your services are no longer required," said the farmer to the horse. "Get out of my stable, and don't come back until you have the strength of the lion!"

With that, the farmer booted the poor old horse out of the only home he'd even known and left him to wander all alone.

The old horse was heartbroken and did not know what to do or where to go, so he just started walking around in the woods. When the wind picked up and the rain began to fall, he started looking for some shelter but could find none. Eventually, cold and wet, the horse ran into the fox.

"Why the long face, friend?" said the fox (Get it?). "What's got you looking like such a sorry mess?"

"Oh, Fox," the horse explained. "My master acts as though the many years I served him faithfully mean nothing! I'm old and can no longer work, so he turned me out and told me never to return unless I have the strength of the lion. How is such a thing possible? It's hopeless!"

"Chin up, buddy," said the fox cheerfully. "I think I can help you out with this. I just need you to lie down on the ground here. Stretch out your legs and be as stiff and still as you can. Think you can do that for me?"

The horse agreed and did as the fox had instructed. As the horse lay there, the fox went to see the lion who lived in a nearby cave.

"Hey, Lion," called the fox from outside the cave. "I found a dead horse not far from here. Let me show you where it is, and you can chow down on it. A horse will make a fine meal, but we need to hurry before it spoils!"

The lion was thrilled when he heard this, and he immediately came out from his cave. He followed the fox, and soon they came to the horse, still lying there as if dead. Before the lion could bite into the horse, however, the fox stopped him.

"You don't want to eat him here, where you'll have to do it quickly. Better to take him back to your cave where you can enjoy a nice, slow meal. I know! I'll tie you to him by his tail, and then you can drag him away."

The lion felt that the fox was offering sound advice. So he lay down beside the seemingly dead animal and allowed the fox to tie him to the horse's tail. However, the fox actually tied the horse's tail around the lion's rear legs. He bound them together so tightly that the lion, even as strong as he was, would never be able to free himself.

As soon as the fox was satisfied with his work, he gave the horse a nice firm smack across his shoulders.

"Giddyup, now!"

Hearing the command to move, as he had his entire life, the horse reacted out of conditioning. He jumped up and took off as fast as he could, dragging the lion behind him. The lion roared and growled, but could do nothing more as the horse trotted on toward his master's house.

"I've brought him for you," the horse announced proudly when he arrived. "I have overpowered the lion and brought him here for you to see, just like you asked!"

The farmer (who apparently saw nothing odd about his horse being able to talk) was impressed by what the horse had accomplished. The farmer thought better of what he'd done and decided he'd been too harsh with the poor old horse.

"You can stay in my stables for the rest of your days," said the farmer to the horse. "I shall always care for you." So the horse was fed well and continued to live . . . until he died, which probably wasn't long in coming. He was pretty old.

The moral of this story, one could say, is that it's sometimes better to be clever than it is to be strong.

The Wedding of Mrs. Fox: A Retelling (two retellings, actually)

There are two versions of this rather brief story, which were both written down by the Brothers Grimm. We might as well tell both of them.

Tasty Morsels

Believe it or not, nine-tailed foxes can also be found in the mythology of both Korea and Japan. The number of tails, between one and nine, denotes the fox's age and power level (more tails = older/more powerful). In Korean myths, these shape-shifting tricksters are called *kumiho*. In Japanese tales these nature spirits are sometimes mischievous and sometimes helpful, depending on the circumstances, and called *kitsune*.

STORY ONE: Once upon a time, there was an old fox (we'll call him Mr. Fox) that had *nine tails*. Mr. Fox was convinced that his wife, Mrs. Fox, was being (or had the potential to be) unfaithful. Therefore, he came up with a clever plan to test his wife's fidelity.

Mr. Fox lay down underneath a bench and stayed so perfectly still that he appeared dead. Mrs. Fox seemed saddened by her husband's (apparent) death and shut herself in her upstairs bedroom. Their maid, Miss Cat, just kept on with her duties and continued cooking beside the fire.

After word of Mr. Fox's death spread through the forest, a number of suitors came to the house in hopes of wooing the recently widowed Mrs. Fox. The first suitor, a young fox, knocked on the door, and Miss Cat opened it.

Their conversation went a little something like this, in poetic verse:

The young fox said, "What may you be about, Miss Cat? Do you sleep or do you wake?"

To which Miss Cat answered:

I am not sleeping, I am waking,
Do you know what I am making?

I am boiling beer with a little butter.
Will you be my guest for supper?

"No thank you," said the young fox. "But I'd like to know what Mrs. Fox is doing."

To which Miss Cat answered:

She is sitting in her room,
Moaning in her gloom,
Weeping until her eyes go red,
Because dear old Mr. Fox is dead.

"Please let her know that a young fox is here to see her, and that I intend to woo her," said the young fox.

"Certainly, sir," replied Miss Cat.

Miss Cat went up to Mrs. Fox's room and tapped on the door.

"Mrs. Fox, are you still in there?"

"Oh, yes. I am here, my dear Miss Cat," Mrs. Fox replied.

"There is a suitor at the door who says he wishes to woo you."

"What does he look like? Does he have nine tails like my dear, late husband?"

"No, he does not. He has but the one, Mrs. Fox."

"Then send him away."

Miss Cat went back downstairs and told the young fox that her lady wanted nothing to do with him and that he should go on about his way.

Not much later, another suitor came knocking. It was another fox, this time with two tails. He, too, was sent away by Mrs. Fox. The suitors kept on coming, though, each with one more tail than the one before. Mrs. Fox sent them all packing.

That is, until a fox with nine tails finally showed up to woo her. When Mrs. Fox heard that he had as many tails as her late husband, she was overjoyed and said to Miss Cat: "Open the gates and doors all wide, and carry the old Mr. Fox outside."

Just as the wedding was about to begin, however, the "old Mr. Fox" came out from beneath the bench. He took up a heavy stick and just started beating the ever-loving crap out of everyone present. Once they'd all been thoroughly pummeled to his satisfaction, he kicked out Mrs. Fox for choosing a new husband so quickly.

So what's the moral of this story?

Poke your husband with a stick to make sure he's dead before you try to get remarried. Yeah . . . that sounds about right.

STORY TWO: One day, old Mr. Fox died (for real, this time). Shortly after, the wolf showed up as a suitor for the widowed Mrs. Fox. The maid, Mrs. Cat (apparently, she's married in this version), opened the door for him and the wolf greeted her cordially:

> Good day, Mrs. Cat of Kehrewit.
> How comes it that alone you sit?
> Are you making something good to eat?

To which Mrs. Cat answered:

> In milk I'm baking bread so sweet.
> Will you be my guest, and eat?

"No thank you," answered the wolf. "Could you tell me if Mrs. Fox is at home?"

To which Mrs. Cat answered:

She sits upstairs in her room,

Bewailing her sorrowful doom,

Bewailing her trouble so terribly sore,

Because dear old Mr. Fox is no more.

The wolf replied:

If she'd like a husband now,

Then would she mind please coming down?

Mrs. Cat went upstairs, knocked on Mrs. Fox's door, and said:

Are you within, good Mistress Fox?

If you're in want of a husband now,

Then would you mind please coming down?

"Does the suitor have a red coat and a pointed mouth?" said Mrs. Fox.

"No, madam."

"Then he won't do. Send him away."

After the wolf left, another suitor came. This time, it was a dog. The new canine suitor, however, was sent away by Mrs. Fox just as quickly as the wolf. The suitors just kept on coming, each just as genetically incompatible as the others—a hare, a stag, a bear, a lion, and one male member of just about every other species in the forest. None of them measured up to her late husband, as far as Mrs. Fox was concerned. So she sent away every single suitor.

The place turned into a revolving door of trans-species suitor rejection . . . until, at last, a young fox suitor came to call at the door. Mrs. Cat came to the parlor to inform her mistress Mrs. Fox of his arrival.

"Does the suitor have a red coat and a pointed mouth?" Mrs. Fox inquired.

"Indeed he does, madam," answered Mrs. Cat.

"Then send him up," said Mrs. Fox:

Sweep the room as clean as you can,
Open the window, fling out my old man!
Though many a fine fat mouse he brought,
Of his wife he never thought,
And ate up every mouse he caught!

So Mrs. Fox married the young Mr. Fox, and their wedding was a joyous occasion. Everyone danced and sang. And if they haven't stopped by now, according to the original story, they are dancing and singing still.

This brings us, once again, to the moral of this story. The Grimm brothers do not really offer one in their writing of the tale. However . . . perhaps one could say the moral is something like, "If your husband dies, you can always just replace him with a younger boy toy. Although, he needs to at least be from the same species as you." Rosalee and Monroe would probably disagree with that one, though.

Shaking Hands with a Fox: A *Grimm* Comparison

By the way, he's a Fuchsbau . . . So count your fingers after you shake hands.
                                                 —Monroe, "Organ Grinder" (1-10)

Fuchsbau characters show up in *Grimm* episodes with a fair amount of frequency, in much the same way that there are many fox-related tales to be found in the Brothers Grimm tradition—not to mention that a plethora of fox stories can also be found in mythology and folklore in general. This makes doing a play-by-play comparison nearly impossible. Therefore, instead of focusing on the episode and stories for this chapter's comparison, we will just take a look at the similarities between foxes in the Brothers Grimm tales and the Fuchsbau of *Grimm*.

In the episode "Organ Grinder" (1-10), Monroe initially warns Nick Burkhardt that Fuchsbau are not trustworthy. This is interesting, considering that he later begins a serious relationship with Rosalee Calvert—a Fuchsbau. Perhaps female Fuchsbau are less mischievous than their male counterparts? This would make sense considering the events of "The Wedding of Mrs. Fox" (story one, at least), in which Mr. Fox pretends to be dead to see how long it takes Mrs. Fox to choose a new husband. Mrs. Fox, however, seems to genuinely grieve her husband's death for a time. This contrast may explain why Rosalee Calvert, one of the only female Fuchsbau regularly seen on the show, seems different from the mischievous and trickster-like males seen in other episodes.

Another interesting point of comparison can be found in the fact that the Fuchsbau of the *Grimm* universe are oftentimes the owners of exotic spice and tea shops, which are actually apothecary shops for Wesen. By season 2 of *Grimm*, it has become fairly obvious that Fuchsbau are portrayed as being the apothecary scholars, merchants, and doctors of the Wesen world. This is very similar to the fox in the Brothers Grimm tale of "The Fox and the Cat," in which the fox claims to have "mastered a hundred arts." That fox is also a snob who looks down on other animals, such as the cat in the story. This attribute is similar to how the Fuchsbau shop owner in "Organ Grinder"

(1-10), Rosalee's late brother Freddy Calvert, is willing to sell human organs. Perhaps male Fuchsbau consider humans (and other types of Wesen) as beneath them, just as the fox in the story considered the cat incapable of teaching him anything of value.

Foxes, Foxes Everywhere: The Mythology of Foxes

The one overlapping element in nearly all of the fox stories already told in this chapter is that foxes are often portrayed as mischievous tricksters. This attribute is actually quite common of fox characters throughout the various mythologies and folklores from all over the world. In many stories, if a fox can find a way to get one over on another character, they won't hesitate to do so. Sometimes, they do such things simply for the joy of it. In certain stories, they do it to teach someone a lesson—often in humility. In still other stories, they do it for personal gain.

Fox-related folklore and mythology can be found in the stories of just about every culture group of the world (as long as they came into contact with foxes, of course). In fact, one could probably fill a book-length text with nothing but fox myths. Since we don't have that much room to discuss all of them here, this section will offer but a tiny sampling of fox mythology.

Among the native Alaskan tribes—namely the Inuit, Iñupiat, and Yupik—there is a myth commonly referred to as "Fox-Woman." The story tells of a man who comes home to find his entire household clean and in order, with a hot dinner already on the table. This is odd because, well, the guy lives alone . . . and he's certain *he* didn't do it. The next day, he pretends to leave home but actually hides himself behind some nearby bushes. Soon, he sees a fox approach. It goes into his home, and he follows it in shortly after. When the man enters, he finds a beautiful woman cleaning and cooking. Hoping she will stay, the man offers to marry her and the two are wed. As the days pass, the man notices a musky scent permeating the air of the house. When he finally asks his wife about the smell, she tells him that the musky scent comes from her. She then removes her human skin and puts back on her fox skin and flees from the house, never to be seen by the man again.

Among the Achomawi tribe, from what is now northeastern California, there is a creation myth known as "Silver-Fox and Coyote." According to the story, Silver-Fox once spent an entire night whittling down sticks from a berry bush. The shavings from Silver-Fox's work were to be made into regular, everyday people, whereas the finely shaven sticks themselves were to be made into the best and most noble people. At sunset they all came to life and Silver-Fox guided them away, sending multiple groups of them walking in various directions. Silver-Fox held a great feast with Coyote, since the two lived together, once the last of the humans were gone. Afterward, Coyote decided he'd like to try the same thing. He whittled sticks, trying to imitate what Silver-Fox had done. And it worked . . . sort of. At sunset, when all the sticks and shavings turned into people, Coyote began lustily chasing after the women. As soon as he'd touch them, however, they transformed back into sticks and shavings.

As mentioned in an earlier sidebar in this chapter, the Japanese view the fox as *kitsune*. Any fox can potentially be one, which is why the Shinto religion of Japan advises treating these animals kindly. Some of them are also said to be the messengers of the Shinto kami Inari, lord of the harvest. Harming one means you risk incurring the wrath of Inari (if this book has taught you anything, it should be that angering deities is never a good idea). These kitsune are often trick-

[17]

WESEN OF THE NEW WORLD

Look out, they ate a baby! That's rude.

—Monroe, "Three Coins in a Fuchsbau" (1-13)

For centuries, the Grimms of both past and present risked their lives in a battle against the rogue Wesen of Europe. However, when some of them inevitably made their way to the New World of the Americas, it stands to reason that they encountered new types of Wesen. Whether it was the incestuous and brutal Coyotl or the human-eating Wendigo, the Grimms who immigrated to the Americas found that evil was not restricted to the lands of the Old World they'd left behind . . . and so they found themselves learning how to hunt and behead a whole collection of dangerous new creatures in order to protect the lives of their fellow New World settlers.

The Coyotl: Ancient Trickster to Modern Wesen

HANK GRIFFIN: *Coyotl, right?*

NICK BURKHARDT: *Yeah, Hank . . . that's the second one today.*

—"Bad Moon Rising" (2-03)

GRIMM WORDS

Coyotl: A coyote. Used in *Grimm* to refer to a coyote-like Wesen. The word comes from the Nahuatl language spoken by the Nahuan Aztecs of central Mexico.

One of the first non-German Wesen to appear in *Grimm* is the Coyotl, in the episode "Bad Moon Rising" (2-03). In this installment of the series, a young female Coyotl named Carly Kampfer (who is also Hank Griffin's goddaughter) is kidnapped by her estranged family— her father's former "pack." And the kind of reunion they have in mind is . . . well . . . icky.

Carly's kidnapping has both Nick and Hank racing against time to rescue her before she is forever traumatized from being subjected to a savage Coyotl initiation ritual called Aseveración. While every horrid detail of this barbaric rite of passage isn't totally explained in the episode (likely because doing so would've given the censors fits), most of the blanks can be filled in by looking at what they *do* explain.

On the first full moon after the seventeenth birthday of a female Coyotl, the girl to be initiated is clothed in a white gown and bound between two poles by her wrists and ankles. A traditional banner made of animal skins is stretched out above her head. What happens after this is only *implied* in the episode—that all the males of the pack would then "have their way" with the girl, which is just a sugarcoated way of saying they planned to rape her.

Needless to say, it is this savage and barbaric Coyotl tradition that prompted Carly's father, Jarold Kampfer, to abandon his pack years before along with his wife and young daughter.

While the Coyotl Wesen portrayed in *Grimm* are a savage and disgusting bunch, the coyote is part of a long-standing mythological

GRIMM WORDS

Aseveración: From Spanish, it can be interpreted to mean "contention," "assertion," or "affirmation." Considering its use in *Grimm*, it can be assumed that it's intended to mean "affirmation" on the show. A ritual referred to by such a label would suggest that it is meant to declare a person as a member of a specific group (in this case, it is meant to "affirm" Carly Kampfer as a female member of their Coyotl pack).

tradition among various Native American culture groups as both a trickster and a culture hero. Since it seems the writers of *Grimm* had the Nahuatl language in mind when they named this Wesen, however, we'll primarily stick to the Uto-Aztec stuff in this section.

When one considers the traits of the ancient Aztec deity called Huehuecoyotl (meaning "Old Man Coyote" or, more literally, "Old, Old Coyote"), it begins to make sense why the writers of *Grimm* chose to associate this species of Wesen with an Aztec dialect. While Huehuecoyotl was primarily a trickster deity and the patron Aztec god of deception and pranks, his role also expanded into many other areas—music, art, dance, poetry, rampant sexuality, and creativity.

Portrayed in ancient Aztec art as having the head of a coyote, Huehuecoyotl was a talented shape-shifter. Similarly to the Norse trickster god Loki, Huehuecoyotl often assumed human form, both male and female.

A coyote-headed shape-shifter who regularly hides behind a human form . . . he's already starting to sound a lot like a Coyotl Wesen, isn't he?

As already mentioned, Huehuecoyotl was the patron deity of unbridled and uninhibited sexual behavior. He'd have sex with just

Tasty Morsels

Hayden Walker, the Coyotl pack leader who orders the kidnapping of Carly Kampfer, is shown as having an apartment—#203. It is interesting to note that this is the same number as the "Bad Moon Rising" episode (2-03).

about anyone and anything, regardless of gender, sex, familial relationships, or even species. He also grew bored rather easily, which could turn out to be a very bad thing for his worshippers since his favorite cure for boredom was to incite wars between humans.

Huehuecoyotl's role as a god of rampant sexuality may have been what inspired the writers of *Grimm* to create the concept of the Aseveración ritual in the episode "Bad Moon Rising" (2-03).

In the cosmological calendar of the Aztecs, called *tonalpohualli* (count of days), Huehuecoyotl rules over the fourth day, called *Cuetzpalin* (lizard) as well as the fourth *trecena* (thirteen-day period, of which there are twenty in the 260-day cycle of the tonalpohualli). This fourth trecena is called *Xochitl* (flower). These Cuetzpalin and *trecena* periods were believed to be an especially appropriate time to let loose with one's creativity, either by inventing new things or just making new objects in new ways. These periods were also considered times for being one's true self and casting aside concerns of what others might think.

It is interesting to note that the Coyotl of *Grimm* are portrayed as being ruled by a "will of the pack" mentality, and yet seem able to break from that pack by the power of their individual free will (as Jarold Kampfer did). Such contradictions are befitting of a trickster figure such as Huehuecoyotl, who could be seen as the potential progenitor of the Coyotl of *Grimm*.

Tasty Morsels

"Bad Moon Rising" (2-03) is a rather unique and noteworthy episode for a number of reasons. First, the increasingly regular character Rosalee does not appear in this episode (the actress, Bree Turner, was pregnant). Secondly, this is the first episode in which Nick reveals his role as a Grimm to a regular human (his partner, Hank Griffin). Lastly, this is one of the first episodes in which a human (Hank) is portrayed as being (albeit unknowingly) friends with a Wesen (Jarold Kampfer).

Balam: One Crazy Cat

With the appearance of the Coyotl in "Bad Moon Rising" (2-03), the writers of *Grimm* set a firm precedent that Wesen are not purely European occurrences. This opened up new opportunities for the writers to pull in even more creatures from non-European folklore and mythology. The second Native American–based Wesen introduced to the *Grimm* audience is the Balam Valentina Espinosa, a former police detective from New Mexico who comes to Nick's Portland turf in search of an unidentified serial kidnapper and child killer in the episode "La Llorona" (2-09). Don't worry, we'll discuss more about La Llorona in the next section. For now let's look at the Balam, which the writers of *Grimm* borrowed from Quiché mythology.

The Quiché (K'iche) people are the ethnical remnants of the once vast and powerful Mayan civilization of South America. These days, however, they live mainly in the country of Guatemala, located between Mexico, Honduras, and El Salvador. The Quiché people observe a plethora of ancient practices, many of which originate from their Mayan roots.

GRIMM WORDS

"Balam" is used in the *Grimm* universe to refer to a jaguar-like Wesen. The term itself, however, comes from the language and myths of the Quiché (sometimes spelled K'iche) people, descendants of the fallen Mayan civilization who now reside primarily in Guatemala. For the Quiché "Balam" could refer to many things, but is primarily a "jaguar." However, this word is also used among the Quiché to refer to supernatural entities or persons believed to possess magical powers.

According to the primal myths of the Quiché, they are descended from four progenitor deities, often called the *Cuatro Balam* (four jaguars). These four deities correspond with what the Quiché see as the four cosmological directions. All four are considered manifestations of the jaguar, as most of their names make evident—Balam-Quitze (Laughing Jaguar), Balam-Agab (Land/Night Jaguar), Iqi-Balam (Jaguar Moon), and Mahu-Cutah (The Sitting One or The Famous/Distinguished Name, depending on whose interpretation you choose to believe). More detailed information on Mayan/Quiché cosmology and myths may be found in the ancient Mayan *Popul Vuh* text.

Balam—whether referred to as gods, general supernatural beings, or magic wielders/spell-casters—are often viewed by the Quiché as protective forces that serve to shield the people, land, family, and children from harm. It would stand to reason that the writers of *Grimm* chose to integrate this protective role of the Cuatro Balam into the attributes of Balam Wesen. This may explain why the Balam Valentina Espinosa becomes so obsessed with avenging the murder of her nephew by the specter La Llorona.

GRIMM WORDS

Cuatro Balam is actually a combination of Spanish (*cuatro* = four) and Mayan/Quiché (*balam* = jaguar/tiger). Obviously, the ancient Mayans did not use Spanish because they didn't even know it existed until after the arrival of the conquistadors in the New World. In modern times, however, their Quiché descendants (most of whom now also speak Spanish in addition to their own native dialect) have come to refer to these four deities with this bilingual title.

La Llorona: The Woman in White

The story of the mysterious figure called La Llorona is one that rides the boundaries between folklore, superstition, the paranormal, and history. Before we continue, one thing needs to be stated—La Llorona is not classified as a Wesen. If anything, a more proper term for her would be "specter" or "ghost." However, since she is among the various New World beings encountered by Nick Burkhardt, it seems only fitting to include her in this chapter.

The tragic story of La Llorona has been told for centuries (if not millennia), in a number of versions, throughout Mexico, many regions of South America, and certain other Spanish-speaking countries. Depending on how it is told, this piece of folklore can serve a number of different mythical functions—as a children's cautionary tale, a warning for young women, or (last but not least) a scary tale meant to keep men from straying into infidelity. This story has a strong message for each of them. Mischievous children are told, "You better behave, or La Llorona will get you." Flirty young women are advised

GRIMM WORDS

La Llorona, translated from Spanish, means "weeping woman." This is more of a title than a name, as she is often heard weeping before she is seen (if she is seen at all . . . according to legends, sometimes she is only heard). In *Grimm*, this word refers to a female specter that lures children to the watery depths.

to take more care in their dealings with men, "Otherwise, you might share La Llorona's fate." Men with wandering eyes are warned, "You may one day encounter La Llorona, and then you'll be sorry."

The equally sad and terrifying story of La Llorona can be found in a number of differing versions, so please understand that no single telling of the story should be considered as any more accurate than another. This is common to such folktales, because they are passed down orally from memory, and human memory is often inconsistent.

Most of the time, however, the story goes something like this:

La Llorona: A Retelling

Long ago, in a tiny village, there lived an exceedingly beautiful young girl (usually, if named at all, she is called Maria . . . perhaps the most common female name in the Spanish-speaking world). Maria, unfortunately, knew all too well how beautiful she was (we all know the type). This caused her to become prideful and arrogant, believing herself better than the other girls in her village as well as too good to even consider marrying any of the young men she knew.

As Maria aged into a woman, she only grew more beautiful . . . and more arrogant. When she reached marrying age, almost every young man in her village became her suitor and all competed to win her hand. She just laughed them all off, of course. How could any simple *villager* be good enough to marry the likes of *her*?

"I will only marry," she finally declared to her suitors, "the most handsome man in the world. I will marry such a man, or I will marry no one."

One day, into the village rode a son of a wealthy rancher who seemed to Maria to be the most handsome man in the world. He was a fine specimen of manliness, to be sure. It was said he always rode a half-wild horse. Once his horse became too tame for his liking, he would go out into the plains and rope a new, wilder one to ride. The rancher's son felt that anything less just wasn't masculine enough. In addition to being handsome and manly, he also had a beautiful singing voice and was skilled at the guitar. It wasn't long before Maria became certain he was the only man worthy of marrying a girl as gorgeous as she. So she began trying to attract his affections by using the old "play-hard-to-get" trick.

When the young ranchero came to her window in the evenings to serenade her with his music, she stayed inside and kept the curtains drawn so he could not see her. When he began sending her expensive gifts, she sent them back. And the poor guy fell for it—hook, line, and sinker.

"That Maria is so uppity and stubborn. She is like a wild horse," he said to himself. "I will win her for my wife, if it's the last thing I do."

So, one evening, the young suitor finally showed up at Maria's house, offering the only thing she was willing to accept from him—a marriage proposal. The two were betrothed and soon became husband and wife.

As is usual for newlyweds, their life together was at first joyous and perfect, full of laughter and lots of lovemaking. They soon had two children and for years lived as a happy family. However, as sometimes happens when the "newness" has worn off, Maria's handsome ranchero husband grew bored with his wife and began spending more and more time away from home. Sometimes, he'd ride out of town and stay gone for days. This was common behavior for a ranchero, of course, but the days he spent away soon outnumbered those he spent at home. On the rare occasions he came home, he'd speak only to the children and almost entirely ignore his wife. It was as if Maria now meant nothing to him.

In town, there were rumors that the young ranchero frequently complained to his friends that he'd made a poor decision in marrying a girl below his station. She was just a poor villager, after all, and her father hadn't even had a dowry of any real value. Some rumors even claimed he was considering casting Maria aside so he could marry a woman from his own class of wealthy landowners.

A proud and arrogant girl like Maria, as one would expect, was furious with her absentee husband. And these rumors only further fueled her spite. Over time, her rage began to extend to her two children. Every time she looked at them, she was reminded of the man who'd sired them . . . the one who now seemed intent on abandoning her for another.

One day, Maria took the children out for a walk along the river near their home. As they strolled along the trail, her husband came upon them in a carriage. Beside him was a beautiful woman. Maria could tell she was obviously a member of a wealthy class, based on her extravagant dress. The ranchero stopped the carriage, stepped out, and took a few moments to speak to his children. He acted, however, as if he didn't even see Maria. Once he was done chatting with his children, he returned to the carriage and spurred the horses down the path.

As Maria watched the man she'd blessed with marriage and two beautiful children ride away with another woman, she was overcome by rage. Unable to carry out vengeance on her wayward husband, she turned her wrath toward the children. Driven mad by her pride and spiteful anger, she grabbed both of them and tossed her own children into the violent current of the water.

As her children were carried downriver, screaming and pleading for their mother to rescue them, Maria suddenly came to her senses and realized with horror what she'd just done. She ran along the riverbank as fast as her feet could carry her. She got ahead of the children, found a downed tree, crawled out on it, and reached out her arms. It was her only chance to rescue her poor children.

She failed.

Maria saw the horror in the terrified eyes of her children as the current stole them swiftly away from her. They were gone, and there was nothing more she could do to save them. And she had no one to blame but herself.

She crawled back to the riverbank, where she died on the spot . . . the victim of a broken heart.

The next day, a traveler came upon her body and rushed to the village to report that he'd discovered the corpse of a beautiful young maiden on the riverbank. The villagers all came running and found Maria there. However, no one could figure out what had become of the children. They searched everywhere, but the little ones were nowhere to be found. A funeral was held that same day, and Maria received a proper burial.

That very night, a number of villagers and townspeople were awoken by what sounded like a woman weeping. Some even claimed to have heard the mournful wails of a woman crying, "What has happened to my children?" (Some versions claim they heard her say, "What have I done to my children?" or "Where are my poor children?"). A band of men decided to follow the sound, which led them to the river. These men swore to have witnessed the ghostly apparition of a crying woman. The woman was wearing the same white gown in which Maria had recently been buried.

Legend states, to this very day, those who walk along a riverbank at night might see La Llorona or hear her weeping for her children. The villagers and townspeople, fearful of the wrathful spirit, decided they would never again speak of the girl they had once called Maria. From that moment on, she would be known only as La Llorona, "the weeping woman."

And what became of Maria after this? Some tell of how her restless spirit still resides in the rivers, waiting for a child to walk by so she can drag them below the waters to join her. Others claim her cursed spirit wanders the land and waits for philandering men (these days, we usually just call such men "cheaters") to happen along her path. When these men approach her, she kills and devours or drowns them. Others still say, whether on land or in water, that she especially hates newlywed and/or pregnant women and will always attempt to kill them, in order to rob them of their joy as she was robbed of hers.

Is the tale of La Llorona a tragic one? Of course. Is it creepy? Most definitely. Is it *true*? Well . . . that's up to you.

Tasty Morsels

This concept of a vengeful female spirit or entity that kills children, seduces and kills men, and/or attacks pregnant women is not a new one. Many similar figures can be found throughout world mythology—Lilith (ancient Mesopotamia and Judaic folklore), Lamia (Greek myths), Yuki-Onna (Japanese myths), and La Malinche (an actual Nahua/Aztec historical figure who was later turned into a legend; also, some believe her to be the root of the La Llorona story), are all examples.

Wendigo: The People-Eaters

In the *Grimm* episode "To Protect and Serve Man" (2-11), Nick comes across a human-eating Wesen call a Wendigo. This is a figure borrowed from the myths of several Native American culture groups—namely the Cree, Anishinaabe, and Ojibwe tribes of the Algonquin tribal group that originally resided in what is now southeast Canada (specifically, the region between the Rocky Mountains and the Atlantic Ocean) and northern Minnesota.

Among members of the previously mentioned native Algonquin tribal groups, the word "Wendigo" was used to refer to any person who resorted to cannibalism . . . for any reason, even if that reason was survival. During the sparse months of winter, tribe members sometimes found themselves growing short on foodstuffs (especially if the warmer months had been lean that year) and unable to travel or easily hunt due to the extreme cold. As a result, there were times when some people gave in to the temptation of cannibalism and chose to feed upon the flesh of dead (or, in some cases, even the living). In cases where a person resorted to cannibalism, even if it was

GRIMM WORDS

While there are various theories regarding where the term came from, no one knows the original root meaning of the term "Wendigo." More or less, one could very roughly interpret it to mean "cannibal." There is definitely a supernatural connotation to the word, however, since Algonquin myths often portray the Wendigo as a kind of evil spirit or demon-like creature. So "cannibal" seems inadequate. "Cannibal Spirit/Demon" might be a more accurate interpretation. Unfortunately, the original definition/ meaning of this word has been lost.

for survival, the Algonquin believed the person had been possessed by the spirit of the Wendigo. When this happened, the person responsible was no longer viewed as human. He or she had become Wendigo and, if not killed quickly, had the potential to undergo a physical transformation into a nearly unstoppable creature that would slaughter any living human it came across. So, in a way, one could view these rules about Wendigo as a mythologized form of an absolute law among the Algonquin—simply put, that the penalty for cannibalism was death.

In later years, certain members of some Algonquin tribal groups undertook the occupation of being professional "Wendigo-slayers-for-hire." No one is sure exactly when this practice began. What is known for certain, however, is that it continued well into the early twentieth century. The last known case of a professional Wendigo slaying among the Algonquin occurred in October 1907.

What you are about to read is neither a myth nor a story. This actually *happened*.

A man from the Cree tribe by the name of Jack Fiddler had grown to become a very highly respected Wendigo slayer among his people, with an impressive career of at least fourteen Wendigo kills. During the case in question, Fiddler had tracked down an elderly Cree woman he suspected of being possessed by the Wendigo (meaning he suspected her of cannibalism). When he finally found her, he confirmed his suspicions and took the old lady out "hit man–style." Unfortunately for Fiddler, the local authorities didn't see things the same way and he was soon arrested for her murder.

Jack Fiddler and his son Joseph, who'd assisted him in the job, were brought before the court. He insisted they'd had no choice but to kill the woman, as she would have soon transformed and become nearly unstoppable. Had they not acted quickly, the Fiddlers explained in court, she would have slaughtered every living human in the nearby village. Their intervention was the only thing that stood between the woman's increasing Wendigo bloodlust and the lives of dozens of innocent villagers.

Any Grimm would probably understand how the whole "But . . . I was killing *monsters!*" claim is a pretty weak defense when you're on trial for murder (as Craig Ferrer, who was convicted for killing the Wendigo who were about to eat him, would attest). At best, it's just going to get you an insanity plea.

This claim didn't work too well for Jack and Joseph Fiddler, either. Both men stood trial for killing the woman they claimed to have been a Wendigo. Neither man ever denied what he'd done. In fact, they openly admitted to killing the woman. *Of course we killed her*, was their general reaction to any questioning, *she was* WENDIGO! They insisted they'd only done what they had to do in order to protect the village. Unfortunately for the Fiddlers (who, in the *Grimm* mythos, would be seen as Grimms themselves), the court didn't believe in Wendigo and the father-son team was convicted of her murder. Both men served prison time. On the day he was sentenced, Jack Fiddler was eighty-seven years old.

Were the Fiddlers Wendigo slayers, Grimms, or just madmen? Who can say? Regardless, people in Canada and northern Minnesota continue to report sightings of Wendigo, from time to time, though most of these sightings do not come from members of the Algonquin tribal groups these days. And these descriptions are completely different from the Wesen of *Grimm*. Most actual Wendigo sightings have not described a creepy, white-haired creature with pointy fangs. Instead, they often describe it as being a tall, hairy creature with antlers protruding from its head (often, they are said to be like moose antlers).

There are various reasons that someone might witness a Wendigo, according to the local lore made up by mostly non-Algonquin settlers. Some claim seeing a Wendigo is a bad omen, and that afterward a death will likely occur. Others claim the Wendigo is a protector of the forest and that to encounter it means you've trespassed into its territory. Lastly, there is the claim that the wrath of the Wendigo is reserved for those who are in some way disrespectful of nature. Needless to say, such "tourist friendly" claims are completely counter to the true depictions of Wendigo in Algonquin myths and seem designed to improve tourism and help vendors sell T-shirts.

No matter why one encounters a Wendigo, one thing is for certain—if you see one, you should start running as fast as you can. Otherwise, you might end up on the dinner plate.

Murciélago: When Wesen Go Batty

My people know them as Geolterblitz. Literally bat out of hell. It's a legendary, liminal being—two distinct states of existence simultaneously within one physical body. The duality of humanity, the yin and the yang . . . the Ike and Tina Turner of it all.

—Monroe, "Happily Ever Aftermath" (1-20)

GRIMM WORDS

Murciélago is Spanish for "bat." Literally translated, however, it actually means "blind mouse."

Geolterblitz: What Monroe says about this word meaning "Literally, bat out of hell" in the episode is a bit odd. In truth, this word's literal translation from German is actually "oiled/greased lightning."

In the episode "Happily Ever Aftermath" (1-20), Nick finds himself drawn into a Cinderella story that's been turned on its head . . . and one that requires him to face a bat-like Wesen called the Murciélago (which, according to Monroe, the Blutbad refer to as *geoletrblitz*). Like a bat-headed banshee, this creature can rupture its victims' internal organs with its air-shattering screech. However, as you learned in Chapter 1, sound is more than just the strength of the Murciélago. It is also their weakness.

The double-edged nature of the relationship between bats and sound isn't just true of the Murciélago in *Grimm*. The same is true of actual bats, as well. Most bats hunt insects and navigate in darkness by using a method call "echolocation," locating their prey and obstacles by emitting high-frequency sounds that (similar to radar) bounce back to them. With their ultrasensitive hearing, the reflected sound waves allow the bats to both hunt and fly in total darkness. However, recent studies have found that sound vibrations can also be harmful to bats.

For example, sudden occurrences of dead bats in large numbers have been showing up around sites where wind farm turbines are in use. Investigations into these dead bats led to the discovery that bats are especially sensitive to the sound vibrations and changes in air pressure commonly caused by the large wind farm turbines. It is possible this fact may have inspired the writers of *Grimm* in creating the Murciélago Matraca, a hand cranked turbine-like siren that emits high-frequency sound waves that are harmful to Murciélago.

As far as what most would consider "traditional" fairy tales go, you would be hard-pressed to find any canonical stories about the Murciélago. However, the fact that this creature's name was taken from Spanish may offer a clue. While there are no Spanish myths of such a creature, there are many among Native American culture groups from Spanish-speaking regions of the southern U.S., Mexico, and South America.

During the archaeological excavation of the Aztec Templo Mayor (High Temple) in the ruins of Tenochtitlan (located in what is now Mexico City), an interesting artifact was uncovered—a life-sized ceramic statue of a tall being with the body of a man and the head of a bat. The hands and feet of the being are also clawed like those of a bat. In fact, the statue looks a heck of a lot like the Murciélago depicted in the *Grimm* television show. This statue is believed to be a representation of some deity, likely one associated with death. One reason for the belief in this death aspect of the being is that another life-sized statue was found in the temple that depicted Mictlantecuhtli—Aztec God of Death and lord of the underworld. Later Mayan myths suggest that the bat was considered a servant of the "devil" (this "devil" title may have been used for figures such as Mictlantecuhtli after the arrival of Christianity), forced into servitude for his misdeeds in life. Whether the Mayan concept has anything to do with the abovementioned Aztec statues is uncertain. However, it is definitely within the realm of possibility since these two civilizations are known to have interacted.

Bat and His Feathers: A Retelling

One myth that comes from the Oaxaca people, of what is now southwestern Mexico, offers an interesting story regarding the bat. In the early days after the creation of the world, Bat originally felt alone and ugly because it had not been blessed with feathers like the other birds. One day, Bat went before the Creator and complained about being cold. Feeling sorry for the creature, the Creator asked all the birds in creation to donate one of their feathers to Bat. Soon after, Bat was covered in feathers of every color and suddenly became beautiful instead of ugly. No longer ashamed of his appearance, Bat was finally able to fly proudly in the daylight as well as at night, filling the sky with colors wherever he went. In the daytime, he created rainbows. At night, he created auroras. However, his newfound magnificence soon caused him to grow proud and arrogant (somewhat like La Llorona, one might say). As time passed, Bat began to look down on the other birds and treated them all as if they were beneath him. After a while, the birds got sick of his uppity attitude. They all went to the Creator to complain and ask for a little divine intervention.

The Creator decided to go down to earth and see Bat's behavior for Himself. When the Creator witnessed how prideful and arrogant Bat had become, he decided to teach the animal a lesson.

"Bat," said the Creator. "Show me how beautifully you can fly."

Bat immediately took to the skies, happy for the opportunity to do a little showing off. As Bat flew, however, his beloved

Tasty Morsels

In many ancient myths, especially Native American ones, a single entity is used as a representation of an entire group or species. When this tale refers to "Bat," it doesn't mean "*a* bat." The Bat character is both a singular entity as well as a representative of *all* bats.

feathers began to fall off, one by one, until he was just as bare and ugly as he'd been before. Bat was so ashamed by how he looked that he flew away and hid in the caves, where he remains even now to avoid the light of day. This is why Bat only comes out at night, in an eternal quest to retrieve his lost feathers.

This wraps up our New World Wesen chapter. However, there remains one last group we have yet to examine, from an area farther south in Europe than the Wesen of the usual German or French traditions of *Grimm*—Greco-Roman Wesen.

[18]

GRECO-ROMAN WESEN

That is quite the history lesson. Do you have a lot of these books, by the way? —Captain Sean Renard, "Volcanalis" (2-18)

While the majority of the European fairy tales from which *Grimm* takes its stories come from such regions as Germany, England, and France, some Wesen originate from the history and mythology of the Greeks and/or Romans. In fact, sometimes it can be hard to tell where the line between fact and fiction should be drawn. In this chapter, we will examine these Greco-Roman Wesen and attempt to discover where the stories end and reality begins.

Löwen: Kings of the Jungle, Lords of the Arena

NICK BURKHARDT: *What do you know about Löwen?*

MONROE: *Ah . . . well, I know they'll rip your face off and then eat it.*

NICK: *Yeah, well . . . what about, uh, combat fighting?*

MONROE: *Oh, You're talking about gladiator Löwen. They're fierce. They're fueled by generations of bitterness. You know? Just imagine.*

One day, you're king of your own jungle—right?—minding your own business. Then suddenly you're in a net, being dragged off to Rome and thrown in a gladiator pit.

—"Last Grimm Standing" (1-12)

Nick Burkhardt encounters a pretty intimidating pride of Löwen while investigating illegal underground fighting events in the episode "Last Grimm Standing" (1-12). These lion Wesen are fearsome warriors with a long-standing tradition of battling it out in the gladiatorial arenas that date back to the days of ancient Rome. Interestingly enough, the connection between lions and the Roman Empire has a basis in both mythology and history.

Let's first take a look at a tale from the ancient Greek fabulist (meaning "storyteller" or "fable-ist") known as Aesop, who is believed to have lived from 620 to 564 BCE. One notable thing about Aesop is that historians can't exactly prove he ever existed. None of his original writings survived the passage of time. In fact, what we now call "Aesop's fables" (*Aesopica* in Greek) is actually a collection of stories that are only known due to the fact they were referenced in the writings of other ancient Greek writers—Herodotus, Plutarch, Aristophanes, and Plato, for example. If Aesop did exist, it is believed he was likely a slave. This is interesting, since the story we are about to discuss involves an escaped slave who encounters a lion.

Monroe pulling a nail from the hand of a Skalenzähne (an alligator/crocodile type of Wesen) as well as the opening quote from the episode "Last Grimm Standing" are both references to an Aesop fable called "The Slave and the Lion" (sometimes called "Androcles and the Lion"). While there have been various translations, retellings, and interpretations of this story over the millennia, it usually goes something like what follows:

GRIMM WORDS

Löwen: This is the German word for "lion." In the universe of *Grimm*, however, it refers to a lion type of Wesen.

The Slave and the Lion: A Retelling

There was once a slave who was treated very cruelly by his master, and so one day he conjured up the courage to escape. In order to avoid being captured and punished, he fled into the wilderness. Once he was certain he was deep enough into the wilderness, he began to seek out food and shelter. He eventually discovered a cave, which he believed to be empty. In truth, though, this cave was home to a great and powerful lion. When the beast revealed himself to the escaped slave, the terrified man was certain he'd be eaten alive. However, much to the man's astonishment, the lion did not attack. Instead, it limped over to him and held out its paw. The slave saw it had become swollen and inflamed because a thorn was imbedded in the pad of the paw. The man removed the thorn and bandaged the lion's wounded paw as best he could. It wasn't long before the lion was healed.

The lion was very grateful to the man for his help, and the two shared the cave for a time. The lion would even share its kills with the man so that he had something to eat. After many months passed, however, the man yearned to be in the company of humans again. So he said good-bye to the lion and returned to the city from which he'd escaped slavery, hoping to slip in and out without being seen. However, someone soon recognized him and he was arrested. The man was put back in chains and dragged before his former master, who decided it was best to make an example of him so his other slaves would not be inspired to escape. The man's former master handed him over to the governor and asked that he be fed to the lions in the arena during the next public games.

Soon enough, the day had come. Wild beasts were set loose into the arena, and the most fearsome among them was a great and powerful lion. Condemned to death, the man was thrown into the pit to be eaten. He abandoned all hope, certain he was about to die a most gruesome death. To the surprise of all the spectators, however, the ferocious lion simply walked up to the man and began to lick his palms. It was the very same lion he'd befriended in the cave, captured while he was gone and forced into the arena. The mob of spectators was so enamored with the spectacle that everyone demanded their lives be spared. The governor was likewise affected by what he'd seen, and was impressed that a wild beast could show such love and loyalty to a man. Therefore, he decreed both the slave and the lion should both be granted their freedom.

While the abovementioned tale is likely just a work of fiction, there is a very real historical relationship between lions and the gladiatorial games of the Roman arena. In fact, many of the oddities and spectacles involving animals that occurred in one particular Roman arena were recorded by a man commonly known as Martial.

Martial and the Lions of the Arena

Marcus Valerius Martialis, or just "Martial" for short, is believed to have lived between 38 and 102 CE (though some sources claim it was 40 to 104 CE). He was a poet from Hispania (Spain) in the Iberian Peninsula, who came to the ancient city of Rome in 64 CE. He is best known for being a writer of epigrams, short poems that are usually satirical in nature and/or cleverly ended.

Martial's work *Liber Spectaculorum* ("Book of Spectacles") has only been translated and published in its entirety in recent years, by the Harvard scholar Professor Kathleen M. Coleman. When it comes to the history of the crazy and violent events witnessed in ancient Roman arenas, Coleman knows more than just about anyone. In fact, she was the chief academic consultant on the Ridley Scott film *Gladiator* starring Russell Crowe.

One need only look to Martial's *Liber Spectaculorum* to see that lions, as well as many other dangerous animals, were a common sight in ancient Roman gladiatorial arenas such as the Amphitheatrum Flavium (commonly called the "Flavian Amphitheater"). Most often, lions and other big cats, such as tigers, were sent into the arena for one of two purposes—as part of a combat spectacle or as "tamed" performers (kind of like a more psychotic version of Siegfried and Roy).

Combat involving animals could be done in any number of chaotic combinations—animal vs. animal, human vs. animal, animal vs. animal vs. human, an animal fighting against multiple humans, and so on. The possibilities were nearly endless. Spectators might view a lion vs. an elephant in one spectacle, and a rhinoceros going up against a bull in the next; or maybe they'd watch a pack of hounds tear a live deer to pieces. When animals were pitted against humans, however, they had to face a gladiator who specialized in doing combat with animals—a *bestiarius*. Sometimes, of course, some poor, untrained person was just thrown into the arena with a bunch of lions in what was more or less just a "fight or die" method of cruel execution, which is what happens in Aesop's tale of "The Slave and the Lion." These people were called *damnati* (or "damned," which they were). While a *damnati* was usually just torn to shreds by the animals, a *bestiarius* was well-trained and properly equipped for the task. However, this doesn't make going toe-to-toe with a wild apex predator, while armed with only close-range melee weapons, any less gutsy or insane. And, most interestingly, the *bestiarii* (plural of bestiarius) weren't just males. There were female gladiators who fought against beasts as well—*bestiariae*. Martial records having seen such a spectacle in Epigram 8 of his *Liber Spectaculorum*:

> Venerable tradition used to sing of the lion laid low in the spreading valley of Nemea, a labor of Hercules. Let ancient testimony fall silent: for now that we have witnessed your games, Caesar, we have seen this feat performed by a woman's hand.

Martial wrote the above cited epigram after witnessing a spectacle of a bestiariae doing battle with a lion in the amphitheater. Since killing a lion was one of the legendary labors of the hero Hercules (or Herakles in Greek), Martial appears to have found it humorous that a woman had been able to do it (please keep in mind, this was a far more sexist time).

Gladiatorial contests, as already mentioned, weren't the only arena spectacles in which lions were used. Sometimes, they were brought in to perform tricks once they'd been trained by special handlers called *magistri* (teachers), or *magistrum* in the singular. Of course, as a modern audience learned back in 2003 when a 600-pound white tiger named Montecore mauled trainer Roy Horn (of Siegfried and Roy) during a show, even dealing with "tamed" or "trained" animals is never 100 percent safe . . . especially when that animal is a natural predator. Montecore was not euthanized after the attack. However, Roy Horn has never fully recovered from his injuries. Similar "accidents" appear to have occurred fairly often in the Flavian Amphitheater as magistri handlers made their lions or tigers perform. In fact, Martial recorded having witnessed two such incidents in his *Liber Spectaculorum*. For example, he writes in Epigram 12 (brackets added for clarification):

> A treacherous lion had wounded its magistrum with its ungrateful maw, daring to desecrate such familiar hands; but it paid a fitting penalty for such a serious crime, and the animal that had not taken a whipping [instead] took a weapon [was killed]. What must the behavior of men be under an emperor that the nature of wild beasts should be made so docile.

Unfortunately for the lion of which Martial wrote, no one argued that its life be spared (as Roy Horn did for Montecore, or the crowd for the lion and slave in Aesop's tale). When the magistrum whipped the lion, it sprang on him in retaliation instead of doing as ordered. Caesar, upon seeing this, immediately had the lion speared to death. The animal was killed for doing nothing more than being what it was—a lion. One could assume that taking a whip to a Löwen would probably get one's face torn off . . . then eaten.

Considering the fact that, in the *Grimm* universe, Löwen are said to have been forced to fight in the gladiatorial games of Rome, it is possible that some would have fought as bestiarii. However, it is hard to know which opponents these Löwen would prefer facing—humans, animals, or other Wesen (perhaps even their fellow Löwen, at times). Considering how they've preserved this gladiatorial tradition using only Wesen vs. Wesen matches, one might assume that the latter is most likely.

Musai: A Kiss of Genius

> *He said she was his inspiration. I thought that was very romantic. But, personally, I think he gave her way too much credit. But I guess that's love, right?* —Landlady, "Kiss of the Muse" (2-20)

What do you get when a Luisant-Pêcheur artist and a human author both fall in love with the same musai? Well . . . you get a dead human author, apparently, as Nick Burkhardt learns in the episode "Kiss of the Muse" (2-20). However, he also learns that musai can destroy the lives of those they inspire to creativity.

In the mythology of the ancient Greeks, the musai are usually known as the Nine Muses (to avoid confusion, we'll refer to the mythical group by the "Nine Muses" title)—Calliope, Clio, Erato, Euterpe, Melpomene, Terpsichore, Urania, Thalia, and Polymnia (sometimes spelled Polyhymnia). Originally, there were said to be only three of them. However, it seems that three just wasn't enough to cover all the various skills, arts, schools, and trades that were so valued in ancient Greek culture.

According to most myths, the Nine Muses were the daughters of Zeus, Greek thunder god and the lord of Olympus, and the female titan Mnemosyne, who was herself considered the personification of memory in Greek mythology. In fact, Mnemosyne's name is the root of the word "mnemonic." Though their father is the highest ranking god in the pantheon and their mother is a powerful titan, the Nine

GRIMM WORDS

Luisant-Pêcheur: Used in *Grimm* to refer to an otter-like Wesen, from French. It translates as something like "shiny fisher," likely a reference to how the coat of an otter grows shiny when wet and, of course, how they like to eat fish.

Musai: In *Grimm*, this refers to a muse-like Wesen. However, it is actually the ancient Greek plural form (usually spelled *musae*) of muse. More specifically, it refers to the Nine Muses of Greek mythology.

Muses are not considered gods themselves. They are more commonly classified as nymphs, beautiful female nature spirits who often inhabit places related to the natural world—springs, rivers, wells, and forests.

The Nine Muses are unique among other nymphs in that they carry out a very specific and useful task—bestowing artistic inspiration, in all its forms. Their gifts are not restricted solely to humans, but sometimes even extend to gods, animals, and even mythical beasts. And their inspirations aren't always beneficial. For example, Greek myths claim it was the Nine Muses who provided the terrible Sphinx of Thebes with its riddle. Many men were killed by the Sphinx after they failed to solve its riddle, which until solved allowed the creature to continue its reign of terror over the people of Thebes. It was not until the tragic hero Oedipus came along and solved the riddle that the Sphinx of Thebes was finally destroyed

The Sphinx's riddle went as follows: *What goes on four legs in the morning, two legs in the day, and three legs in the evening?*

Oedipus's answer was a work of clever simplicity: *A man . . . who crawls on all fours as a baby, walks on two legs as an adult, and uses a cane during old age.*

GRIMM WORDS

Mnemonic: A method or device used to assist a person with remembering something or recalling information, often in the form of a set of letters, word association, and/or conceptual comparisons.

Collectively, all of the Nine Muses preside over the art of poetry. Individually, though, each muse has her own particular fields of interest. Sometimes these fields overlap. It is also important to note there is no real consensus among mythology scholars as to which muse does what. However, the most common arrangement for the Nine Muses is as follows:

Calliope: epics and heroic poetry

Clio: historical records and lyre-playing

Erato: love poetry, religious hymns, lyre-playing, and theater/pantomime

Euterpe: flute-playing, lyrical poetry, and tragedies

Melpomene: tragedies and lyre-playing

Terpsichore: group dancing, choral singing, and flute-playing

Urania: astrology and cosmological poetry (poetry about the arrangement of the cosmos/universe)

Thalia: comedies and idyllic poetry (rural or nature poetry)

Polymnia/Polyhymnia: hymns, religious dance rites, and theater/pantomime

Unlike the musai of *Grimm*, the Nine Muses of the ancient Greeks do not have to use a kiss to inspire (though they certainly *could*, one would assume). Also, being inspired by a muse was not

GRIMM WORDS

Lyre: a stringed instrument, often handheld and U-shaped from base to neck, that somewhat resembles a strange mix between a guitar and a harp. Such instruments were common in the ancient world, especially among the Greeks and Egyptians.

usually a death sentence. A muse could use her powers of inspiration for either creative or destructive purposes, depending on her choice of action in a particular situation. One thing the writers of *Grimm* definitely got right, however, is that making an enemy of a muse is a *very* bad idea. One myth regarding the Nine Muses provides a rather graphic example of what befell one guy who dared to cross these daughters of Zeus.

The story, which can be found in the *Iliad* of Homer (among other works), explains how a talented Thracian musician named Thamyris arrogantly boasts of how he is so freaking awesome at his craft that he can outsing and outplay the muses themselves. Well guess what happens next? That's right: the muses themselves show up. All nine of them. And they are *not* a-*muse*-d.

Thamyris is prideful to a fault, and refuses to back down on his ridiculous boast. The musician even has the nerve to challenge the muses to a wager—to compete against each of them in music, singing, and poetry. If he wins, he gets to have sex with *all* of them. If he loses, then the muses can do whatever they wish with him. This turns out to be an unwise move on his part. The muses, needless to say, defeat Thamyris . . . and *epically* so.

Now free to do whatever they wish to the defeated Thamyris, as per the wager he was dumb enough to propose himself, the Nine Muses start by blinding him and smashing his lyre to pieces. However, their wrath doesn't stop here. They also rob him of all his musical and poetic abilities, leaving him unable to make music or even write lyrical poetry. After all, who did he think gave him those abilities in the first place?

For a man like Thamyris, who has always made his living with his creative talents, this is a terrible fate. The guy eventually dies after spending his last years wandering, broke and destitute, because of his own stupid pride. Even after death, the Nine Muses aren't done with him. Thamyris spends eternity in the Greek underworld, ruled by the god Hades, still blind and just sitting there alone next to his smashed up lyre.

The moral of this story? Don't mess with the musai. They will mess up your life (and, if you really make them mad, they'll even mess up your afterlife).

Taureus-Armenta: Taking the Wesen by the Horns

> *Listen to this. Known for stubbornness and courage in the face of adversity, many have been found in the front lines. The first to volunteer; willing to face down any enemy, they have nerves of steel under fire.*
> —Nick Burkhardt, read from the "books",
> "Volcanalis" (2-18)

When Nick Burkhardt finds himself on a case in which he must solve the strange murder of a local geologist, he comes face to face with Markus Hemmings, a bullheaded (literally) Wesen he's never seen before—Taureus-Armenta. Nick manages to take this powerful Wesen into custody (with a little help from Wu, of course), only to discover he is not the killer. The true killer is a creature called Volca-

GRIMM WORDS

Taureus-Armenta: The first half of this term comes from the Latin *taurus/taureus*, which in turn comes from the Greek word *tauros*. The meaning is the same in both languages—"bull." The second term comes from the Latin *armenta*, a term used to refer to an individual head of livestock (more specifically, livestock used as beasts of burden for work such as plowing) and could refer to cows, horses, and (of course) bulls/oxen. In *Grimm*, this term refers to a bull-like Wesen.

nalis (but more on that in the next section). The name of Taureus-Armenta comes from both Latin and Greek, which is fitting since it is in ancient Greek mythology that one finds myths of a bullheaded creature known as the Minotaur.

The Minotaur is one of the crazier figures to be found in the Greek mythos (however, he's probably not the *craziest*. The ancient Greeks came up with all sorts of weirdness). If nothing else, his story is definitely among the most colorful myths in the Greek tradition. The Minotaur's tale is a strange one, indeed, involving blasphemy, war, betrayal, a mutant baby, and human sacrifice, with just a hint of bestiality thrown in for good measure.

The Minotaur: A Retelling

You have taken what isn't yours! You've not shown respect, and now you're gonna die! You can't stop it! You're all gonna die! You've not shown respect!

—Markus Hemmings, "Volcanalis" (2-18)

The story begins back in the days when a man named Minos was king of Crete, a large, powerful, and prosperous trade island empire located in the Mediterranean. Few things were more important to Minos than his kingship, aside from perhaps his very sexy wife, Pasiphae, daughter of the sun god Helios. Sometime either before or after he became king of Crete, the validity of Minos's right to rule came into question. In order to set things straight once and for all, Minos appealed to the sea god Poseidon to send a miraculous sign of his choosing. So, in front of a large group of witnesses (his doubters among them), he asked Poseidon to bless him with a bull of pure white from the sea. The bull immediately emerged from the waves, and any doubts about his right to be king were put to rest. In return, Poseidon asked for only one thing—the bull had to be sacrificed to him once all was said and done.

Minos, it seems, was a greedy man. The white bull was such a magnificent beast that the king decided it'd be a waste to kill it as a sacrifice. Hoping to fool Poseidon, Minos replaced it with one from his own herd. The sea god, of course, saw right through his deception. Unfortunately for Minos, the Greek gods were not known to react well when they felt they were being disrespected. They did not forget . . . and they were *not* forgiving. Minos's greed earned him the wrath of Poseidon, perhaps one of the most spiteful gods among all the Olympians (just read Homer's *Odyssey*, if you have doubts).

In retribution for Minos's blasphemy, Poseidon caused Queen Pasiphae to fall in love with the white bull. Her feelings were not restricted to just emotional love, mind you, but sexual lust as well. Queen Pasiphae, the poor thing, was overcome with desire to get it on with the white bull. Of course, doing so presented a bit of a problem when it came to the mechanics of how to get it done. So she went to the legendary Minoan engineer, Daedalus, and requested his help. Daedalus used his skills to construct a cow from wood. He then had a real cow skinned and covered the wooden one in the hides. Pasiphae crawled inside the false cow, strategically positioned herself, and had it placed in the fields where the white bull grazed. The white bull, upon seeing what appeared to be a cow, mounted the contraption and got his bovine freak on with the queen.

Shortly thereafter, Pasiphae became pregnant and her husband Minos, along with the entire kingdom of Crete, rejoiced at the upcoming birth of a possible heir to the throne. When she delivered the child, however, Minos's joy turned to horror when he beheld a half-bull, half-human monstrosity. Though the baby's true given name was Asterius (or Asterion, in some versions), he came to be referred to as the Minotaur (bull of Minos).

King Minos wanted this abomination hidden from his sight forever. However, Poseidon forbade him from killing Asterius as a punishment for that whole "bull switch" debacle. So instead Minos orders Daedalus to construct an immense labyrinth, an inescapable maze in which to confine the creature. However, starving the Minotaur would be the same as killing it, which Poseidon already forbid. But what to feed such a monster, which had quickly grown from a disgusting baby into a voracious and murderous beast?

King Minos found his answer when, later on, he defeated the Athenians in battle. In the terms of the Athenian surrender, the king demanded a tribute of fourteen youths each year (some versions say it was every nine years)—seven young men and seven young women. These tributes would continue until the Minotaur was killed by one of them. The doomed groups of young tributes, like an even more homicidal version of *The Hunger Games*, were to be thrown unarmed into the labyrinth. Once inside, none could find their way back out. Some versions of the myth claim this was because the labyrinth changed its configuration regularly, making it impossible to memorize. The first two groups of young tributes met their deaths in this way, unable to survive unarmed against the powerful Minotaur. Among the third group of tributes sent to Crete, however, the Athenians were blessed with a warrior savior—Theseus.

Theseus, the prince of Athens, had watched helplessly for years as on two separate occasions his fellow Athenian youths were sent to their deaths. Theseus, one must understand, was no ordinary young man. He was a hero half-god, and the son of three parents—Poseidon, King Aegeus, and the mortal Queen Aethra. (Aethra was married to Aegeus but had sex with both Poseidon and Aegeus in the same night when Theseus was conceived. Roughly speaking, this made Theseus the "half-son" of King Aegeus.)

No longer willing to stand idly by as his fellow young Athenians were sent to die in the labyrinth, Theseus went to King Aegeus and volunteered himself as the seventh male tribute to Crete. Mere mortals stood no chance fighting unarmed against such a creature. As a half-god, however, Theseus knew he had a better chance of defeating the monster than any young man in Athens. Alongside thirteen other Athenian youths—six male and seven female—he journeyed by sea to Crete in a black-sailed ship. However, Theseus brought with him a white sail for the return journey to let his parents know that he had been successful when they came back.

Minos wanted as little to do with the Minotaur as possible. Therefore, he put his daughter Ariadne in charge of matters related to both it and the labyrinth. When the ship carrying the

Athenian tributes arrived in Crete, Ariadne was required to greet it. When she caught sight of Theseus, however, it was love at first sight . . . for her, at least.

Just as Theseus was about to be thrown into the labyrinth, Ariadne came to him and presented him with two very important items—a sword and a ball of thread. As Theseus entered the labyrinth, he told Ariadne that if he survived he would take her home to Athens as his bride.

Theseus hid the sword under his clothes and, once inside, tied one end of the thread at the entrance. He then took off to battle the beast alone, leaving the other tributes to stay put. As he navigated the winding halls of the labyrinth, he allowed the thread to roll out behind him so he could find his way back out. However, first he had to kill the Minotaur and put an end to the Athenian tributes once and for all. Only the creature's death would release Athens from its terrible agreement with Crete.

Theseus traveled through the labyrinth until he finally found himself at the center of the maze, confronted by the sleeping Minotaur. The creature awoke and immediately attacked. Theseus reacted, pulling the sword from his tunic. The hero and the beast engaged in an epic battle, which ended with the Minotaur dead. In some versions, Theseus is said to have beat it to death with his bare hands like an even more-psychotic version of Mike Tyson! Theseus then took the defeated beast's head and used the thread to find his way back out of the labyrinth.

Tasty Morsels

Ariadne, after being abandoned by Theseus on the deserted island, didn't fare so badly. She was eventually found there by Dionysus, the god of wine, merriment, sex, and madness. Hearing her heartbroken sobs, he took pity on the forlorn princess and made her his wife.

Free of the labyrinth, Theseus met up with Ariadne, her sister Phaedra, and the rest of the Athenian tributes. They wasted no time setting sail for home. Exhausted, they stopped briefly at a nearby island to rest for the night. According to some versions of the myth, Theseus was awoken that night by Athena, patron goddess of Athens. She told him he needed to set sail at first light, and that he should leave behind his Minoan passengers—Ariadne and Phaedra. Theseus followed Athena's suggestions, violating his promise and abandoning the woman who'd given him the tools he needed to kill the Minotaur and save his people.

On his way home, Theseus forgot to put up the white sail he'd brought to let his parents know of his success. Seeing the black sails, King Aegeus was grief stricken and immediately threw himself off a cliff into the sea.

Theseus: What a tool.

The comparison between the Minotaur and the Taureus-Armenta of *Grimm* is a fairly simple one. The idea of a Wesen with a man's body and a bull's head is pretty similar to the Greek figure of the Minotaur. In truth, there are few if any other myths that are as properly comparable to the Taureus-Armenta. So . . . take the Wesen by the horns, strap yourself in, and get ready to face the incredible, apocalyptic terror of the creature known as Volcanalis!

Volcanalis: Keep Your Hands off His Rocks!

> *I'll tell you what, dude . . . this looks a little bit like what, in my book, is known as "El Diablo."*   —Monroe, "Volcanalis" (2-18)

Nick Burkhardt's investigation into the murder of a local geologist, who was herself investigating the appearance of a *fumarole* on Mount Hood—an actual stratovolcano located just east of Portland, which is part of Oregon's Cascade Volcanic Arc, leads him to the Taureus-Armenta Markus Hemmings. However, he soon learns this Taureus-Armenta is nothing compared to the creature he serves—Volcanalis.

> *One question: what's a fumarole?*   —Sergeant Wu, "Volcanalis" (2-18)

Before going any further in this chapter, one thing should be made clear—Volcanalis is *not* a Wesen. So *what* is he? According to what Captain Renard tells Nick in this episode, Volcanalis was once human, a priest of the Roman god Vulcan. His service to Vulcan seems to have long ago transformed him into the being now known as Volcanalis.

Hoping to learn more, Nick and Monroe decide to consult "the books." Trusty old Monroe finds a sketch of a fiery being, accompanied by an inscription in Latin. Unfortunately, neither he nor Nick can read it. Renard, luckily, is educated in Latin and is able to translate:

GRIMM WORDS

Fumarole: This is a crack or opening in a volcano, or in the surrounding area, from which hot, often sulfurous, gases escape.

Having encountered the molten beast twice before, I enlisted the help of the high priest before I had the courage to return up the mountain. Many of the dwellers of Pompeii had removed rocks. When we discovered the bodies of these villagers, burnt and blistered, the priest uttered one word before he ran for his life—Volcanalis. Too frightened to face it on my own, I retreated just in time as Vesuvius sought revenge, erupting and burying Pompeii. I returned to Rome, where I was to learn that Volcanalis had often been mistaken for that ancient serpent, Satana.

—Captain Renard, read from "the books", "Volcanalis" (2-18)

Based on the abovementioned excerpts from this episode, the show offers us at least two clues as to the mythology and history used to create the Volcanalis figure of *Grimm*—the Roman God Vulcan and the destruction of Pompeii. Let's start by taking a look at Vulcan then we will examine Pompeii, an entire city wiped off the map in one of the most catastrophic volcanic events in human history.

Worship of the Roman god of fire and destruction, Vulcan, can be traced to well before 900 BCE. Some have claimed the practice of Vulcan worship is even older, pointing to preexisting evidence of worship for the Greek god Hephaestus, who is often seen as the Greek equivalent of Vulcan. While such Greek-to-Roman comparisons are often nearly identical when it comes to the Olympian gods, this is not the case with Vulcan and Hephaestus. The god Hephaestus, as he was worshipped by the ancient Greeks, was viewed as a kindly *creator* deity. He was portrayed as the blacksmith and artisan of the gods, fashioning their incredibly powerful weapons (Zeus's lightning bolt), armor (Athena's shield, Aegis, and the winged helm of Hermes), and other useful gadgets (the girdle of Aphrodite, which made her irresistible to any man).

Vulcan, on the other hand, is a *destroyer*, plain and simple. He is neither an artisan nor a blacksmith, and he is certainly not portrayed as an ally to humankind. In fact, Vulcan was considered perhaps the most unlikeable god in the ancient Roman pantheon. However, it was believed that disrespecting Vulcan by not properly worshipping him or failing to make sacrifices in his name risked incurring his fiery wrath, which most often came in the form of wildfires, burned storehouses, or (if he got mad enough) volcanic eruptions. While Vulcan is decidedly different from Hephaestus, it is believed the Romans integrated certain aspects of the Greek god, to at least a small degree, in later ages.

Vulcan was honored at an annual festival known as *Volcanalia* (sometimes spelled *Vulcanalia*), every August 23. This was during the hottest and driest part of the year, when fire became a very real and always present danger to agricultural fields, forests used for timber, and foodstuffs stored in granaries. So this festival was meant to appease Vulcan in an attempt to avoid his destructive flames. This role of appeasement in the festival becomes even more apparent when one considers that the most prominent temple of the Vulcan *cult* was located in Ostia Antica, the ancient harbor city which was home to the main storehouse of the Roman Empire.

While Ostia Antica was the ancient center of the Vulcan cult, it was by no means the only place where he was worshipped. In the capital of Rome, there was the Volcanal (roughly, "Palace of Vulcan"). This temple dates back to the eighth century BCE. According to legend, it was built upon the very spot where Romulus, one of the two mythical brothers who founded Rome, signed a peace accord with

GRIMM WORDS

The term *cult* has a different meaning when used to refer to ancient religions. In modern days the term has come to refer to destructive or exploitative religions. However, when used in reference to ancient religions, it simply means a specific religious group.

Titus Tatius, king of the nearby city-state of Cures, uniting their people for a time. Later the daughter of Titus, Tatia, married the son and heir of Romulus, Numa Pompilius. Their marriage created a strong and unified empire with a national identity and their people came to be called by one name—*Quirites* (meaning "people of the spear," which was the original ancient name for the people who would later be called "Roman citizens").

During the Volcanalia festival, sacrifices and libations were overseen by a Vulcan priest called a *flamen*. The chief overseeing priest bore the title *flamen Volcanalis*. Existing records suggest that large bonfires were burned during Volcanalia. The patriarchs of various Roman families would venture to the Tiber River to each catch a fish. These fish would then be thrown into the bonfires as sacrifices to Vulcan. Some scholars have theorized that these fish were used as substitutions for human lives, either to replace a preexisting practice of human sacrifice or just as symbolic victims to appease Vulcan's wrathful fire.

Needless to say, Vulcan was not considered a god to be trifled with (not that any of the Roman gods *were*, of course). So perhaps it should be no surprise that, in *Grimm*, Volcanalis is unforgiving when folks take his precious rocks from Mount Hood. Seriously . . . the guy gets pretty crazy when it comes to his rocks. Just look at Pompeii,

---

Tasty Morsels

During the height of the cult's influence, the high priest of the Vulcan temple in Ostia Antica bore the title *Pontifex Vulcani et Aedium Sacrarum* (High Priest of the Vulcan Cult and the Sacred Temple). This was a lifelong appointment and he who held it was considered equal in power to the *Pontifex Maximus* (High Priest), head of the entire official religion of Rome.

---

which, according to the mythos of the *Grimm* universe, was the work of Volcanalis in retribution for the theft of his rocks by some locals.

Near what is now Naples, Italy, there was once a small city known as Pompeii. It sat on the western Roman coast near the base of Mount Vesuvius. In or around 79 CE, the whole place was wiped off the face of the planet when this nearby "mountain" turned out to be a volcano and violently erupted. Interestingly enough, the Vesuvius eruption that destroyed Pompeii is recorded as having occurred on August 24, just a day after the annual August 23 festival of Volcanalia. It is a fair assumption that this odd coincidence may have inspired the writers of *Grimm* with the idea that Volcanalis was responsible for the event.

Whether or not the eruption of Vesuvius had anything to do with Vulcan or his cult, the horrific reality of what occurred there remains unchanged. Some believe a series of tremors may have foreshadowed the eruption to come, but were ignored. In those times, it's likely no one in Pompeii believed these tremors had anything to do with Vesuvius. This may explain why, when it finally erupted, no one had evacuated the area. When the volcano blew, raining down ash and debris, many people in Pompeii ran to their homes for shelter. This was futile. When all was said and done after the Vesuvius eruption,

Tasty Morsels

One might assume that the word "volcano" comes directly from the name of Vulcan. In truth, this is not the case. The root of "volcano" actually comes from *Vulcano*, the name for a chain of volcanically active islands off the coast of Italy. However, the name of Vulcan was the root word for the naming of these islands.

everyone still in Pompeii was dead. Even nearby city-towns, such as Herculaneum, sustained damage.

The citizens of Pompeii died in one of two ways, for the most part, neither of which sound very pleasant. Most of the people who remained in the city were killed by the intense heat, which scientists have estimated as having reached roughly 480 degrees Fahrenheit. They were cooked alive. Those who tried to escape found they couldn't get out of the city fast enough and the majority of people were asphyxiated by the ash and sulfurous-gas-choked air. By the time Vesuvius grew quiet once more, Pompeii was gone, buried beneath roughly eighty-two feet of molten rock and volcanic ash. When people from the surrounding areas were finally able to return to the site, it must have appeared to them as if Pompeii had just vanished. In reality, the entire city was so well buried that no trace of it could be seen.

Most of what is now known about the catastrophe at Pompeii has been learned from the writings of Pliny the Younger (born in roughly 61 CE and died in 112 CE). This young Roman, likely about eighteen years old at the time, was visiting an uncle who lived near Pompeii when Vesuvius erupted. Pliny went along with his uncle, who mounted a rescue mission to save as many Romans from the danger zone as he could. According to the following account of Pliny the Younger, they weren't able to save many (brackets have been added for clarity):

> He [Pliny's uncle] hurried headlong toward a place from which most were fleeing, taking his vessel into the heart of danger. He was fearless, and spoke to me all he observed so that I might note his words down. Ashes fell, hotter and thicker as our ships grew close. Pieces of pumice and black stones, cracked by the heat, came down behind the ash. The water grew shallow. The shore was blocked with debris, spewed out by the mountain . . . The wind favored my uncle, however, and he was able to bring in his ship. He embraced his friends [fellow Romans who'd requested aid], who were terrified. He cheered and encouraged them and, hoping to calm their fears, ordered them to be taken to the bath.

Later, Pliny describes the sounds as the air becomes so clouded that none could see:

> You could hear the wailings of women and infants, as well as the cries of men. Some called out for their parents. Others cried out the names of children and wives, hoping to find them in the dark by their voices. Some cursed their fates . . . some prayed for death, overcome by the fear of dying. So very many called out to the gods, while so many more claimed there must be no gods remaining and that the cosmos had been plunged into eternal darkness.

Finally, however, they managed to escape and, in the below excerpt from his account, Pliny describes the moment when light broke through the darkness:

> A shimmer of light returned. We at first mistook this as a sign of approaching flames. However, we saw the flames were still far off. Darkness fell. The ashes fell once more, this time in heavy sheets. We had to get up and shake off the ashes, every now and then, or we'd have been buried in them and crushed by their weight. I could say that I never gave a cry or shout of fear during these perils, but I must confess I got some comfort from my mortal belief that the entire world was dying and I with it.

Pliny the Younger, of course, did not die. He survived to convey his harrowing account and, because of this, the modern world knows far more about what happened at Pompeii than it would otherwise. Whether due to a god's wrath or the shifting of the earth, Pliny the Younger was able to let future generations know of how an entire city came to an end nearly overnight. If not for his writings, who's to say if the ruins of Pompeii would have ever been found again?

A GLOSSARY OF WESENOLOGY

Balam (baa-LAM): Yucatec/Mayan/Quiché term for "jaguar." In *Grimm*, this refers to a jaguar-type Wesen. First seen in "La Llorona" (2-09).

Bauerschwein (BOW-er-schvyn): German for "farmer pig." In *Grimm*, this refers to a pig-type Wesen. First seen in "The Three Bad Wolves" (1-06).

Blutbad (BLOOT-baat): German for "bloodbath." In *Grimm*, this refers to a wolf-type Wesen. First seen in "Pilot" (1-01).

Coyotl (koh-YOH-tuhl): Nahuatl for "coyote." In *Grimm*, this refers to a coyote-type Wesen. First seen in "Bad Moon Rising" (2-03).

Cracher-Mortel (CRAH-shay mor-TEL): French for "deadly/mortal spit." In *Grimm*, this refers to a puffer-fish-type Wesen. First seen in "The Waking Dead" (2-21).

Dämonfeuer (DAY-mon-foy-er): German for "demon fire." In *Grimm*, this refers to a dragon-type Wesen. First seen in "Plumed Serpent" (1-14).

Dickfellig (DIK-fay-lig): German for "thick skin." In *Grimm*, this refers to a rhino-type Wesen. First seen in "Last Grimm Standing" (1-12).

Drang-Zorn: (drahng-tzorn) German for "stress-wrath." In *Grimm*, this refers to a badger-type Wesen. First seen in "The Bottle Imp" (2-07).

Eisbiber (ICE-bee-ber): German for "ice beaver." In *Grimm*, this refers to a beaver-type Wesen. First seen in "Danse Macabre" (1-05).

Fuchsbau: (FOOKSH-bow): German for "fox burrow." In *Grimm*, this refers to a fox-type Wesen. First seen in "Organ Grinder" (1-10).

Fuchsteufelwild (FOOKSH-too-fuhl-vilt): German for "wild fox devil" or "wild as a fox devil." In *Grimm*, this refers to a goblin-type Wesen. First seen in "Nameless" (2-16).

Geier (GUY-er): German for "vulture." In *Grimm*, this refers to a vulture-type Wesen. First seen in "Organ Grinder" (1-10).

Gefrierengeber (geh-FREYR-ehn-geh-bur): German for "freezing giver." In *Grimm*, this refers to an as yet unseen and unknown Wesen (as of season 2) that appears to be their equivalent of Santa Claus. First referred to by Monroe in "Let Your Hair Down" (1-07).

Genio Innocuo (JEE-nee-oh in-NAH-koo-oh): Latin for "harmless genius." In *Grimm*, this refers to a tortoise-type Wesen. First seen in "The Other Side" (2-08).

Glühenvolk (GLOH-en-folk): German for "glowing people." In *Grimm*, this refers to a rare type of Wesen with bioluminescent skin (often mistaken for aliens by non-Wesen). First seen in "Endangered" (2-19).

Hässlich (HAYS-lick): German for "nasty" or "ugly." In *Grimm*, this refers to a troll-type Wesen. First seen in "Pilot" (1-01).

Hexenbiest (HEK-sen-beest): German for "Hex beast" or "spell-casting beast." In *Grimm*, this refers to an evil female Wesen that uses potions and curses to harm others. See also Zauberbiest.

Hundjäger (HOONT-yay-ger): German for "hunting hound." In *Grimm*, this refers to a dog/hound-type Wesen. First seen in "Cat and Mouse" (1-18).

Jägerbar (YAY-ger-bar): German for "hunter bear." In *Grimm*, this refers to a bear-type Wesen. First seen in "Bears Will Be Bears" (1-02).

Jinnamuru Xunte (JIN-ah-muh-ROO CHOON-tay): Eastern Maninkakan for "limping evil spirit." In *Grimm*, this refers to a fly-type Wesen. First seen in "Mr. Sandman" (2-15).

Klaustreich (KLOW-shtryk): German for "claw stroke" (interpretations differ). In *Grimm*, this refers to a domestic- or alley-cat-type Wesen. First seen in "The Thing With Feathers" (1-16).

Königschlange (KOH-nig-shlaan-guh): German for "king snake." In *Grimm*, this refers to a king cobra–type Wesen. First seen in "Over My Dead Body" (2-06).

La Llorona (lah yor-OH-nah): Spanish for "weeping woman." In *Grimm*, this refers to a non-Wesen, ghost/specter-like entity that drowns children. First seen in "La Llorona" (2-09).

Lausenschlange (LOW-zin-shlan-guh): German for "louse/unpleasant snake." In *Grimm*, this refers to a snake-type Wesen. First seen in "Of Mouse and Man" (1-09).

Lebensauger (LAY-bin-zow-ger): German for "life sucker." In *Grimm*, this refers to a vampire/lamprey-type Wesen that feeds off the life force of others. First seen in "The Hour of Death" (2-10).

Löwen (LØ-ven): German for "lion." In *Grimm*, this refers to a lion-type Wesen. First seen in "Last Grimm Standing" (1-12).

Luisant-Pêcheur (lu-WEE-zahn pesh-UR): French for "shiny fisher." In *Grimm*, this refers to an otter-type Wesen. First seen in "Kiss of the Muse" (2-20).

Mauvais-Dentes (MOH-vay dont): French (poorly translated) for "bad teeth." In *Grimm*, this refers to a saber-toothed-tiger-type Wesen. First seen in "Bad Teeth" (2-01).

Mauzhertz (MOWTS-hairts): German for "mouse heart." In *Grimm*, this refers to a mouse-type Wesen. First seen in "Of Mouse and Man" (1-09).

Mellifer (MELL-i-fer): German for "honey maker" or "to bear honey." In *Grimm*, this refers to a bee-type Wesen. First seen in "Beeware" (1-03).

Mellischwuler (MELL-ish-vool-er): To be honest, this translates from German as "gay honey." Most likely, the writers looked up "queen" in a German translator and were given this word (which is a slang term for "queen/gay"). So, in the *Grimm* universe, it's the term for a "queen bee." In reality, however, the word would mean something more like "honey drag queen."

Minotaur: a monster from Greek mythology. In the Grimm universe, a Wesen appears in the comic book adaptation that is said to be a "Minotaur." However, it makes more sense that this is simply a Taureus-Armenta and that this was a typo on the part of the comic book writers.

Mordstier (MORT-shteer): German for "murder bull." In *Grimm*, this refers to one bull-type Wesen. It has yet to be seen on the show as of season 2, but is referenced in the Grimm Journals in "Game Ogre" (1-08).

Murciélago (mur-see-EL-ah-go): Spanish for "bat" (literally "blind mouse"). In *Grimm*, this refers to a bat-type Wesen. Among some Wesen, they are referred to in German as Geölterblitz ("greased lightning"). First seen in "Happily Ever Aftermath" (1-20).

Musai (moo-ZA-yee): In ancient Greek, this referred to the Nine Muses. In *Grimm*, this refers to a muse-type Wesen. First seen in "Kiss of the Muse" (2-20).

Nuckelavee (noo-keh-LAH-vee): Scottish Gaelic word that refers to a centaur-like creature that was considered among the most terrible of the race of Scottish elves. In *Grimm*, this refers to a horse-type Wesen. First seen in "Quill" (2-04).

Raub-Kondor (ROWB kon-dor): German for "consuming condor." In *Grimm*, this refers to a condor-type Wesen. First seen in "Endangered" (2-19).

Reinigen (RYE-nee-gin): German for "to clean." In *Grimm*, this refers to a rat-type Wesen (some of whom can control rats with music). First seen in "Danse Macabre" (1-05).

Rißfleisch (RIS-flysh): German (rough translation) for "flesh ripping predator." In *Grimm*, this refers to a tiger-type Wesen. First seen in "Game Ogre" (1-08)

Rotznasig Carcaju (ROTS-nah-zig kar-KAH-zhoo): This is a mix of German and Portuguese, meaning "dirty/snot-nosed wolverine." In *Grimm*, this refers to a wolverine-type Wesen that has yet to be seen on screen. The first reference to this creature is in "Bad Teeth" (2-01) when Nick Burkhardt learns that an ancestor of his once castrated one with the "castration blade" knife.

Schakal (SHAHK-ahl): German for "jackal." In *Grimm*, this refers to a jackal-type Wesen. First seen in "Three Coins in a Fuchsbau" (1-13).

Scharfblicke (SHARF-blik-uh): German for "sharp eyes." In *Grimm*, this refers to an owl-type Wesen. First seen in "Face Off" (2-13).

Schneetmacher (SHNEET-mah-ker): German for "snow maker." In *Grimm*, this refers to an as yet unseen and unknown type of Wesen. First referenced in "Tarantella" (1-11), no one is certain what this Wesen might be. However, the general consensus is that it's very dangerous.

Seelengut (ZEE-luhn-goot): German for "kindhearted." In *Grimm*, this refers to a sheep-type Wesen. First seen in "The Good Shepherd" (2-05).

Seltenvogel (ZEL-ten-voh-gul): German for "rare bird." In *Grimm*, this refers to a very rare songbird-type Wesen that produces golden eggs. First seen in "The Thing With Feathers" (1-16)

Siegbarste (ZEEG-bars-tuh): German for "broken victory." In *Grimm*, this refers to an ogre-type Wesen. First seen in "Game Ogre" (1-08).

Skalengeck (SKAH-lin-geck): A mistranslation of German, this really means "measuring scale fop." However, it's likely supposed to mean a "scaled fop." In *Grimm*, this refers to a lizard-type Wesen. First seen in "Pilot" (1-01).

Skalenzahne (SKAH-lin-tsah-nuh): Another mistranslation of German, this really means "measuring scale teeth." However, it's likely supposed to mean "scaled teeth" or "scaly teeth." In *Grimm*, this refers to a crocodile-type Wesen. First seen in "Last Grimm Standing" (1-12).

Spinnetod (SPIN-nuh-toht): German for "death spider." In *Grimm*, this refers to a spider-type Wesen. First seen in "Tarantella" (1-11).

Stangebär (SHTAHN-guh-bair): German for "spear bear." In *Grimm*, this refers to a porcupine-type Wesen. First seen in "Quill" (2-04).

Steinadler (SHTYN-ahd-ler): German for "stone eagle." In *Grimm*, this refers to a hawk/eagle/raptor-type Wesen. First seen in "Three Coins in a Fuchsbau" (1-13).

Taureus-Armenta (TAH-ree-oos ar-MIN-tuh): Latin (with some Greek origins) for "plough bull/ox." In *Grimm*, this refers to a bull/Minotaur-type Wesen. First seen in "Volcanalis" (2-18).

Volcanalis (vol-kuhn-AL-is): An ancient Latin term for a high priest in the cult of Vulcan (god of fire and destruction) that oversaw sacrifices during the Volcanalia festivals dedicated to the god. In *Grimm*, this refers to a non-Wesen fire being that is similar in appearance to a demon/devil from the Judeo-Christian tradition. First seen in "Volcanalis" (2-18).

Waage (VAH-guh): German for "scales of weight." In *Grimm*, this refers to an as yet unseen and unknown type of Wesen. First referred to by the Grimm Journals in "Pilot" (1-01).

Waschbär (VAASH-bair): German word for "raccoon." In *Grimm*, this refers to an as yet unseen raccoon-type of Wesen. This Wesen has been seen in the *Grimm* comic book adaptation. On the show, it is first referred to by Monroe in "Organ Grinder" (1-10).

Wendigo (win-DEE-go): This term comes from Algonquin and refers to an evil spirit that is believed to take over the body of any person who resorts to cannibalism. In *Grimm*, this refers to a voracious, fanged, human-eating type of Wesen. First seen in "To Protect and Serve Man" (2-11).

Wildermann (VIL-der-mahn): German for "wild man" or "man of the forest." In *Grimm*, this refers to a hair-covered, sasquatch-like type of Wesen. First seen in "Big Feet" (1-21).

Zauberbiest (TSOW-bur-beast): German for "magic beast." In *Grimm*, this refers to male counterparts of the Hexenbiest type of Wesen. Hence, there is no real "first episode" for this. However, clues are first given that Sean Renard is a Zauberbiest in the episode "The Kiss" (2-02).

Ziegevolk (TSEE-guh-folk): German for "goat people" or "goat folk." In *Grimm*, this refers to a goat-type Wesen with the ability to influence people by releasing pheromones they gain from eating special frogs. First seen in "Lonelyhearts" (1-04).

A GLOSSARY OF *GRIMM* TERMINOLOGY

Blau Teuful (BLAU TOO-ful): German for "Blue Devil." First mentioned in the *Grimm* comic book adaptation (#2). "The best single malt whiskey Deutschland has to offer."

Endezeichen Grimm (END-eh-ZAI-shen): German for "end sign." In *Grimm*, this referred to a group of more violent and intolerant Grimms of days past. They would kill any Wesen they came across and preferred to do so in slow, brutal, and torturous ways, branding the Wesen with their symbol—Gterbestunde—regardless of whether or not those Wesen were living peacefully and not harming humans. These sorts of Grimms are mentioned by Monroe in "The Hour of Death" (2-10), and he expresses that he is glad they are no longer around.

Freidenreden (FRY-din-ray-din): German for "peace talk." In *Grimm*, this is a concept seemingly created by the Verrat to refer to meetings in which truces or terms are discussed between enemies. There are two rules—no weapons and absolutely no fighting for any reason. First mentioned on the show in "Cat and Mouse" (1-18).

Gallenblase (GAH-lin-blaze): German for "gallbladder." In *Grimm*, human gallbladder is valued for its effects on certain types of Wesen. First mentioned in "Organ Grinder" (1-10).

Gebirgeleutewortfuhrerin (geh-BIR-geh-LOY-tuh-VORT-FYUR-er-in): Broadly translated from German, this rather long word means "First/Head (female) Speaker of the Mountain Clans." In *Grimm*, this is the title of the queen of the Schwarzwald roma (a clan of Romani gypsies). See also, Zigeunersprache.

Gterbestunde (geh-TUR-beh-SHTOON-duh): A combined term that refers to the *Sterbestunde* (Hour of Dying) *G*, which was the symbol of the brutal Endezeichen Grimm. Members of this old sect of Grimms often branded this symbol into the flesh of their Wesen victims with a red-hot iron.

Jay (JAY): Short for the "jacine" mold spores from which it is made, in *Grimm* this refers to an extremely addictive narcotic used by some Wesen. Rosalee Calvert is known to have once been addicted to Jay, but has since kicked the habit.

Kehrseite (KEHR-zy-tuh): German for "other side" or "reverse side." In *Grimm*, this refers to humans who are not aware of the existence of Wesen.

Kehrseite-Schlich-Kennen (KEHR-zy-tuh-SHLISH-kin-in): Translated from German, this means something like "awareness of the other side" or "sneaked knowledge of the other side." In *Grimm*, this refers to humans who know the truth about the Wesen world's existence.

Laufer (LOW-fur): German for "runner." In *Grimm*, this refers to a group of Wesen (sometimes called "The Resistance") who battle against the Verrat and oppose the idea of them returning to the power they once had in the days of old.

Nilpferd Furzen (NILP-fairt fur-tsen): German for "hippo fart." This appears to be an insult among Wesen. It is first used by Monroe in the *Grimm* comic book adaptation, just before he tears a few Hundjägers to pieces.

Purewelt Orden: From German, this is somewhat poorly translated as "Pure World Order," or PWO for short. In the *Grimm* universe, this refers to a purist/racist organization that forbids interspecies relationships between Wesen and believes that all species should keep to their own. This group first appears in the *Grimm* comic book adaptation, in which members interrupt a marriage between a Fuchsbau and a Löwen, kidnap the bride and groom, and attempt to burn them alive (thankfully, they are saved by Nick Burkhardt, Hank Griffin, and Monroe).

Roh-Hatz (ROH-hots): German for "raw hunt" or "barbarous hunt," depending on interpretation. In *Grimm*, this refers to an old rite of passage once performed by male Jägerbars in which they would hunt down humans. It is rarely practiced by modern Jägerbars.

Verrat (fur-RAHT): German for "betrayal" or "treason." In *Grimm*, this refers to a syndicate made up of the Seven Houses of royals in the Wesen world. Established in 1945, this group seems to have two primary goals—to maintain the balance of power in the Wesen world and, among some, to return to the old days of monarchy rule. Members are often identified by a tattoo of two interlocking diamonds. The writers of *Grimm* took the name of this group from a series of texts (widely considered conspiracy theory by most scholars) written by Sebastian Haffner called *Der Verrat*.

Wesen (VEHS-sin): German for "creature" or "being." In *Grimm*, this refers to a race of human-appearing beings with special (often animal-like) traits. For the most part, the only non-Wesen (see Kehrseite) people who can see their true forms when they don't wish to be seen are Grimms.

Wider (VEE-der): German for "against/contrary to" or "to go against." In *Grimm*, this refers to a Wesen who has learned to control his/her natural tendencies so as to live a peaceful coexistence among humans. This word could also be spelled as "wieder," which means "again" or "to go back," on certain *Grimm* fan websites. Depending on one's interpretation, either term could fit the label.

Wieder: See *Wider*.

Woge (VOH-guh): German for "wave" or "a powerful, wavelike motion." Normally, this term is a noun. In *Grimm*, however, it is used as a verb and refers to when Wesen transform from their human appearances to their true forms.

Zaubertrank (TSOW-bur-tronk): German for "magic drink/potion." In *Grimm*, this word's meaning remains more or less the same. It is normally used in the *Grimm* universe to refer to the destructive concoctions used by

Hexenbiests/Zauberbiests, though it has also been used to refer to medicines and potions made by Fuchsbau.

Zigeunersprache (ZEE-geh-UN-er-SPRA-kuh): German for "gypsy language." While the term appears in certain *Grimm* circles as a matriarchal gypsy title, this is likely a misinterpretation/mistranslation. In the German language, this word clearly refers to the spoken language of Romani gypsies and nothing more.

BIBLIOGRAPHY

Works Cited or Consulted

The following bibliography provides a list of all source materials that were consulted during research for and/or cited throughout the writing of this book.

Aesop. *Aesop's Fables; A New Translation*. Translated by V. S. Vernon Jones. 1912. Reprint, Seattle: Amazon Digital Services, 2012. Kindle Edition.

Asbjørnsen, Peter Christian, and Jörgen Møe. *Popular Tales from the Norse*. Translated by Sir George Webbe Dasent. 1859. Reprint, Seattle: Amazon Digital Services, 2012. Kindle Edition.

Ashley, Mike, ed. *The Giant Book of Myths and Legends*. London, UK: Magpie Books, 1995.

Bettelheim, Bruno. *The Uses of Enchantment: The Meaning and Importance of Fairy Tales*. New York: Vintage Books, 2010.

Cunningham, Scott. *Cunningham's Encyclopedia of Magical Herbs: Expanded and Revised Edition*. Woodbury, MN: Llewellyn Publications, 2012.

Grimm, Jacob, and Wilhelm Grimm. *Deutsche Sagen*. 1818. Reprint, Seattle: Amazon Digital Services, 2011. Kindle Edition.

——. *Kinder- und Hausmärchen*. 1812. Reprint, Seattle: Amazon Digital Services, 2011. Kindle Edition.

Haase, Donald, ed. *The Greenwood Encyclopedia of Folktales and Fairy Tales*. Volumes 1–3. Westport, CT: Greenwood Press, 2008.

Jacobs, Joseph. *English Fairy Tales*. Lexington, KY: Seven Treasures Publications, 2008.

Leach, Maria, ed. *Funk and Wagnalls Standard Dictionary of Folklore, Mythology, and Legend*. New York: Harper and Row, 1984.

Martial. *Martial: Liber Spectaculorum*. Edited and translated by Kathleen M. Coleman. Oxford, UK: Oxford University Press, 2012.

Mondschein, Ken. *The Knightly Art of Battle*. Los Angeles: Getty Publications, 2011.

Oakeshott, Ewart. *A Knight and His Weapons*. 2nd edition. Chester Springs, PA: Dufour Editions, 1997.

Opie, Iona, and Peter. *The Classic Fairy Tales*. New York: Oxford University Press, 1980.

Perrault, Charles. *The Fairy Tales of Charles Perrault*. Lexington, KY: Amazon CreateSpace, 2012.

Pliny the Younger. *The Complete Letters*. Translated by P. G. Walsh. New York: Oxford University Press, 2009.

Rybandt, Joe, ed. *Grimm: Comic Adaptation*. #0-3 (July 2013). Written by Marc Gaffin, David Greenwalt, Jim Kouf, Kyle McVey. Mt. Laurel, NJ: Dynamite Comics.

Tatar, Maria, ed. *The Annotated Brothers Grimm: Bicentennial Edition*. New York: W. W. Norton and Company, 2012.

Further Reading

For even more information on folklore, fairy tales, mythology, and/or the works of the Brothers Grimm, readers should consider consulting any of the following titles:

Birkhäuser-Oeri, Sybille. *The Mother: Archetypal Image in Fairy Tales*. Toronto: Inner City Books, 1988.

Bottigheimer, Ruth B. *Grimms' Bad Girls and Bold Boys: The Moral and Social Vision of the Tales*. New Haven, CT: Yale University Press, 1987.

Bulfinch, Thomas. *Bulfinch's Mythology*. New York: Gramercy Books/Random House, 2003.

Campbell, Joseph. *The Hero with a Thousand Faces*. Princeton: Princeton University Press, 1973.

Frazer, James G. *The Golden Bough: The Roots of Religion and Folklore*. New York: Gramercy Books/Random House, 1993.

Graves, Robert. *The White Goddess*. New York: The Noonday Press, 1994.

Hettinga, Donald R. *The Brothers Grimm: Two Lives, One Legacy*. New York: Clarion Books, 2001.

Sproul, Barbara C. *Primal Myths: Creating the World*. New York: Harper and Row Publishers, 1979.

Tatar, Maria, ed. *The Classic Fairy Tales: A Norton Critical Edition*. New York: W. W. Norton and Company, 1999.